Water Informatics for Water Resource Management

The primary focus of the book series is to understand digital technologies and solutions thereby enabling them to correlate the solutions with their region-specific problems and finally apply them to the Water Resource Management. This will help to generate novel research and innovative solutions. This domain of Water Informatics is growing at a very fast rate and its potential has been realized since it harnesses the use of digital technologies to leverage the applications offered for Water Resource Management.

The book series is tailored to meet the following learning objectives:

- Learn Machine Learning Techniques for data-driven modeling for management of Water Utilities.
- Learn IOT technologies for Smart Water Management.
- Learn Artificial Neural Networks for decision making in Water Utilities.
- Learn Risk Analysis, Fuzzy Logic and management of uncertainty in Water Utilities.
- Learn Block-Chain Technology for effective allocation of Water Resources.
- Learn Cyber-Security essential techniques for Smart Water Services.
- Learning Evolutionary Methods for Water Management.

Sur Singh Rawat · Nitima Malsa ·
Gyanendra Kumar · Vimal Gupta
Editors

Unleashing the Power of Blockchain and IoT for Water Informatics

Springer

Editors
Sur Singh Rawat
Department of Computer Science
and Engineering
JSS Academy of Technical Education
Noida, Uttar Pradesh, India

Nitima Malsa
Department of Computer Science
and Engineering
JSS Academy of Technical Education
Noida, Uttar Pradesh, India

Gyanendra Kumar
Department of IoT and Intelligent System
Manipal University Jaipur
Jaipur, Rajasthan, India

Vimal Gupta
Department of Computer Science
and Engineering
JSS Academy of Technical Education
Noida, Uttar Pradesh, India

ISSN 2731-9105 ISSN 2731-9113 (electronic)
Water Informatics for Water Resource Management
ISBN 978-981-96-3885-7 ISBN 978-981-96-3886-4 (eBook)
https://doi.org/10.1007/978-981-96-3886-4

This Springer imprint is published by the registered company Springer Nature Singapore Pte Ltd.
The registered company address is: 152 Beach Road, #21-01/04 Gateway East, Singapore 189721, Singapore

Preface

In an era where technology is continuously evolving, the fusion of Blockchain and the Internet of Things (IoT) offers unprecedented opportunities for enhancing water informatics. This book, *Unleashing the Power of Blockchain and IoT for Water Informatics*, explores the synergistic potential of these technologies to revolutionize water resource management. By integrating Blockchain's secure and transparent data handling capabilities with IoT's real-time monitoring and automation, we can pave the way for innovative solutions to contemporary water management challenges.

Water informatics is an emerging interdisciplinary field that integrates data science, artificial intelligence, and modern technologies to enhance water management and conservation practices. The chapters in this book delve into various aspects of water informatics, offering insights into how these technologies are revolutionizing the field.

"A Comparative Study of IoT-Based Water Quality Monitoring Systems (IoT-WQMS) and the Potential of Machine Learning in Water Quality Assessment": This chapter explores the potential of IoT-based systems in monitoring water quality and assesses how machine learning can enhance the accuracy and efficiency of these systems.

"IoT and Blockchain in Smart Water Management: A Comprehensive Review": This comprehensive review highlights the integration of IoT and blockchain technologies in smart water management, showcasing their combined benefits and applications.

"An Integrated Water Management System for Smart Cities Using an IoT and Secure Blockchain Framework": Focusing on smart cities, this chapter presents a framework that combines IoT and blockchain for secure and efficient water management.

"Transfer Learning and Transformer for Multi-parameter Water Quality Assessment: A Novel Framework": This chapter introduces a novel framework utilizing transfer learning and transformers to enhance multi-parameter water quality assessment.

This book also addresses the pivotal role of IoT in monitoring and managing water consumption and detecting leaks. Effective water management requires advanced methods for tracking and detecting leakage and contamination. The chapters in this part present innovative solutions leveraging IoT, machine learning, and blockchain technologies.

"An Integrated Water Tracking and Leakage Detection System Using Blockchain Technology": This chapter discusses the integration of blockchain technology in tracking water usage and detecting leaks, ensuring transparency and security.

"The Role of Machine Learning and IoT in Early Detection of Water Contamination": Highlighting the synergy between machine learning and IoT, this chapter examines their role in the early detection of water contamination.

"Arduino IoT Platform with Bayes Theorem-Based Water Contamination Detection System": This chapter explores the development of an Arduino IoT platform that uses Bayes theorem for detecting water contamination, showcasing its efficiency and reliability.

Regulatory compliance and effective auditing are crucial for sustainable water resource management. These chapters of the book focus on the application of modern technologies to ensure efficient water usage and regulatory adherence.

"Efficient Utilization of Water Using the Internet of Things and Blockchain Technology": This chapter discusses how IoT and blockchain technologies can be leveraged to optimize water usage and ensure regulatory compliance.

"IoT-Based Smart Water Resource Management": This chapter presents strategies for smart water resource management to enhance efficiency and sustainability.

"Agriculture Production Optimization": This chapter explores methods to optimize agricultural water use, ensuring productivity and sustainability.

"Conservation of Water Using Smart IoT-Based Sensors: A Methodical Study": This chapter presents a methodical study on the use of smart IoT sensors for water conservation, highlighting practical applications and benefits.

"The Future of Water Informatics Lies in its Potential to Drive Sustainability and Innovation": This book also explores forward-thinking approaches and future prospects in water management.

"Intelligent Water Management: Implementing IoT and AI for Enhanced Efficiency and Sustainability": This chapter discusses the implementation of IoT and AI in water management to achieve enhanced efficiency and sustainability.

"Synergising Water Management with Blockchain and Artificial Intelligence: Empowering Sustainable Solutions for the Future": This chapter explores the synergy between blockchain and AI in water management, proposing sustainable solutions for future challenges.

"Sustainability Through Water Informatics Using Blockchain and Future Prospects": The final chapter examines the role of blockchain in water informatics, offering insights into its future prospects and potential for driving sustainability.

Noida, India — Sur Singh Rawat
Noida, India — Nitima Malsa
Jaipur, India — Gyanendra Kumar
Noida, India — Vimal Gupta

Contents

Editors and Contributors

About the Editors

Sur Singh Rawat holds a Ph.D. in Computer Science and Engineering from Govind Ballabh Pant Engineering College, Pauri Garhwal, which is affiliated with Uttarakhand Technical University, Dehradun, India. He earned his Master of Technology degree in Information Technology from IIIT, Allahabad, India, in 2010, and his Bachelor of Technology degree in Computer Science and Information Technology from UPTU, Lucknow, in 2004. Currently, he serves as an assistant professor at JSSATE, Noida, India. His research areas include digital image processing, pattern recognition, and deep learning.

Nitima Malsa is also an assistant professor in the Department of Computer Science and Engineering at JSSATE, Noida, India. Her research interests encompass blockchain technology, machine learning, smart contracts, and cryptocurrency. She has published over 30 papers in various journals and conference proceedings, and has served as an editorial and review member for academic journals and conferences. Dr. Malsa has chaired numerous conference sessions and conducted many special sessions at international conferences. She has received funding for a project focused on blockchain technology from the CSTUP, Government of India.

Gyanendra Kumar earned his B.Tech. in Computer Engineering and Information Technology from Uttar Pradesh Technical University, Lucknow, in 2004, followed by an M.Tech. in Information Technology from J. C. Bose University of Science and Technology, YMCA, Faridabad, Haryana, in 2011. He completed his Ph.D. in Computer Engineering from the same institution in 2023. Dr. Kumar is currently an assistant professor at Manipal University Jaipur, Rajasthan. With over 18 years of academic experience across various engineering colleges and universities, he has published numerous research papers in reputable journals and conferences. Dr. Kumar serves as a reviewer for esteemed publishers such as Elsevier, Springer, MDPI, and Tech Science Press. He has been an invited speaker, session chair, and track chair at various international conferences, and is a professional member of IEEE and ACM.

Vimal Gupta obtained his B.Tech. degree in Computer Science and Engineering from Maharishi Dayanand University, Rohtak, and his M.Tech. in Computer Science and Engineering from Guru Gobind Singh Indraprastha University, New Delhi. He is currently pursuing a Ph.D. from Dr. A. P. J. Abdul Kalam Technical University, Lucknow. His research interests focus on medical image processing, data compression, and deep learning.

Contributors

Nikunj Agarwal Department of Mathematics, JSS Academy of Technical Education, Noida, India

Ritesh Agarwal Department of Computer Application, School of Engineering and Technology (UIET), CSJM University, Kanpur, UP, India

Vishal Awasthi Department of Electronics and Communication Engineering, School of Engineering and Technology (UIET), CSJM University, Kanpur, UP, India

Hiti Bansal Shiva Shiksha Sadan, Sonepat, Haryana, India

R. S. Chaithra SJB Institute of Technology, Bengaluru, India

Sachin Chaudhary School of Computer Science and Applications, IIMT University, Meerut, UP, India

Parul Dixit Department of Law DAV PG College, Dehradun, India

B. C. Girish Kumar RV Institute of Technology and Management, Bengaluru, India

Abhinav Gupta Moradabad Institute of Technology, Moradabad, UP, India

Kashika Jain Amity University, Noida, India

Rachna Jain JSS Academy of Technical Education, Noida, India

Kalpana Dronacharya Group of Institutions, Greater Noida, Uttar Pradesh, India

Harleen Kaur Jaypee Institute of Information Technology, Noida, India

Alok Kumar Department of Computer Science and Engineering, School of Engineering and Technology (UIET), CSJM University, Kanpur, UP, India

Bhupendra Kumar School of Computer Science and Applications, IIMT University, Meerut, UP, India

Gyanendra Kumar Department of IoT and Intelligent Systems, Manipal University Jaipur, Jaipur, Rajasthan, India

Shishir Kumar Babasaheb Bhimrao Ambedkar University, Lucknow, UP, India

Shravan Kumar School of Liberal Arts Uttaranchal University, Dehradun, India

Sunil Kumar Department of Information Technology, School of Engineering and Technology (UIET), CSJM University, Kanpur, UP, India

C. A. Latha RV Institute of Technology and Management, Bengaluru, India

Komal Malsa Lingaya's Vidyapeeth, Faridabad, India

S. Nagamani SJB Institute of Technology, Bengaluru, India

Aziz Nanthaamornphong University of Alabama, Alabama, USA

Rajneesh Panwar School of Computer Science and Applications, IIMT University, Meerut, UP, India

Pragya Department of Computer Science & Engineering, School of Computer Science and Engineering, Galgotias University, Greater Noida, UP, India

Namrata Prakash Graphic Era Hill University, Dehradun, India

G. Puspha R N S Institute of Technology, Bengaluru, India

Arman Raj Galgotias University, Greater Noida, India

Reeta Rautela School of Liberal Arts Uttaranchal University, Dehradun, India

Sur Singh Rawat Department of Computer Science and Engineering, JSS Academy of Technical Education, Noida, India

Ruchi Saraswat Department of Civil Engineering, JSS Academy of Technical Education, Noida, India

Neelaksh Seel Moradabad Institute of Technology, Moradabad, UP, India

Kewal Krishan Sharma School of Computer Science and Applications, IIMT University, Meerut, UP, India

Vikas Sharma School of Computer Science and Applications, IIMT University, Meerut, UP, India

Bishnu Kant Shukla Department of Civil Engineering, JSS Academy of Technical Education, Noida, India

Hans Kumar Singh Department of Civil Engineering, JSS Academy of Technical Education, Noida, India

Harikesh Singh Professor, CSE(AIML), GL Bajaj Institute of Technology & Management, Noida, UP, India

Mahesh Kumar Singh Dronacharya Group of Institutions, Greater Noida, Uttar Pradesh, India

Nitya Singh Department of Civil and Environmental Engineering, University of Liverpool, Brownlow Hill, Liverpool, UK

Prabal Pratap Singh Department of Physics, School of Basic Science (UIET), CSJM University, Kanpur, UP, India

Pushpendra Singh SRMIST Delhi-NCR Campus, Modinagar, Ghaziabad, Uttar Pradesh, India

Suhani Dronacharya Group of Institutions, Greater Noida, Uttar Pradesh, India

Priyanka Thapa Dronacharya Group of Institutions, Greater Noida, Uttar Pradesh, India

Vishu Tyagi Graphic Era Deemed to be University, Dehradun, Uttarakhand, India

Tarun Kumar Vashishth School of Computer Science and Applications, IIMT University, Meerut, UP, India

K. M. Veeresh SJB Institute of Technology, Bengaluru, India

Lal Pratap Verma Manipal University Jaipur, Jaipur, Rajasthan, India

Shivam Verma Department of Mechanical and Industrial Engineering, New Jersey Institute of Technology, Newark, New Jersey, USA

Chapter 1
A Comparative Study of IoT-Based Water Quality Monitoring Systems (IoT-WQMS) and the Potential of Machine Learning in Water Quality Assessment

Bishnu Kant Shukla, Ruchi Saraswat, Nikunj Agarwal, Hans Kumar Singh, and Shivam Verma

Abstract The severe concerns regarding water scarcity and pollution necessitate the implementation of novel methods for monitoring and managing these challenges. This study investigates the utilisation of Internet of Things (IoT) in Water Quality Monitoring Systems (WQMS), with a specific emphasis on its fundamental elements, operational capabilities, and the incorporation of sensor technology and machine learning. The Internet of Things (IoT) enables the connection of equipment equipped with sensors to gather and analyse real-time data, hence improving the effectiveness of water quality monitoring. The IoT-WQMS functions by utilising modules for sensing, transmitting data, processing, and interfacing. Intelligent sensors oversee crucial water characteristics such as pH, temperature, turbidity, and Dissolved Oxygen (DO), with data analysed and presented through user interfaces. The development of sensor technology has resulted in the creation of small, real-time data-generating intelligent sensors, which are essential for IoT-WQMS. Precision and durability are crucial. Machine learning, specifically Artificial Neural Networks, aids in forecasting water quality parameters based on linked data, hence contributing to the development of a

B. K. Shukla (✉) · R. Saraswat · H. K. Singh
Department of Civil Engineering, JSS Academy of Technical Education, Noida, India
e-mail: bishnukantshukla@gmail.com

R. Saraswat
e-mail: rsaraswat@jssaten.ac.in

H. K. Singh
e-mail: hanskumarsingh4@gmail.com

N. Agarwal
Department of Mathematics, JSS Academy of Technical Education, Noida, India
e-mail: nikunjagarwal@jssaten.ac.in

S. Verma
Department of Mechanical and Industrial Engineering, New Jersey Institute of Technology, Newark, New Jersey, USA
e-mail: ssv8@njit.edu

S. S. Rawat et al. (eds.), *Unleashing the Power of Blockchain and IoT for Water Informatics*, Water Informatics for Water Resource Management,
https://doi.org/10.1007/978-981-96-3886-4_1

comprehensive Water Quality Index (WQI). Nevertheless, machine learning necessitates significant computational and large training data, both of which might be alleviated by utilising robust computing systems and dependable data sources. Conclusively, the utilisation of IoT in water quality monitoring offers a highly effective and immediate method for managing water resources. Advanced sensors and machine learning provide precise and practical information about water quality. This research establishes a foundation for future advancements in smart water monitoring and environmental monitoring technology. *abstract* environment.

Keywords Water quality monitoring (WQM) · Wireless sensor network (WSN) · Internet of things (IoT) · Machine learning techniques (MLT) · Water quality index (WQI)

1.1 Introduction

Life on earth depends on water. However, there are freshwater shortages in many countries [1–3]. Gulf nations use a laborious desalination process to draw fresh water from the sea [4, 5]. However, the increased development along the coast and the resultant water contamination are making this process much more difficult. Other nations treat rainwater to produce freshwater [6], however, the alteration in climate has recently showed an influence on rainfall, endangering this possibility [7–9]. For years, water pollution has been noted as a major issue [10–12]. For instance, in 2003, the Clean Water Foundation of America created the Earth Echo Water Challenge, a day dedicated to water monitoring [13] with a goal of raising public awareness of water contamination. Freshwater is frequently becoming an industrial commodity on the verge of such a water crisis. It is frequently kept in overhead or subterranean tanks under municipal management in metropolitan settings, sometimes for extended periods of time before consumption [14]. Environmental Protection Agency of the United States (USEPA) and WHO (World Health Organisation) both often offer updates and suggestions on how to deal with freshly discovered water diseases and toxins [15–18]. Consequently, the current fashion is to manage and observe the readily available natural water supply in order to prevent water shortage issues during dry periods [19, 20]. Due to the rising population, limited water resources, and effects of global warming, it is difficult to evaluate water quality in real time. Therefore, improved approaches for real-time monitoring of water quality indicators are required [21]. The parameters governing water quality, the hydrogen ion concentration, is gauged by pH. The pH level is a measure of the acidity or alkalinity of water. Water with a pH of 7 is considered neutral, while pH levels below 7 indicate acidity and values over 7 suggest alkalinity. The optimal pH range for drinking water is typically between 6.5 and 8.5 on a scale that spans from 0 to 14. Turbidity measures the concentration of small particles that are suspended in water and cannot be seen. High turbidity levels can raise the risk of water-borne illnesses like diarrhea and cholera. Lower turbidity levels indicate water that is clearer. Temperature sensors measure the thermal condition of water, while flow sensors monitor the quantity of water flowing through a system. The manual collecting of water samples from various locations is one of the classic techniques of monitoring water quality. Since the employed systems have the ability to replace manual monitoring, water monitoring technologies have prepared a revolutionary advance and gained acceptance for water sources and water plant management. Online water monitoring systems are required since current laboratory-based solutions are ineffective and do not provide the same level of real-time public safety [22]. Numerous Internet-of-Things (IoT) driven water monitoring resolutions have recently been developed, driven by the advancements in IoT [23–26]. The bulk of commercial systems have shown higher efficiency compared to earlier systems built on outdated technologies [27]. However, these technologies are either extremely expensive or their architectures are unavailable to the general public [23–29]. As a reason, only developed nations have had access to such commercial systems. This action sparked numerous research to develop an affordable and trustworthy, smart water monitoring solution powered by the Internet of Things that aims to make use of the existing communication infrastructure for smart applications [30, 31].

1.2 Water Existing Concerns

Oceans contain 97% of the earth's water, however, due to its high salt content, this water is not directly beneficial for agriculture, people, or plants [16]. Freshwater makes up just 3% of the total amount of water on Earth [32]. Around 69% of it is also contained in glaciers and the polar ice caps. Additionally, groundwater makes up around 30% of all the water resources. As a result, only 1% of freshwater is usable by people [33, 34]. Freshwater is currently under extreme stress due to numerous issues, including its scarcity [36–38].

1.2.1 Groundwater Depletion

There is groundwater everywhere on Earth, although it is dispersed unevenly by nature, according to the literature [33, 35]. Under the surface of the earth, there is groundwater that is kept in and gently travels through the formations of geology (aquifers) of the sand, gravel, rocks, and soil [38, 39]. The water table is naturally discharged from the surface of the earth at springs and seeps in addition to being replenished by rain and the melting of snow, glaciers, and icecaps. Pumps, bores, and tube wells are also used to remove water from the water table for use in municipal, agricultural, and industrial applications. Notably, numerous nations including India, Pakistan, Oman, and Saudi Arabia are experiencing a major decline in their water table levels [35–40]. This problem arises when water is removed from the water table quicker than it is restocked by precipitation. The act of taking more water out of the water table than it is replenished also causes land to sink, increased costs of pumping, quality of water to deteriorate, dry wells, and a decrease in water in streams and lakes. Notably, if public knowledge of the water shortage is raised, this problem may be somewhat reduced.

1.2.2 Water Pollution

Water is the most contaminant-prone liquid because it may dissolve the most chemicals of any other liquid that is readily available [41, 42]. When hazardous substances (such as microbes and chemicals) contaminate a water body, water pollution occurs (e.g. river, pond). It impairs the quality of the water and renders it harmful [42]. When pollutants (such as pesticides, industrial waste, and fertilisers) reach an aquifer, groundwater pollution occurs. Typically, sandstone, gravel, or broken rock make up an aquifer. Due to this action, the aquifer in question is dangerous for human use. Notably, it may be highly expensive and difficult, if not impossible, to remove such toxins from groundwater. It has been noted that a polluted aquifer may remain unusable for a considerable amount of time, most likely for thousands of years [35]. Contamination from the original polluting location can go further thanks to groundwater. It can seep into lakes, streams, and oceans, which causes it to occur [16, 38, 39].

Nutrient pollution, such as that caused by nitrates and phosphates, is one of the most significant contaminants in surface water contamination, according to well-known sources. Undoubtedly, all animals and plants require these minerals to grow correctly, but their overuse in agricultural practices can contaminate water supplies. Additionally, garbage discharged from factories, as well as municipal and private dumps, pollutes surface water [16]. Additionally, natural pollutants can taint water. For instance, when it travels through the rocks, it becomes mineral contaminated (such as manganese, iron, calcium, and arsenic). Volcanoes, animal feces, sediment from storms, algae blooms, and floods are the main causes of natural pollution. Nutrients, pesticides, matter and particles in a suspended state, viruses/bacteria, organics, heavy metals, synthetic chemicals, turbidity, updraft pollution, anti-fouling chemicals, and petroleum hydrocarbons are just a few examples of the many water contaminants that pollution from all sources can cause [42–44]. These contaminants may cause eutrophication and nutrient enrichment, as well as increased stress on the life of animals and plants living in water, a reduction in oxygen levels, habitat modification, and light availability.

1.2.3 Water Quality

Water that has been contaminated can harm aquatic life and plants as well as endanger humans [45]. It might contain pathogenic bacteria, viruses, and other germs. The

WHO [22, 39] estimates that millions of people perish each year as a result of water-borne illnesses. More pathogenic bacteria could develop and spread through water in the future, according to the literature [16]. Some sources of freshwater, including groundwater, may generally be suitable for home use. For different types of sources, for example, water from lakes, ponds, rain, or rivers, it might not be true. For this reason, it is essential to regularly monitor water quality in order to promptly stop any damage from spreading to customers [22, 43–49]. To screen water quality metrics in real time, technical development must be improved [19]. The selection of parameters depends on the physical, biological, or chemical characteristics of the water that is being used [49, 50]. These parameters each include a sensor since it's crucial to help with the right treatment and prevent contamination [51]. As a system for supporting sustainable water management, monitoring of quality of water in real time has been developed. It uses embedded sensors and integrates Geographical Information Systems (GIS) for data collection [50]. It has the ability to collect, update, analyse, store, and present all types of geographic data to aid in decision-making [52, 53].

Smart system for water quality was created by Nikhil et al. [54] to monitor the water quality in a reservoir as explained in Fig. 1.1(prepared based on the comprehensive discussion detailed in [54]). The system helped to protect the water resources' ecological surroundings. It was made up of a number of covertly positioned sensors that allowed users to check on the monitored area from a distance. Arduino is used to wirelessly connect and present sensors through the Internet of Things. They came to the conclusion that the smart system may reduce both the time and the cost of measuring the water quality in reservoirs.

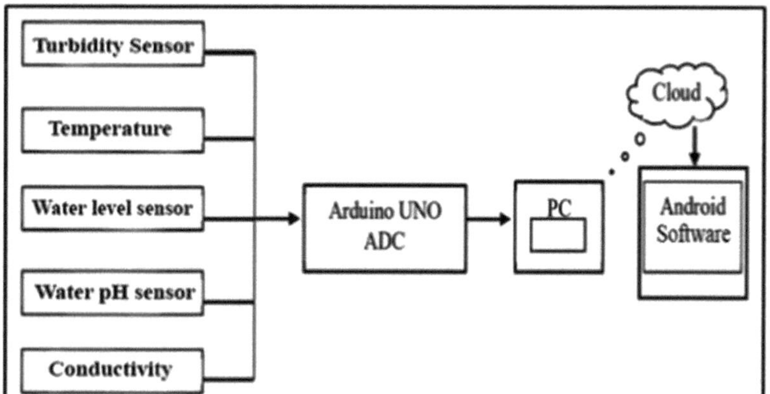

Fig. 1.1 IoT environment embedded smart monitoring system for quality of water

1.3 Water Quality Index

Numerous organisations, like the WHO and USEPA, are continually developing standards and guidelines for water quality. Despite the fact that there is a fairly long list of quality of water monitoring parameters (WQM) [16], To monitor water quality, a select few significant WQM metrics are typically used [22, 54–59]. Based on these features, an index of water quality generates a solitary value that indicates the comprehensive quality of water collected from a particular region at a particular time. It seems somewhat logical that a single number would not accurately capture the full picture of water quality since the major goal of WQI is to convert complex data of water quality into some comprehendible form of information. It's because when computing it, a significant number of WQM factors are typically neglected. It essentially provides a broad overview of the total water quality.

1.3.1 Common WQI Parameters for Domestic Water

To calculate the WQI of drinking water, communities around the world employ various sets of USEPA and WHO-recommended WQM criteria [22, 43]. When determining the water quality using traditional laboratory-based techniques, some WQI metrics [22–25] include, Faecal Coliform (FC), Chloride (Cl), Total Coliform (TC), Aggregate Suspended Solids (TSS), Reduction-Oxidation Potential (ORP), Total Dissolved Solids (TDS), Aggregate Hardness (TH), Aggregate Solids (TS), Electrical conductivity (EC), Temperature (T), Potential of Hydrogen (pH), Turbidity (Turb), Free Chlorine (F-Cl), Total Chlorine (T-Cl), Combined Chlorine (C-Cl), Dissolved Oxygen (DO).

1.4 Water Quality Monitoring Sensors

Surroundings and transmit the data or information it has collected to other electronic devices, including implanted microprocessors [51]. Water has chemical, biological, and physical characteristics that can all be detected by WQM sensors. It is known that the WQI contains about 100 water quality-related metrics [18]. WHO/USEPA recommends a limited number of these measures to assess the quality of drinking water [22–25, 43]. This makes sense because the commercial market cannot possibly provide sensors for every characteristic. Fortunately, there is a high connection between most WQM measures in Table 1.1.

Table 1.1 Sensors of water quality monitoring for IoT-WQMS

Comments	Parameters	References
A Xylem brand, completely condensed electronics	T	[60]
A Xylem brand, completely condensed electronics	DO	
A Xylem brand, completely condensed electronics	ORP	
A Xylem brand, completely condensed electronics	Turb	
A Xylem brand, completely condensed electronics	EC	
A Xylem brand, completely condensed electronics	pH	
Product of electro-chemical devices	Free-Cl	[61]
Multi algorithmic probe. It slanders fluorescence to screen C.O.D., T.O.C., B.O.D. and total coliforms (and disparities there upon) in real time.	E-Coli.	[62]

According to this reasoning, the WQM parameters that are most frequently employed in IoT-WQMS are pH, Turb (turbidity), reduction-oxidation potential, free-Cl, electrical conductivity, DO, E-Coli and temperature (T). Table 1.1 lists various available WQM sensors that are suggested for these parameters. Besides individual sensors, multiparameter sensor modules are also available on the market [24, 25].

1.5 Methodology

Environmental telemonitoring has significantly advanced thanks to recent breakthroughs in technology, detecting improvements, and Internet of Things (IoT). Research institutes have generally organised stationary stations or drifts with capacities for computerised estimation, logging of data, and wireless broadcast in the field of aquatic monitoring [63, 64]. Since WQI primarily depends on characteristics like turbidity, pH, temperature, salinity, and dissolved oxygen, these are measured. First, we interact with Arduino by connecting sensors (turbidity, pH, dissolved oxygen, temperature, and electrical conductivity). ADC is a procedure that transforms analogue data obtained from sensors into digitalized data (real-world data) (analogue-digital converter). Arduino is used to process this data. Then, using serial communication between Arduino and NodeMCU, all processed data is sent to NodeMCU.

Character-by-character transmission is how we conveying data. After that, divide the entire string of data into individual data. Parameter data is processed before being sent to Firebase's Realtime database. We export data in json format from the Firebase cloud store and display it on our own website. The web system handles the statistical and decision-making components.

pH Sensor: The pH of an allowing users to find whether it is alkaline or acidic. The scale of pH is a logarithmic scale with a nonaligned point of 7, and its range is 0–14. A basic solution is indicated by a number over 7, whilst an acidic solution is indicated by a value below 7. It runs on a 5 V power supply and is easy to connect to an Arduino. pH levels should be between 6 and 8.5.

Turbidity Sensor: Turbidity measures the opacity or lack of clarity in water, showing the degree to which visibility has been diminished. This attribute is frequently employed as a gauge of water quality. Increased turbidity can hinder the transmission of light, which is crucial for the development of submerged vegetation. Moreover, the proximity of particles in the vicinity can intensify the assimilation of solar heat, potentially resulting in an elevation of the water's surface temperature.

Temperature Sensor: Warmness or coldness of the water is evaluated by monitoring the temperature. The temperature gradient of the DS18B20 temperature probe is –55 to +125 °C. The findings from this digital temperature sensor are precise.

Flow Sensor: The measurement of water flow rate is determined by utilising a flow sensor, which commonly consists of a plastic valve casing, a rotating rotor, and a Hall Effect sensor. When water flows through the valve, it induces the rotor to rotate. The rotational speed of the rotor is directly proportional to the rate of water flow—an increase in water flow results in a corresponding increase in the speed of the rotor. Similarly, the Hall Effect sensor produces an electric signal for every full turn of the rotor, allowing for the quantification of flow rate.

Arduino Uno: The Arduino microcontroller board is modelled on the ATmega328P. It has a power jack, a USB port, a reset button, an ICSP header, six analogue inputs, a 16 MHz quartz crystal, 16 input/output pins, and 6 of which can be used as PWM outputs. The microcontroller is accompanied by every component that is essential. The software (IDE) for Arduino has since evolved from its older iterations to its more prominent releases. The Uno board, the first of a succession of USB Arduino boards, serves as the baseline design for the ecosystem.

Wifi Module: The ESP8266 Wi-Fi Module is, a conscience SOC with an integral TCP/IP protocol, that enables any microcontroller to interface to the Wi-Fi network. The ESP8266 is capable of accommodating an application or delegating all Wi-Fi networking operations to another application processor. Each ESP8266 module comes pre-programmed with an AT command set firmware. An affordable pricing board with a large and constantly expanding community is the ESP8266 module.

1.6 Systems For Monitoring of Water Quality

The first layer of the Internet of Things system, Layer 1, is primarily responsible for the collection and generation of data about things via sensor nodes. An overview of water monitoring methods, from WSN through WSN and machine learning to smart monitoring, is provided in this section.

1.6.1 Water Quality Monitoring Schemes

As previously elaborated, humans place a great demand on keeping water quality at a suggested level. Humans have created a variety of water quality monitoring programmes in this context, which are highlighted in the text that follows.

WSN-Based Water Quality Monitoring: The following describes how WSN-based water quality monitoring systems [22, 65] operate:

- First, a mobile sensor (such as a pH sensor) put on-site is read by an embedded microprocessor-based device (also known as a node).
- The obtained data is then processed locally if necessary.
- Via a wireless communication medium (such as ZigBee, Wi-Fi, or LoRaWAN), it transports data to a core station (such as a server computer), where all the needed processing followed by analysis is then finished.
- The results must then be updated, and if necessary, feedback must be sent to the appropriate customers or water authorities.

Machine Learning (ML) and WSN Technology Driven Water Quality Monitoring: Although WSN has improved various problems with earlier systems, modern systems still have drawbacks, such as high energy needs, slow communication speeds, lax security, high installation/maintenance costs, storage problems, etc. Researchers used ML algorithms in parallel to evaluate water quality using a limited set of WQM metrics and forecast future changes [22, 27, 66, 67]. Without a doubt, this action significantly increased the effectiveness of WSN systems, but the majority of the aforementioned problems-such as infrastructure costs and spatial resolution remain unaddressed.

- IoT technology application was used by researchers. Using a mix of mobile sensor devices, communication medium (such protocols of TCP/IP), devices for digital computing and internet amenities, water may be scrutinised in real time from any point in the sphere with IoT [68, 69]. IoT-based water quality analysis is also referred to as "smart water quality monitoring" [70, 71]. These systems have been put in place to keep an eye on the quality of water used for home purposes [25, 72–78], water used in agriculture [79, 80] and aquaculture [79–83], and municipal trash recycling [80], among other things. These structures also keep an eye on the eminence of the water in lakes [?], rivers [91] etc. IoT-WQMS visually fixed numerous problems compared to earlier water monitoring systems. Its principal contributions are highlighted in the text below:

- Low-cost: Because this technology makes use of already-existing, commercially available communication infrastructure, creating an IoT-WQMS is less expensive overall.
- Greater spatial resolution: Since the Internet serves as the foundation of IoT technology, there should ideally be no spatial restrictions.
- Low computational costs: Cloud servers, such as the Ubidots IoT-Platform [92], typically handle heavy computational workloads. This law allows for the use of any common processor-based node instead of a high-tech computer such as the Raspberry Pi 4 Model-B, DE1-SoC FPGA board, etc. by developers [58].
- Low energy needs: Local nodes must execute little activities and spend the most of their time in sleep mode after shifting the bulk of their computing workload to a cloud server. This action made it simple for a modest battery to run Sensor's nodes in outlying locations.
- Real-time feedback provision: These systems are capable of giving real-time feedback by SMS, email, Twitter, Facebook, and other channels to both end users and the appropriate water authority.
- Better quality of water: Developers can quickly incorporate analytical tools (such machine learning techniques) into a cloud server to deduce certain WQM characteristics evaluated from measured values of parameters of WQM utilising sensor devices. Additionally, ML approaches could be used to forecast future water trends [90].

1.6.2 A Typical Model of IoT-WQMS

A common IoT-WQMS encompasses of four elementary modules as described subsequently.

Sensors Layer Module (SLM): It is essential to an IoT-WQMS' overall effectiveness because the output of all other succeeding modules is very dependent on it. As a result, any issue (such as sensor biofouling) with this module could result in erroneous reporting of the water quality [24]. When sensors are submerged in water, biofouling, also known as biological fouling, occurs on the surface of the devices. Typically, an SLM has three submodules: the Communication-module (SLM-CM), the Digital based module (SLM-DM), the Sensors based module (SLM-SM), and SLM-SM momentarily reads information and data from sensors of WQM first (e.g. Turb), then analyses data, updates any local demonstration tool and directs it to the SLM-CM, which leads data and information to a target server of cloud (for example Ubidots IoT-Platform [91]) using a GSM/GPRS modem or a nearby Wi-Fi network. Be aware that many kits available commercially, feature SLM-SM, SLM-CM, and SLM-DM modules that are altogether assembled on the same board of printed circuit. Otherwise, another microprocessor-based electronic kit, such as an Arduino, might be connected to a communication shield (such as a SIM900 GPRS/GSM shield with DTMF capabilities or an ESP8266 transceiver module).

Gateway Module (GWM): Since SLM is in charge of sending data to a local gateway, or GWM, A gateway enables communication from one network or device to another or from one network to the cloud. Although it could be expensive, developers are urged to adopt freshly created IoT gateways for best performance and excellent security [93]. These gateways have the capacity to carry out a wide range of crucial tasks, including device connectivity, protocol translation, upgrading, security, data filtering, management, processing, etc. Developers can also utilise a DTMF-empowered SIM900 GSM/GPRS safeguard to send data to a cloud-based server if a local gateway is not available.

Cloud Services Module (CSM): It offers a versatile, effective, and scalable paradigm for delivering the infrastructure and services needed to power IoT-enabled applications and devices. Multiple cloud services are even now available on the market for this issue, like the Adafruit, Blynk, and Ubidots IoT-Platforms. These available platforms make it simple for developers to store, view, and analyse sensor data. Additionally, IoT devices (like a water pump) could be accessed and handled more easily [92]. In the event that an anomaly is found, servers are able to forecast future water quality trends and alert users (for example, via social media platforms). Notably, the majority of these cloud services are chargeable to consumers.

User Interface Module (UIM): The majority of modern cloud IoT platforms offer end users an interface. These platforms enable message sending via Facebook, Twitter, email, SMS, and other networks. Additionally, these service providers assist customers through their mobile apps, which are simple to add to a smart handset-based phone. For instance, operators can easily monitor, connect, and operate their own IoT (such as sensors) from any place in the world by installing the Arduino IoT cloud software [93] on a smartphone.

1.6.3 Enhancing IoT Security and Optimization

The security of Internet of Things (IoT) systems is of utmost importance, particularly when handling highly sensitive environmental data. Singh et al. [94] proposed an advanced adaptive optimisation technique to enhance information security in IoT-enabled systems. Implementing this strategy is crucial for protecting the accuracy of data and the dependability of the system from possible cyber-attacks, highlighting the importance of strong security measures. In addition, the utilisation of advanced optimisation algorithms, such as the enhanced Harris Hawks optimisation proposed by Gharehchopogh [95], has the potential to significantly improve the effectiveness and analytical capabilities of IoT systems, especially in intricate network settings like social and environmental monitoring.

1.7 Review of Domestic Water IoT-WQMS

First, using any search engine, the websites of various journals, and other sources, the writers downloaded a collection of articles for the study. In this case, a variety of keywords and phrases were used for investigating, including IoT-dependent monitoring systems for water quality, water monitoring using IoT-based technologies, water seepage surveys, reviews of water quality, smart monitoring systems of water, surveys of water quality, IoT-enabled domestic monitoring of water quality and Internet of Things-based monitoring systems of water quality. The authors then went over each of these articles by hand, one by one. Three different water quality indices-the DWQI, HWQI, and AWQI-were proposed by the WHO and USEPA. In general, these indices include a wide range of water quality-related characteristics. Numerous such criteria are typically employed while evaluating water quality using standard laboratory-based techniques. Though it might. In order to make use of this fact, the majority of researches [43, 48, 78] concurred on the use of the most well-known parameters of WQM in IoT-WQMS for urban water. The following are these criteria:

- Turbidity (Turb)
- Potential of hydrogen (pH)
- Electrical conductivity (EC)
- Oxidation potential reduction (OPR)
- Temperature (T).

Based on the evaluated values of these parameters, several pertinent WQM parameters might also be deduced using ML techniques. For instance, ORP strongly correlates with the ability of any oxidising/reducing agents to sanitise an environment [96] ORP measurement is an empirical, accurate method that does not require human interpretation. Additionally, based on evaluated values of T, pH, and ORP, the concentration of free chlorine can be deduced [48]. Similar to this, it is possible to determine the dissolved oxygen amount in water by looking at its correlation with T. Similarly, using observed values of suspended total solids (TSS), turbidity and total dissolved solids in water might be deduced [91, 96, 98, 99]. The authors provide the empirical criterion reflected by Eq. 1.1 based on WQM parameters and analytical methods (such as ML approaches).

$$\lambda = \left(2x_0 + 2x_1 + 2.5x_2 + x_3 + 2x_4\right) + 1.5 \tag{1.1}$$

where λ is the overall score of a modern IoT-WQMS. The characters x_0, x_1, x_2, x_3, x_4, respectively, refer to pH, Turb, ORP, T, and EC. These attributes are all binary [99].

Due to the lack of a Thump-rule to ratify modern IoT-WQMS in the literature, the authors empirically gave weights to the variables utilised in Eq. (1.1) that were solely based on their significance. Given that not all WQM factors contribute equally to the calculation of water quality, it appears practical. For instance, turbidity (or TDS/TSS) and pH could be sensed while drinking or seeing the sight of water through a glass. We also gave ORP a larger weight because people who consume water contaminated with pathogenic microorganisms cannot feel it. We gave higher weight than T and EC because ML approaches can infer other significant parameters (such as salinity, coliform bacteria, and DO) from measured values of a small number of WQM parameters. Undoubtedly, this rubric can be improved or modified further, and we intend to look into this in our upcoming work.

An IoT-based approach to track biological and chemical steadiness in systems of supply of water was published by Carminati et al. [100]. The authors placed a focus on monitoring silt deposits on the inner pipe surface in addition to measuring temperature, pH, conductivity for electricity, flow rate (FR), and pressure (PR) (Table 1.2). The water quality can be damaged by slime (which is connected with turbidity), which can also cause the sensors to biofoul. In this study, a new sensor (based on impedance) and several traditional sensors were combined to create a sensing device that could track the inner pipe surface fouling. Additionally, it has the ability to determine the origin of the slime and estimate its thickness. The technical specifications for each sensor include calibration procedures. Notably, the authors included thorough explanations of every circuit, electrical component, communication device, turbine-powered power source, and computing equipment.

This system's editing and simulation were carried out using the Arduino IDE. The whole system architecture can be summed up as follows: The primary parts of this portion are an ATmega328 (8-bit MCU), a sealed lead-acid battery (1200 mAh, 6 V), an LCD, an electric current sensing chip device (MAX4373) and a buck-boost convertor device. Energy is produced from pipe water flow utilising turbine technology.

A smartphone-based water quality monitor system with access to data on location via the Google Maps app was published by Srivastava et al. [107]. The authors included pH, TDS, and temperature in this investigation. Using statistical modelling techniques, other crucial WQM parameters like EC, ORP, and salinity were taken from evaluated values of these strictures. On datasets for pH and TDS as well as other observed parameters stated above, learning models (such as Artificial Neural Networks) were trained. The authors created an interface unit with a front-end using industry-standard components such as HC-05 Bluetooth module, a pH sensor (LMP01200), an exclusive 8-bit MCU, EEPROM memory chips rather than depending on pre-made commercial electrical kits. This module is in charge of reading data from sensors, doing local processing, and logging it. A smartphone serves as the interface between the IoT platform utilising Google Firebase and the front-end device. To address this issue, the authors created a specialised programme for cloud-based analysis. The inferred and measured parameters of WQM were united into a solitary, effortlessly understood WQI value by means of machine learning procedures. The created smartphone application may also automatically calibrate delicate parts for on-site use. Users can receive emails, WhatsApp messages, and SMSes. On comparison of this system's complete conclusions to current work, they are satisfactory. However, if this structure needs to be implemented at numerous locations, such as in a smart city, one major barrier may be the cost of the device. However, using a SIM900 GPRS/GSM modem in place of a smartphone for data transfer between a

Table 1.2 Comparison of modern-day IoT-WQMS

Parameters of WQM	IoT-WQMS SLM	References
Turb, pH,T and TSS	ZigBee kit and Arduino Uno kit	[23]
Turb, pH, T and EC	Built-in Wi-Fi segment of TI CC3200, TI CC3200 Wi-Fi Launchpad board	[43]
pH and Turb	NodeMCU (ESP8266) kit and Arduino Uno kit	[28]
Turb, pH, T and DO	SX1278 Ra-02 LoRa component, ATmega328 MCU and ESP32 Wi-Fi segment	[97]
Turb	ESP8266 Wi-Fi transceiver element and Arduino Intel Galileo board	[97]
pH, T, EC, and Slime	LoRaWAN device and ATmega2560 MCU	[100]
Turb, pH, T and EC	ESP8266 Wi-Fi combined radio transmitter and receiver segment and Arduino Uno R3 kit	[54]
Turb, pH, T and ORP	Arduino Uno R3, Arduino Mega2560 kit and ESP8266 Wi-Fi segment	[67]
Turb and pH	Raspberry Pi (built-in Wi-Fi) and Raspberry Pi kit	[101]
pH only	SIM900 GPRS modem with PIC16F877 based board and PIC16F877 based board	[102]
Turb and pH	ESP8266 Wi-Fi combined radio transmitter and receiver segment and Arduino Uno kit	[74]
Turb, pH, T, EC and ORP	ZigBee kits and Atmega328 MCU based board	[78]
TDS and pH	Raspberry Pi 3, Arduino Uno type card and Raspberry Pi 3 to PC	[103]
Turb, T, pH	ESP8266 Wi-Fi combined radio transmitter and receiver segment and Arduino Uno kit	[104]
pH, ORP, T and EC	GSM element and Waspmote MCU card	[75]
Turb and pH	NodeMCU (ESP8266) kit and Arduino Mega2560 kit	[105]
pH, TDS,T, EC, ORP via machine learning and Salinity	Bluetooth and MCU, but not specified	[106]
Turb, pH, T and CO_2	ESP8266 Wi-Fi combined radio transmitter and receiver segment and Arduino Pro Mini card	[107]
Turb, pH, T, ORP and EC	Ethernet components ZigBee GPRS/3G segment and Raspberry Pi kit and	[48]
Turb, pH, T and CO_2	ZigBee PRO S1 802.15.4 and DE1-SoC development kit	[108]

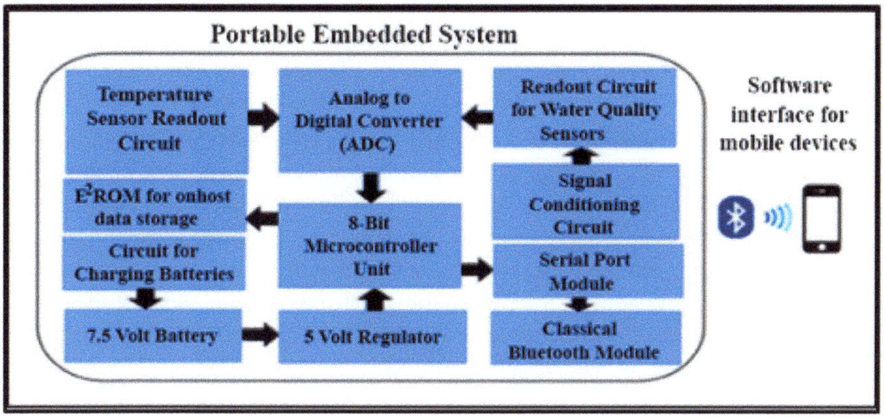

Fig. 1.2 Block diagram of self-powered wireless detection network for monitoring quality of water

Fig. 1.3 DE1-SoC development kit (top view)

cloud server and a sensor module could reduce the overall system cost as depicted in Fig. 1.2 (constructed based on the detailed discussion extracted from [100]).

An Internet of Things enabled method for monitoring water quality was presented by Cho-Zin et al. [109]. The authors took into account CO_2, turbidity, pH, and temperature. Additionally, they used a sonar sensor called the LV-MAXSONAR-EZ1 to monitor the level of water. The authors employed DS18B20, SKU: SEN0219, and SKE: SEN0189 sensors for measuring temperature, CO_2, and turbidity, respectively. The pH model, however, is not made explicit. The DE1-SoC FPGA Development Kit is used to deploy the full system as represented by Fig. 1.3 (constructed based on the detailed discussions presented in [99]). A platform of hardware design centred on an Altera System-on-Chip (SoC) FPGA is provided by this board. A dual-core CPU (ARM cortex-A9) with an 800 MHz clocking frequency, peripheral interfaces, and memory are all integrated into this SoC through a high-bandwidth connection backbone and connected to an FPGA module. The Altera Quartus-II IDE was used by the authors for simulations and coding. The processor of Nios-II softcore found in the Quartus-II Qsys Tools was used to create the control unit that monitors and records data from sensors and communicates with an FPGA fabric-embedded ZigBee transceiver. The control unit was operated using VHDL and C-code running over the Nios-II CPU. The wireless transceiver modules' WQM parameters and directives were processed using code created in Nios-II Eclipse using the C language-driven VHDL languages. On a desktop computer running the Linux operating system, the authors installed the Grafana package for data visualisation. Additionally, every sensor and device pin connections are thoroughly described. Using an integrated ADC module, analogue signal conditioning is accomplished. The authors used a ZigBee PRO S1 module to enable wireless communication between this board and a distant PC. In point-to-point, peer-to-peer, and star/multipoint arrangements, this radiofrequency module can offer reliable communication. In addition to environmental monitoring, IoT systems have demonstrated their effectiveness in several industrial applications, showcasing the wide range of uses for this technology. Kumar and Tomar [110] effectively integrated the SENSEnuts IoT platform with the Bayes decision theorem in a mine control system to improve safety and operational efficiency. This example not only emphasises the versatility of IoT solutions in different industries but also showcases their capacity to greatly enhance safety protocols and operational efficiencies. Research conducted by Kumar Shakya et al. [111] has demonstrated the potential of IoT technologies to be applied in various safety-critical applications, such as environmental disaster response. Their study focused on developing an intelligent ontology model for safety using wireless networks. This adaption demonstrates the potential of IoT systems not only in regular monitoring but also in crisis management when the availability of real-time data and quick response are essential.

1.8 Machine Learning Techniques

As was previously noted, it might not be possible to compute WQI while taking into account all WQM factors. Additionally, the commercial market could not provide a sensor for every characteristic. Fortunately, the majority of these characteristics have significant connections between them (Table 1.2). It suggests that it is possible to monitor some parameters (such as pH, turbidity, and ORP) using a limited number of sensors, and then apply mathematical models to infer other significant parameters based on the measured values of these measures. Researchers turned to machine learning to address this problem [48, 55, 75, 94, 95]. AI is thought of as a subcategory of machine learning (AI). ML algorithms produce a model based on mathematical parameters that are capable of making judgements or predictions based on sample data (referred to as training data) without being explicitly programmed to do so [58]. Supervised ML algorithms are a good fit for IoT-WQMS. Although ML approaches significantly improve IoT-overall WQMS's effectiveness, they have several drawbacks.

- An increase in the demand for technological resources, such as more memory or faster CPU performance.
- The performance of ML algorithms increases with training data amount. The performance of ML algorithms increases with the training data amount.

There are two ways to deal with the problem of extra resources. Developers should first employ a straightforward 8-bit MCU-based card (such as the NodeMCU (ESP8266)) before shifting recorded data to a cloud-based server for ML algorithms-based analysis. The TI CC3200 Wi-Fi Launchpad, Raspberry Pi4 Model-B, DE1-SoC FPGA board, or Arduino Intel Galileo board are a few examples of ready-made kits that they might employ. Developers could ask the international/local authorities responsible for the control of water quality to give them data for training, if accessible, in order to address the second issue. The integration of IoT and machine intelligence is making substantial progress in waste management. Singh et al. [112] investigated the efficacy of deep learning architectures based on transfer learning for garbage classification. Their research suggests that combining IoT with sophisticated machine learning techniques can improve data analysis and decision-making in urban trash management systems, leading to increased efficiency and sustainability. These integrations demonstrate how machine learning may improve the processing of data and the ability to make predictions within IoT frameworks. Machine learning has made notable strides in improving IoT applications beyond conventional monitoring systems in recent developments. An example of how Generative Adversarial Networks (GANs) can be used is in creating artificial data to train machine learning models. This helps address the problem of not having enough labelled datasets for environmental monitoring. Empirical evidence has demonstrated that this approach enhances the predicted precision of models in situations where there is a scarcity or high cost associated with obtaining real-world data [113]. Moreover, reinforcement learning has become a potent technique for making dynamic decisions in IoT systems. Recent research has employed reinforcement learning to enhance the performance of IoT devices by using real-time environmental data. This approach aims to decrease energy usage and enhance response times in smart water management systems [114]. These advancements not only enhance the capabilities of IoT in environmental applications but also create new opportunities for sustainable and effective resource management.

1.9 Conclusion

This study introduces readers to the concerns related to existing water on the globe, including its source, contaminant levels, subsurface water shortages, and seawater desalination. Additionally, it provides information on the WHO-recommended water quality index, widely used index parameters of water quality and permitted potable water standards. After that, it briefs about the WQM sensors and details about water monitoring from WSN-based monitoring intelligent water monitoring

It briefly describes a typical IoT-depended monitoring system of water quality for the comfort of readers and its four basic modules. After that, it provides a thorough analysis of current IoT-WQMS for home water. In this matter, numerous crucial factors are discussed and compared. Regarding IoT-WQMS, a thorough technical description and analysis are provided. Finally, the authors provided a series of practical suggestions for developing an effective IoT-WQMS for residential water. This study is beneficial for the research community focusing on smart water monitoring or engineers to develop possible technologies or applications for smart monitoring of the environment.

References

1. Yaroshenko, I., Kirsanov, D., Marjanovic, M., Lieberzeit, P.A., Korostynska, O., Mason, A., Frau, I., Legin, A.: Real-time water quality monitoring with chemical sensors. Sensors **20**(12), 3432 (2020)
2. Sambito, M., Freni, G.: Strategies for improving optimal positioning of quality sensors in urban drainage systems for non-conservative contaminants. Water **13**(7), 934 (2021)
3. Piazza, S., Sambito, M., Feo, R., Freni, G., Puleo, V.: Optimal positioning of water quality sensors in water distribution networks: comparison of numerical and experimental results. In: Proceedings of the CCWI (2017)
4. Nassrullah, H., Anis, S.F., Hashaikeh, R., Hilal, N.: Energy for desalination: a state-of-the-art review. Desalination **491**, 114569 (2020)
5. Viola, A., Curto, D., Franzitta, V., Trapanese, M.: Sea water desalination and energy consumption: a case study of wave energy converters (WEC) to desalination applications in Sicily. In: OCEANS 2016 MTS/IEEE Monterey, pp. 1–5. IEEE (2016)
6. Hofman-Caris, R., Bertelkamp, C., de Waal, L., van den Brand, T., Hofman, J., van der Aa, R., van der Hoek, J.P.: Rainwater harvesting for drinking water production: a sustainable and cost-effective solution in the Netherlands? Water **11**(3), 511 (2019)
7. Gao, G., Xiao, K., Chen, M.: An intelligent IoT-based control and traceability system to forecast and maintain water quality in freshwater fish farms. Comput. Electron. Agric. **166**, 105013 (2019)
8. Franco, J.D., Ramirez-delReal, T.A., Villanueva, D., Gárate-García, A., Armenta-Medina, D.: Monitoring of Ocimum Basilicum seeds growth with image processing and fuzzy logic techniques based on Cloudino-IoT and FIWARE platforms. Comput. Electron. Agric. **173**, 105389 (2020)
9. Zhu, X., Li, D., He, D., Wang, J., Ma, D., Li, F.: A remote wireless system for water quality online monitoring in intensive fish culture. Comput. Electron. Agric. **71**, S3–S9 (2010)
10. Shukla, B.K., Bhowmik, A.R., Raj, R.B., Sharma, P.K.: Physico-chemical parameters and status of ground water pollution in Jalandhar-Phagwara region. Green Eng. **9**(2), 212–23 (2019)
11. Shenoy, A., Shukla, B.K., Bansal, V.: Sustainable design of textile industry effluent treatment plant with constructed wetland. Mater. Today: Proc. **61**, 537–542 (2022)
12. Shukla, B.K., Bashir, M., Sharma, P.K., Abhimanyu, P.K.: An analytical investigation of surface water quality and pollution status in Srinagar, Jammu and Kashmir, India. J. Green Eng. **11**, 952–962 (2021)
13. Daraghmi, Y.A., Daadoo, M.: Smart water leakage detection using wireless sensor networks
14. Min-Allah, N., Farooqui, M., Alwashmi, A., Almahasheer, S., Alsufayyan, M., Altulaihan, N.: Smart monitoring of water tanks in KSA. In: 2018 International Conference on Computational Science and Computational Intelligence (CSCI), pp. 1044–1047. IEEE (2018)

15. Priadi, C.R., Suleeman, E., Darmajanti, L., Putri, G.L., Genter, F., Foster, T., Willetts, J.: Policy and regulatory context for self-supplied drinking water services in two cities in Indonesia: priorities for managing risks. Environ. Dev. **49**, 100940 (2024)
16. de Mars, H., Van Dijk, G., van der Weijden, B., Grootjans, A.P., Wołejko, L., Farr, G., Graham, J., Oosterlynck, P., Smolders, A.J.: The threat of groundwater pollution for petrifying springs; defining nutrient threshold values for an endangered bryophyte dominated habitat. Environ. Pollut. 123324 (2024)
17. Naderian, D., Noori, R., Heggy, E., Bateni, S.M., Bhattarai, R., Nohegar, A., Sharma, S.: A water quality database for global lakes. Resour. Conserv. Recycl. **202**, 107401 (2024)
18. Rickwood, C.J., Carr, G.M.: Development and sensitivity analysis of a global drinking water quality index. Environ. Monitor. Assess. **156**, 73–90 (2009)
19. Sukanya, S., Joseph, S.: Alternative water resources in rural areas: smart solutions for a sustainable future. In: Water Resources Management for Rural Development, pp. 107–116. Elsevier (2024)
20. Shenoy, A., Bansal, V., Shukla, B.K.: Treatability of effluent from small scale dye shop using water hyacinth. Mater. Today: Proc. **61**, 579–586 (2022)
21. Yang, Z., (ed.).: Environmental Science and Technology: Sustainable Development: International Conference on Environmental Science and Technology. Springer Nature (2023)
22. Lambrou, T.P., Anastasiou, C.C., Panayiotou, C.G., Polycarpou, M.M.: A low-cost sensor network for real-time monitoring and contamination detection in drinking water distribution systems. IEEE Sens. J. **14**(8), 2765–2772 (2014)
23. Ahmed, U., Mumtaz, R., Anwar, H., Mumtaz, S., Qamar, A.M.: Water quality monitoring: from conventional to emerging technologies. Water Supply **20**(1), 28–45 (2020)
24. Zijie, F., Al-Shareeda, M.A., Saare, M.A., Manickam, S., Karuppayah, S.: Wireless sensor networks in the internet of things: review, techniques, challenges, and future directions. Indones. J. Electr. Eng. Comput. Sci. **31**(2), 1190–1200 (2023)
25. Syafrudin, S., Sarminingsih, A., Juliani, H., Budihardjo, M.A., Puspita, A.S., Mirhan, S.A.A.: Water quality monitoring system for temperature, pH, Turbidity, DO, BOD, and COD parameters based on internet of things in Garang Watershed. Ecol. Eng. Environ. Technol. **25**(2), 1–16 (2024)
26. Zeng, H., Dhiman, G., Sharma, A., Sharma, A., Tselykh, A.: An IoT and block-chain-based approach for the smart water management system in agriculture. Expert Syst. **40**(4), e12892 (2023)
27. Singapore, Public Utilities Board.: Pan_Ju_Khuan@ pub. gov. sg.: Managing the water distribution network with a Smart Water Grid. Smart Water **1**(1), 4 (2016)
28. Abba, S., Wadumi Namkusong, J., Lee, J.A., Liz Crespo, M.: Design and performance evaluation of a low-cost autonomous sensor interface for a smart IoT-based irrigation monitoring and control system. Sensors **19**(17), 3643 (2019)
29. Nawandar, N.K., Satpute, V.R.: IoT based low cost and intelligent module for smart irrigation system. Comput. Electron. Agric. **162**, 979–990 (2019)
30. Alahi, M.E.E., Sukkuea, A., Tina, F.W., Nag, A., Kurdthongmee, W., Suwannarat, K., Mukhopadhyay, S.C.: Integration of IoT-enabled technologies and artificial intelligence (AI) for smart city scenario: recent advancements and future trends. Sensors **23**(11), 5206 (2023)
31. Bouramdane, A.A.: Optimal water management strategies: paving the way for sustainability in smart cities. Smart Cities **6**(5), 2849–2882 (2023)
32. Singh, D., Mishra, P.: Smart city mission and urban environmental sustainability in India. In: The Impact of Environmental Emissions and Aggregate Economic Activity on Industry: theoretical and Empirical Perspectives, pp. 291–312. Emerald Publishing Limited (2023)
33. Nasirudin, M.A., Za'bah, U.N., Sidek, O.: Fresh water real-time monitoring system based on wireless sensor network and GSM. In: 2011 IEEE Conference on Open Systems, pp. 354–357. IEEE (2011)
34. Ottoni, F.P., South, J., Azevedo-Santos, V.M., Henschel, E., de Bragança, P.H.N.: Freshwater biodiversity crisis: multidisciplinary approaches as tools for conservation. Front. Environ. Sci. **11**, 246 (2023)

35. Mishra, R.K.: Fresh water availability and its global challenge. Br. J. Multidiscip. Adv. Stud. **4**(3), 1–78 (2023)
36. Shukla, B.K., Gupta, A., Sharma, P.K., Bhowmik, A.R.: Pollution status and water quality assessment in pre-monsoon season: a case study of rural villages in Allahabad district, Uttar Pradesh, India. Mater. Today: Proc. **32**, 824–830 (2020)
37. Shukla, B.K., Goel, A., Sharma, P.K.: An experimental study on oxygenation performance of rectangular shaped solid jet aerator having rounded edges. J. Green Eng. **10**(06), 2728–2745 (2020)
38. Iqbal, U., Nabi, G., Iqbal, M., Masood, M., Arshed, A.B., Saifullah, M., Shahid, M.: Groundwater age and origin and its relation with anthropogenic and climatic factors. Water **16**(2), 287 (2024)
39. Ezugwu, C.N., Apeh, S.: Ground water and surface water as one resource: connectivity and interaction. IOSR J. Mech. Civ. Eng. **14**, 54–59 (2017)
40. Schwartz, F.W., Zhang, H.: Fundamentals of Groundwater. Wiley (2024)
41. Reljić, M., Romić, M., Romić, D., Gilja, G., Mornar, V., Ondrasek, G., Bubalo Kovačić, M., Zovko, M.: Advanced continuous monitoring system-tools for water resource management and decision support system in salt affected delta. Agriculture **13**(2), 369 (2023)
42. Prayag, A.G., Zhou, Y., Srinivasan, V., Stigter, T., Verzijl, A.: Assessing the impact of groundwater abstractions on aquifer depletion in the Cauvery Delta. India Agric. Water Manag. **279**, 108191 (2023)
43. Mumtaz, T., Cheema, A.T.: Causes and effects of water and environmental pollution: a way forward. J. Pol. Stud. **30**, 83 (2023)
44. Shukla, B.K., Khan, A., Saikiran, G., Sriram, M.: A comparative study on effect of variation in opening shape on oxygenation performance of surface jet aerators used in water and wastewater treatment. J. Green Eng. **9**(3), 427–440 (2019)
45. Shukla, B.K., Kumar, R., Goel, A.: Experimental studies on the effect of variation in jet length on oxygenation performance of elliptical shaped solid jet aerator. J. Adv. Res. Dyn. Control Syst. **10**, 1037–44 (2018)
46. Geetha, S., Gouthami, S.J.S.W.: Internet of things enabled real time water quality monitoring system. Smart Water **2**(1), 1–19 (2016)
47. Parks, P.J.: Waterborne Illnesses. Greenhaven Publishing LLC (2013)
48. Shahra, E.Q., Wu, W.: Water contaminants detection using sensor placement approach in smart water networks. J. Ambient Intell. Hum. Comput. **14**(5), 4971–4986 (2023)
49. Lambrou, T.P., Anastasiou, C.C., Panayiotou, C.G., Polycarpou, M.M.: A low-cost sensor network for real-time monitoring and contamination detection in drinking water distribution systems. IEEE Sens. J. **14**(8), 2765–2772 (2014)
50. Sridharan, S.: Water quality monitoring system using wireless sensor network. Int. J. Adv. Res. Electron. Commun. Eng. (IJARECE) **3**(4), 399–402 (2014)
51. Ungureanu, F., Lupu, R.G., Stan, A., Craciun, I., Teodosiu, C.: Towards real time monitoring of water quality in river basins. Environ. Eng. Manag. J. (EEMJ) **9**(9), 1267–1274 (2010)
52. Adu-Manu, K.S., Tapparello, C., Heinzelman, W., Katsriku, F.A., Abdulai, J.D.: Water quality monitoring using wireless sensor networks: current trends and future research directions. ACM Trans. Sens. Netw. (TOSN) **13**(1), 1–41 (2017)
53. Shaban, M., Urban, B., El Saadi, A., Faisal, M.: Detection and mapping of water pollution variation in the Nile Delta using multivariate clustering and GIS techniques. J. Environ. Manag. **91**(8), 1785–1793 (2010)
54. Nikhil, R., Rajender, R., Dushyantha, G.R., Jagadevi, N.: Smart water quality monitoring system using IoT environment. Int. J. Innov. Eng. Technol **10**(4), 29–31 (2018)
55. Pule, M., Yahya, A., Chuma, J.: Wireless sensor networks: a survey on monitoring water quality. J. Appl. Res. Technol. **15**(6), 562–570 (2017)
56. Ajith, J.B., Manimegalai, R., Ilayaraja, V.: An IoT based smart water quality monitoring system using cloud. In: 2020 International Conference on Emerging Trends in Information Technology and Engineering (IC-ETITE), pp. 1–7. IEEE (2020)

57. Babu Loganathan, G., Mohan, E., Siva Kumar, R.: IoT based water and soil quality monitoring system. Int. J. Mech. Eng. Technol. (IJMET) **10**(2), 537–541 (2019)
58. Vinod, G.V., Peter, A.V., Rao, I.S., Babu, Y.S.: IoT based water quality monitoring system using WSN. Indian J. Public Health Res. Dev. **9**(12) (2018)
59. Jabbar, W.A., Ting, T.M., Hamidun, M.F.I., Kamarudin, A.H.C., Wu, W., Sultan, J., Al-sewari, A.A., Ali, M.A.: Development of LoRaWAN-based IoT system for water quality monitoring in rural areas. Expert Syst. Appl. **242**, 122862 (2024)
60. Jan, F., Min-Allah, N., Düştegör, D.: IoT based smart water quality monitoring: recent techniques, trends and challenges for domestic applications. Water **13**(13), 1729 (2021)
61. Arepalli, P.G., Naik, K.J.: An IoT based smart water quality assessment framework for aqua-ponds management using Dilated Spatial-temporal convolution neural network (DSTCNN). Aquac. Eng. **104**, 102373 (2024)
62. Nassereddine, M., Khang, A.: Applications of internet of things (IoT) in smart cities. In: Advanced IoT Technologies and Applications in the Industry 4.0 Digital Economy, pp. 109–136. CRC Press (2024)
63. Alippi, C., Camplani, R., Galperti, C., Roveri, M.: A robust, adaptive, solar-powered WSN framework for aquatic environmental monitoring. IEEE Sens. J. **11**(1), 45–55 (2010)
64. Adu-Manu, K.S., Tapparello, C., Heinzelman, W., Katsriku, F.A., Abdulai, J.D.: Water quality monitoring using wireless sensor networks: current trends and future research directions. ACM Trans. Sens. Netw. (TOSN) **13**(1), 1–41 (2017)
65. Karim, L., Hossain, N., Khan, N., Shorfuzzaman, M., Almhana, J., Nasser, N.: Sensor-based wastewater monitoring framework to detect COVID-19. In: 2023 19th International Conference on Wireless and Mobile Computing, Networking and Communications (WiMob), pp. 387–392. IEEE (2023)
66. Gite, P., Shrivastava, A., Krishna, K.M., Kusumadevi, G.H., Dilip, R., Potdar, R.M.: Under water motion tracking and monitoring using wireless sensor network and machine learning. Mater. Today: Proc. **80**, 3511–3516 (2023)
67. Velayudhan, N.K., Devidas, A.R., Ramesh, M.V.: Delay and energy efficient offloading strategies for an IoT integrated water distribution system in smart cities. Smart Cities **7**(1), 179–207 (2024)
68. Chowdury, M.S.U., Emran, T.B., Ghosh, S., Pathak, A., Alam, M.M., Absar, N., Andersson, K., Hossain, M.S.: IoT based real-time river water quality monitoring system. Procedia Comput. Sci. **155**, 161–168 (2019)
69. Rawat, S., Shukla, B.K., Sihag, P., Srivastav, Y., Singh, H.K.: Environmental effects and sustainable hydropower development: a review of deployment research, environmental valuation and IoT sensors integration. AIP Conf. Proc. **3050**(1) (AIP Publishing) (2024)
70. Jan, F., Alrashed, S., Min-Allah, N.: Iris segmentation for non-ideal Iris biometric systems. Multimed. Tools Appl. 1–29 (2021)
71. Kumar, S., Yadav, S., Yashaswini, H.M., Salvi, S.: An IoT-based smart water microgrid and smart water tank management system. In: Emerging Research in Computing, Information, Communication and Applications: ERCICA 2018, vol. 2, pp. 417–431. Springer, Singapore (2019)
72. Kawarkhe, M.B., Agrawal, S.: Smart Water monitoring system using IoT at home. IOSR J. Comput. Eng. **21**(1) (2019)
73. Spandana, K., Rao, V.S.: Internet of things (Iot) based smart water quality monitoring system. Int. J. Eng. Technol. **7**(3.6), 259–262 (2018)
74. Madhavireddy, V., Koteswarrao, B.: Smart water quality monitoring system using IoT technology. Int. J. Eng. Technol. **7**(4.36), 636 (2018)
75. Pasika, S., Gandla, S.T.: Smart water quality monitoring system with cost-effective using IoT. Heliyon **6**(7) (2020)
76. Arepalli, P.G., Naik, K.J.: An IoT based smart water quality assessment framework for aqua-ponds management using Dilated Spatial-temporal convolution neural network (DSTCNN). Aquac. Eng. **104**, 102373 (2024)

77. Overmars, A., Venkatraman, S.: Towards a secure and scalable IoT infrastructure: a pilot deployment for a smart water monitoring system. Technologies **8**(4), 50 (2020)
78. Cardoso Dos Santos, L.: Design, Cryptanalysis and Protection of Symmetric Encryption Algorithms (Doctoral dissertation, University of Luxembourg, Luxembourg) (2022)
79. Priya, S.K., Shenbagalakshmi, G., Revathi, T.: Design of smart sensors for real time drinking water quality monitoring and contamination detection in water distributed mains. Int. J. Eng. Technol. **7**(1), 47–51 (2018)
80. Suwaileh, W., Johnson, D., Hilal, N.: Membrane desalination and water re-use for agriculture: state of the art and future outlook. Desalination **491**, 114559 (2020)
81. Khatri, N., Sharma, A., Khatri, K.K., Sharma, G.D.: An IoT-based innovative real-time pH monitoring and control of municipal wastewater for agriculture and gardening. In: Proceedings of First International Conference on Smart System, Innovations and Computing: SSIC 2017, Jaipur, India, pp. 353–362. Springer, Singapore (2018)
82. Sharma, D., Bhondekar, A.P., Ojha, A., Shukla, A.K., Ghanshyam, C.: A technical assessment of IOT for Indian agriculture sector. Int. J. Comput. Appl. **80**, 11–21 (2016)
83. Lin, Y.B., Tseng, H.C.: FishTalk: an IoT-based mini aquarium system. IEEE Access **7**, 35457–35469 (2019)
84. Raju, K.R.S.R., Varma, G.H.K.: Knowledge based real time monitoring system for aquaculture using IoT. In: 2017 IEEE 7th International Advance Computing Conference (IACC), pp. 318–321. IEEE (2018)
85. Lindholm-Lehto, P.: Water quality monitoring in recirculating aquaculture systems. Aquac. Fish Fish. **3**(2), 113–131 (2023)
86. Encinas, C., Ruiz, E., Cortez, J., Espinoza, A.: Design and implementation of a distributed IoT system for the monitoring of water quality in aquaculture. In: 2017 Wireless Telecommunications Symposium (WTS), pp. 1–7. IEEE (2017)
87. Rani, S.S., Balakrishnan, S., Sundari, V.K., Ramya, K.C.: IoT based water level monitoring system for lake in a cloud environment. Int. J. Lakes Rivers (IJLR) **12**(1), 21–25 (2019)
88. Huang, L., Cheng, S.: Unmanned monitoring system of rivers and lakes based on WSN. In: 2012 International Conference on Systems and Informatics (ICSAI2012), pp. 495–498. IEEE (2012)
89. Zhu, G., Zhao, G., Zhang, Z., Lu, X.: Water quality of water source area in Taihu Lake and effect on water treatment process. In: 2011 International Conference on Consumer Electronics, Communications and Networks (CECNet), pp. 3783–3786. IEEE (2011)
90. Liao, R., Shen, Y., Zhan, N., Liu, C., Huang, Y.: Research on the water purification for reclaimed water resource supply-type lakes by the method of recirculation filtration. In: 2011 International Conference on Remote Sensing, Environment and Transportation Engineering, pp. 5271–5275. IEEE (2011)
91. Yang, C., Wang, X.: The water quality and pollution character in Qing-ShuiHai lake valley-typical urban drinking water sources. In: 2011 International Conference on Remote Sensing, Environment and Transportation Engineering, pp. 7287–7291. IEEE (2011)
92. Jing, W., Tingting, L.: Application of wireless sensor network in Yangtze River basin water environment monitoring. In: The 27th Chinese Control and Decision Conference (2015 CCDC), pp. 5981–5985. IEEE (2015)
93. Shukla, B.K., Maurya, N., Sharma, M.: Advancements in sensor-based technologies for precision agriculture: an exploration of interoperability. Anal. Deploy. Strateg. Eng. Proc. **58**(1), 22 (2023)
94. Singh, S.P., Alotaibi, Y., Kumar, G., Rawat, S.S.: Intelligent adaptive optimisation method for enhancement of information security in IoT-enabled environments. Sustainability **14**(20), 13635 (2022)
95. Gharehchopogh, F.S.: An improved Harris Hawks optimization algorithm with multi-strategy for community detection in social network. J. Bionic Eng. **20**(3), 1175–1197 (2023)
96. Medvediev, D., Khotskina, V., Khodukin, M., Dashko, A., Kravchuk, M.: Development of an Android application for controlling the device on Arduino. Econ. Tech. Eng. **2**, 98–114 (2023)

97. Novianta, M.A., Firman, B., Purnawan, P., Muchlis, M.: Development of embedded system for water quality monitoring using multi-sensors for multi-nodes. AIP Conf. Pro. **2706**(1) (AIP Publishing) (2023)
98. Simitha, K.M., Raj, S.: IoT and WSN based water quality monitoring system. In: 2019 3rd International conference on Electronics, Communication and Aerospace Technology (ICECA), pp. 205–210. IEEE (2019)
99. Zainurin, S.N., Wan Ismail, W.Z., Mahamud, S.N.I., Ismail, I., Jamaludin, J., Ariffin, K.N.Z., Kamil, Wan Ahmad, W.M.: Advancements in monitoring water quality based on various sensing methods: a systematic review. Int. J. Environ. Res. Public Health **19**(21), 14080 (2022)
100. Carminati, M., Turolla, A., Mezzera, L., Di Mauro, M., Tizzoni, M., Pani, G., Zanetto, F., Foschi, J., Antonelli, M.: A self-powered wireless water quality sensing network enabling smart monitoring of biological and chemical stability in supply systems. Sensors **20**(4), 1125 (2020)
101. Ibrahim, S.N., Asnawi, A.L., Abdul Malik, N., Mohd Azmin, N.F., Jusoh, A.Z., Mohd Isa, F.N.: Web based water turbidity monitoring and automated filtration system: IoT application in water management. Int. J. Electr. Comput. Eng. **8**(4), 2088–8708 (2018)
102. Rao, K.R., Srinija, S., Bindu, K.H., Kumar, D.S.: IOT based water level and quality monitoring system in overhead tanks. Int. J. Eng. Technol. **7**(2), 379–383 (2018)
103. Sha, S.A., Pavethra, M.: Smart tank water monitoring system using IOT cloud server at home/office. Int. J. Eng. Comput. Sci. **8**(4), 16748–16751 (2018)
104. Velammal, M., Rakesh, V., Kartheeban, K., Qidwai, K.A., Shyamala, G., Thulasimani, T.: Intelligent IoT-based water quality monitoring system using TD-CNN-LSTM approach. In: 2023 International Conference on Self Sustainable Artificial Intelligence Systems (ICSSAS), pp. 1300–1305. IEEE (2023)
105. Sabari, M., Aswinth, P., Karthik, T., Kumar, B.: Water quality monitoring system based on IoT. In: 2020 5th International Conference on Devices, Circuits and Systems (ICDCS), pp. 279–282. IEEE (2020)
106. Pasika, S., Gandla, S.T.: Smart water quality monitoring system with cost-effective using IoT. Heliyon **6**(7) (2020)
107. Srivastava, S., Vaddadi, S., Sadistap, S.: Smartphone-based system for water quality analysis. Appl. Water Sci. **8**(5), 130 (2018)
108. Bhagat, P.S., Gulhane, D.V.S., Rohankar, P.T.S.: Implementation of internet of things for water quality monitoring. Int. J. Trend Sci. Res. Dev. **3**, 306–311 (2019)
109. Cho-Zin, M., Lenin, G., Huo Chong, L., Prassana, M.V.: Real-time water quality system in internet of things. IOP Conf. Ser.: Mater. Sci. Eng. **495**, 012021 (IOP Publishing) (2019)
110. Kumar, G., Tomar, P.: SENSEnuts IoT platform and Bayes decision theorem based mine control system. J. MESA **12**(4), 901–914 (2021)
111. Kumar Shakya, H., Sundar, R., Kushwaha, A., Thakur, R., Rai, A.S., Reddy, P.K., Sivasubramanian, M., Jaikumar, R., Venkataramanan, V., Chandragandhi, S., Abera, W.: Internet of things-based intelligent ontology model for safety purpose using wireless networks. Wirel. Commun. Mob. Comput. **2022**(1), 1342966 (2022)
112. Singh, S., Gautam, J., Rawat, S., Gupta, V., Kumar, G., Verma, L.P.: Evaluation of transfer learning based deep learning architectures for waste classification. In: 2021 4th International Symposium on Advanced Electrical and Communication Technologies (ISAECT), pp. 01–07. IEEE (2021)
113. Akkem, Y., Biswas, S.K., Varanasi, A.: A comprehensive review of synthetic data generation in smart farming by using variational autoencoder and generative adversarial network. Eng. Appl. Artif. Intell. **131**, 107881 (2024)
114. Campoverde, L.M.S., Tropea, M., De Rango, F.: An IoT based smart irrigation management system using reinforcement learning modeled through a markov decision process. In: 2021 IEEE/ACM 25th International Symposium on Distributed Simulation and Real Time Applications (DS-RT), pp. 1–4. IEEE (2021)

Chapter 2
IoT and Blockchain in Smart Water Management: A Comprehensive Review

Gyanendra Kumar, Pragya, and Sur Singh Rawat

Abstract The Internet of Things (IoT), as the next-generation intelligent network, empowers devices to independently service requests or responses, making it a crucial and inevitable technology for modern-day water management. This chapter of the book provides a comprehensive review of existing state-of-the-art IoT solutions that harness the potential of IoT technologies in water management. The chapter delves into various applications, highlights encountered challenges, identifies research gaps, and proposes future research directions in this domain. Furthermore, the chapter explores the integration of blockchain technology as a solution to manage water services. By utilizing blockchain, water consumption by consumers can be accurately tracked, enabling them to view and pay bills while ensuring the security of their online transactions. The blockchain functions as a shared ledger among different parties, fostering transparency in water management practices. Its adoption facilitates trust-building among diverse entities, offers robust control over the blockchain network, and validates transactions effectively. With this holistic exploration of IoT and blockchain in smart water management, this book chapter aims to shed light on the transformative potential of these technologies in ensuring sustainable and efficient water resource management for the future.

Keywords IoT · Blockchain technology · Water conservation · Water treatment technology · Water utilization

G. Kumar
Department of IoT and Intelligent Systems, Manipal University Jaipur, Jaipur, Rajasthan, India
e-mail: maurya.gyanendra@gmail.com; gyanendra.kumar@jaipur.manipal.edu

Pragya (✉)
School of Computer Science and Engineering, Galgotias University, Greater Noida, UP, India
e-mail: agrawal.pragya11@gmail.com

S. S. Rawat
Department of Computer Science and Engineering, JSS Academy of Technical Education, Noida, India
e-mail: sur.rawat@jssaten.ac.in

S. S. Rawat et al. (eds.), *Unleashing the Power of Blockchain and IoT for Water Informatics*, Water Informatics for Water Resource Management,
https://doi.org/10.1007/978-981-96-3886-4_2

2.1 Introduction

In the future, water will become one of the key resources for sustaining life. As per the United Nations, if water resources are not efficiently managed, they will cause catastrophic effects on life on Earth [1]. Water resources are crucial for many domains, such as agriculture, healthcare, manufacturing, etc. Mismanagement of water supply, exploitation, treatment, and consumption of polluted water may cause serious effects on life [2]. Using IoT and Blockchain with Artificial Intelligence, Cloud Computing, Data Analysis, Robotics, and Machine Learning can become a boon for managing natural resources, especially air, water, electricity, transportation, etc. [3–6].

IoT technology may become a key enabler in smart water management (SWM) because of the self-operating nature of things connected with IoT networks. In IoT, sensing devices collect data and automatically send it to remote processing servers or the cloud for further analysis and decision-making. A typical IoT system consists of devices with power sources (smart sensors and actuators), a communication network (Wi-Fi, ZigBee, Bluetooth, 6LowPAN), data storage (Cloud, Server), user interface, security, and analytics. Figure 2.1 depicts the general components of an IoT system [7, 12].

IoT-based system consists of the following components.

IoT devices: These devices include sensors, actuators, and communication devices. Sensors are primarily used to sense the stimuli of the environment, initial processing, transmission to remote devices, and cooperating with other sensors. Actuators are devices that perform actions on receipt of instructions remotely or locally. Communicating devices help transmit data from sensors to servers and actuators and vice versa.

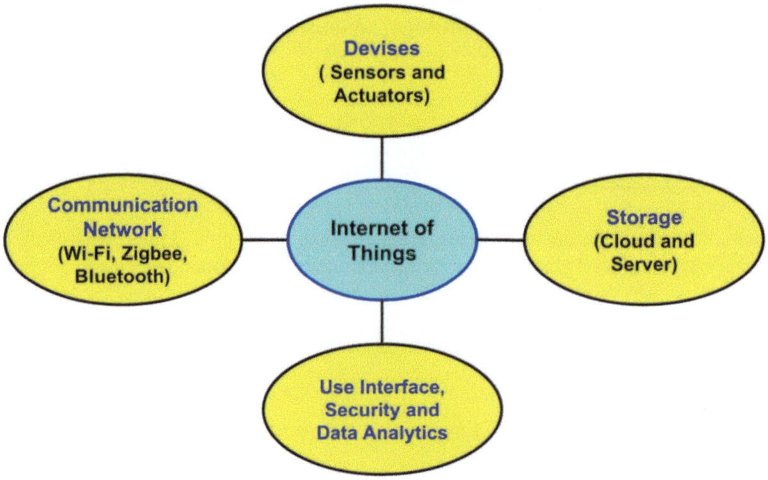

Fig. 2.1 Components of IoT

Communication Network: In the IoT system, deployed devices communicate with each other using any of the latest wireless technologies. These technologies include Wi-Fi, Zigbee, 5G/6G, GSM, LORA, Bluetooth, etc. [10].

Storage: The sense data are processed and stored locally and remotely. This storage may be cloud, centralized servers, distributed servers, or local small storage of devices. User Interface, Security, and Analytics: The end users interact with the IoT applications via user interface in the form of data visualization, secure data transfer between entities, personalization, authentication, and security [11]. One can get meaningful insights from the collected data using analytics in an IoT system.

IoT Applications: Many IoT-enabled applications are available, including smart homes, smart water management, transportation, logistics, Industrial IoT, etc.

Blockchain—In the context of an IoT system designed for sensing, controlling, and facilitating communication among various entities, the integration of blockchain technology serves as a robust foundation for ensuring trusted transactions among system participants. In this scenario, blockchain is defined as a network of distributed entities that engage in transactions and collectively maintain a secure and decentralized repository to record transaction history. This approach guarantees transparency and accountability among the participants in the blockchain. When applied to SWM, deploying blockchain technology can effectively minimize risks, enhance transparency, safeguard data privacy, mitigate security threats, and bolster trust within the system. Agencies deploying such systems can leverage blockchain to establish a secure and tamper-resistant framework, reducing the likelihood of fraudulent activities. This, in turn, fosters a more reliable and trustworthy environment for managing and optimizing SWM processes [8].

Components and Actors: The blockchain system consists of several components and actors, as shown in Figs. 2.2 and 2.3. Establishing a blockchain-based system requires the following components to make it fully functional. These components include smart contracts, peer networks, wallets, distributed ledgers, Event handling systems, etc., as shown in Fig. 2.2. Several actors also play important roles in making it a reliable and trustworthy system; they may be architecture, users, developers, network operators, regulators, etc., as shown in Fig. 2.3 [9].

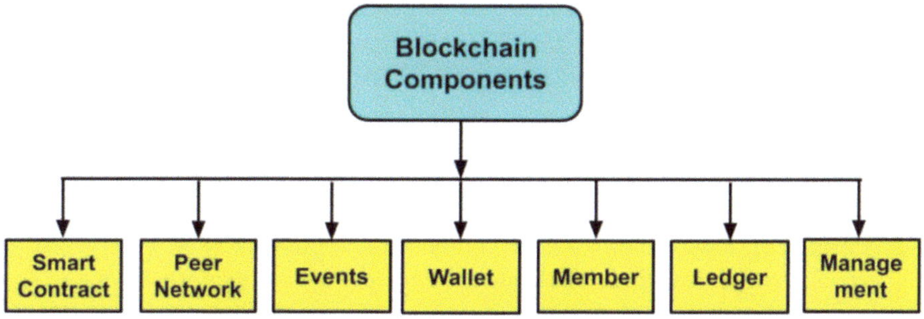

Fig. 2.2 Blockchain components

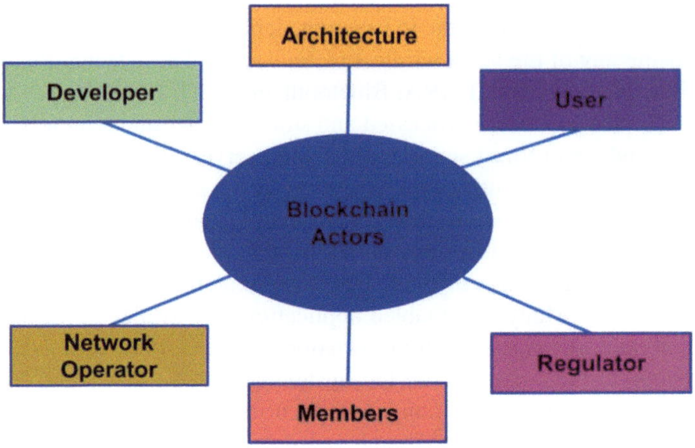

Fig. 2.3 Blockchain actors

Integrating IoT and Blockchain in SWM offers a powerful solution to address several critical challenges and enhance the efficiency of water-related processes. Key issues like Real-time Monitoring, Data Collection, Improved Accuracy, Efficiency, Tamper-Resistant Data, Smart Contract Automation, Enhanced Transparency, Accountability, Water Trading, Resource Optimization, etc. are manageable with IoT and Blockchain. Combining IoT and blockchain in water management creates a sophisticated and secure ecosystem that improves data accuracy, transparency, and efficiency while enabling automated responses to changing conditions. This integrated approach can revolutionize monitoring, managing, and conserving water resources [13–15].

Water resource management faces multifaceted challenges, demanding innovative solutions to ensure sustainability, efficiency, and resilience. This research addresses critical issues in this domain by exploring the applications of IoT and blockchain technologies in SWM. The contributions of this study are threefold, each aimed at advancing the understanding and implementation of IoT and blockchain in the context of water resource management:

1. This chapter comprehensively analyzes contemporary challenges in water resource management, laying the groundwork for targeted interventions leveraging cutting-edge technologies.
2. Building on identified challenges, we explore IoT and blockchain applications in SWM, proposing novel solutions to enhance data accuracy, operational efficiency, and accountability.
3. It critically reviews existing IoT and blockchain implementations in SWM, synthesizing insights from literature and case studies to offer a nuanced understanding of successes and challenges in integrating these technologies.
4. This chapter charts future research directions at the intersection of IoT, blockchain, and SWM, providing a roadmap for researchers and practitioners to shape the

future of water resource management through innovative technological interventions.

The rest of the chapter is organized as follows: Section 2.2 presents the current challenges in SWM, Sect. 2.2.1 outlines the possible applications of IoT and blockchain in SWM, Sect. 2.3 presents the key existing integration of IoT and blockchain in SWM, finally, Sect. 2.4 presents the future research direction, and Sect. 2.5 concludes the whole work outline in the chapter.

2.2 Challenges and Application of IoT and Blockchain in SWM

Managing water resources is a critical endeavor within our current ecosystem, fraught with challenges that span social, economic, technical, and environmental domains. The traditional challenges associated with water resource management have been comprehensively outlined in [16], as illustrated in Fig. 2.4. These challenges encapsulate a spectrum of issues, and addressing them is pivotal for ensuring sustainable water use and availability. From the intricate interplay of societal needs and economic factors to the complex technical hurdles and the delicate balance of environmental concerns, the landscape of water resource management demands a multifaceted approach. This involves innovative solutions, collaborative efforts, and a holistic understanding of the intricate web of challenges that shape the sustainable management of our precious water resources.

To confront the multifaceted challenges in water resource management, modern technologies, notably IoT and Blockchain, emerge as powerful tools to streamline and enhance resource utilization efficiency. However, it is crucial to acknowledge that deploying IoT and Blockchain solutions is not without its complexities. While

Fig. 2.4 Challenges of conventional water resource management

they offer substantial benefits, they may not be a panacea for all the challenges. Here are specific technical challenges that IoT and Blockchain applications can address.

2.2.1 Application of IoT in SMW

Real-time Monitoring: To overcome this challenge, leveraging the capabilities of the IoT is instrumental. We can establish a robust system for real-time monitoring of critical water parameters by deploying a network of IoT sensors. These sensors can be strategically placed across water sources, distribution networks, and key infrastructure points. They continuously collect and transmit data on water quality, consumption patterns, and the condition of essential infrastructure [17].

Leak Detection: One of the critical challenges in water resource management stems from inefficient water usage practices and the aging of infrastructure. As infrastructure deteriorates, it becomes susceptible to leaks, leading to significant water wastage. Identifying and promptly addressing these leaks is crucial for preserving water resources and maintaining the integrity of the overall water supply system. Integrating IoT-enabled smart meters and sensors emerges as a proactive and efficient solution to tackle the challenge of inefficient water use and aging infrastructure. Smart meters can be strategically deployed throughout the water supply network to monitor usage patterns in real time. Simultaneously, sensors can detect anomalies, such as leaks, in the infrastructure [18].

Smart Irrigation: Agriculture accounts for a substantial portion of global water consumption, and inefficient irrigation practices contribute to water wastage and environmental stress. Traditional irrigation methods often lack precision, leading to overuse or underuse of water resources. Addressing this challenge is crucial for sustainable agriculture and responsible water management. Implementing IoT-enabled smart irrigation systems emerges as a transformative solution to combat the inefficiencies in agricultural water use. These systems leverage real-time data from sensors to optimize irrigation practices based on specific environmental conditions, ensuring that crops receive the right amount of water at the right time [19].

Water Quality Monitoring: The pollution and contamination of water sources pose a severe threat to public health and the environment. Identifying and mitigating these issues promptly is crucial to ensure access to safe and clean water for communities. Traditional water quality monitoring methods may have limitations in providing real-time information, making it challenging to respond promptly to emerging threats. To address the challenge of water pollution and contamination, deploying IoT sensors for continuous water quality monitoring offers an effective and proactive solution. These sensors are strategically placed in water sources, enabling real-time data collection and early detection of pollutants [20].

Flood Monitoring and Early Warning: Vulnerability to floods and extreme weather events poses a significant risk to communities and infrastructure. The timely identification of rising water levels and adverse weather conditions is crucial for issuing early warnings and implementing necessary evacuation measures. Traditional monitoring systems may have limitations in providing real-time data, making it challenging to mitigate the impact of flooding events effectively. To address the challenge of flood vulnerability, deploying IoT devices for flood monitoring and early warning systems offers a proactive and technologically advanced solution. These devices, including sensors and weather monitoring equipment, are strategically placed in flood-prone areas to provide real-time data for accurate and timely warnings [21].

Smart Water Grids: The aging of water distribution infrastructure poses challenges such as leaks, inefficiencies, and a potential decrease in overall reliability. Traditional systems may struggle to cope with the demands of growing populations and changing environmental conditions. Upgrading and modernizing these systems are essential for ensuring efficient water distribution and minimizing losses. Implementing IoT-enabled smart water grids presents a forward-thinking solution to address the challenges associated with aging water distribution infrastructure. These smart grids utilize advanced technologies to monitor, control, and optimize water distribution in real time, enhancing efficiency and reliability [22].

Rainwater Harvesting: Traditional rainwater harvesting systems may face challenges such as insufficient data monitoring, leading to suboptimal performance. Inefficient utilization of collected rainwater can result in underutilization or, in some cases, contamination, impacting the overall effectiveness of these systems. Implementing IoT in rainwater harvesting systems provides an intelligent solution to maximize efficiency and performance. IoT transforms traditional systems into smart, adaptive, and data-driven infrastructure by integrating sensors and data analytics [23].

2.2.2 Application of Blockchain in SMW

Data Security and Integrity: Ensuring the security and integrity of water-related data is paramount, especially when dealing with critical information about water quality, infrastructure conditions, and usage patterns. Conventional data storage systems may be susceptible to unauthorized access or tampering, raising concerns about the reliability of the information. Implementing blockchain technology offers a robust solution to enhance data security and maintain the integrity of information throughout the water resource management process. As a decentralized and tamper-resistant ledger, blockchain provides a secure and transparent framework for recording and verifying data transactions [24].

Transparent Transactions: Traditional water transactions may suffer from opacity and a lack of transparency, leading to potential disputes, inefficiencies, and challenges in tracking the allocation and usage of water resources among stakeholders. Implementing smart contracts on a blockchain introduces transparency and automation into water transactions, providing a secure and unalterable ledger for managing agreements between stakeholders in the water management ecosystem [25].

Decentralized Water Trading: Traditional water allocation and trading systems may suffer from inefficiencies, lack of transparency, and centralized control, leading to suboptimal utilization of water resources and potential disputes among stakeholders. The implementation of blockchain technology facilitates the creation of decentralized water trading platforms. These platforms leverage smart contracts and a transparent ledger to enable efficient, secure, decentralized water marketplaces [26].

Traceability of Water Sources: Lack of clarity about the origin and quality of water sources can lead to concerns about the safety and reliability of the water supply. Traditional systems may face challenges in maintaining a transparent and traceable record of water sources. Implementing blockchain technology offers a solution by creating a transparent and traceable record of water sources. This ensures accountability in the water supply chain, providing stakeholders and the public with verifiable information about the origin and quality of water [26].

Smart Contracts for Agreements: Water agreements and contracts can be intricate, involving multiple stakeholders, conditional clauses, and various parameters. Managing and enforcing these agreements manually can lead to inefficiencies, delays, and a higher likelihood of disputes. Smart contracts, as self-executing contracts with predefined rules encoded in code, offer an innovative solution to simplify and automate water agreements. These contracts operate on blockchain technology, providing transparency, security, and automated execution of agreed-upon terms [27].

Tokenization of Water Rights: Traditional water rights systems may lack liquidity, making it difficult for stakeholders to transfer or trade water assets efficiently. Additionally, the lack of transparency in water rights transactions can lead to inefficiencies and difficulties in managing water resources effectively. Tokenization involves representing ownership or rights as digital tokens on a blockchain. Applying this concept to water rights can create a system where these rights are more liquid, transparent, and easily tradable [26].

By combining IoT and blockchain technologies, water resource management can become more efficient, transparent, and resilient, addressing many of the technical challenges faced by traditional systems.

2.3 Existing IoT and Blockchain-Based SWM

Many water resource management systems based on IoT and blockchain have recently been proposed. In these systems, the different parameters of water resources are captured with the help of IoT-enabled sensors. Furthermore, the captured data are analyzed, and appropriate actions are taken either by actuating devices deployed or with the help of operators. The concept of blockchain is also used in managing the different services related to water resource management. These SMW systems are classified into four categories based on their uses: irrigation, domestic, industrial, and miscellaneous [13].

This section of the book chapter outlines a review of key SWM systems in Table 2.1. This table describes the systems based on their category, use of IoT and blockchain, its main functionality, and limitations.

Table 2.1 Systematic review of existing IoT and blockchain-based SWM systems

SWM System/year	Hardware/ sensors/software	Application	Functionalities	Limitations
[28] 2018	Arduino Uno & Raspberry Pi	Agriculture	The smart irrigation system was designed using photovoltaic panels and a combination of control devices	Limited assessment of real-world scalability and comparative analysis between Spruce controllers and Arduino Uno
[29] 2019	Arduino micro-controller	Agriculture	A low-cost automated irrigation system for green walls has been designed. The system reduces energy consumption, increases irrigation efficiency and saves time	Sensor precision issues with low-cost sensors, sensor precision issues with low-cost sensors and lack of comprehensive exploration of environmental variability's impact
[30] 2020	AgriSens	Agriculture	Design of a dynamic irrigation scheduling system based on IoT (farmer-friendly user interface). Based on farmer requirements, an algorithm for autonomous dynamic-cum-manual irrigation is designed	Cost breakdown lacks depth, hindering a comprehensive understanding of economic viability and scalability
[31] 2020	TelosB and the IRIS motes	Agriculture	The full-scale smart irrigation system was developed in a strawberry greenhouse environment in Greece. Reference network architecture aimed primarily toward smart irrigation	Lacks extensive validation in various environmental conditions and fails to address potential scalability challenges for larger agricultural settings
[32] 2021		Agriculture	Implementing a cost-effective smart irrigation system simplifies garden care and reduces water and energy use	Insufficient emphasis on security and privacy considerations
[33] 2023		Agriculture	Implements lightweight cryptography to create secure communication, safeguard data and irrigation decisions, and optimize for IoT-constrained devices	Focuses solely on the Expeditious Cipher (X-cipher) without exploring multiple encryption options

(continued)

Table 2.1 (continued)

SWM System/year	Hardware/ sensors/software	Appli-cation	Functionalities	Limitations
[34] 2022		Agriculture	Implementing hybrid remote-controlled devices integrating GPS and radial function network (RFN) for irrigation system control and prediction	Economic feasibility and scalability of the proposed intelligent irrigation system on various agricultural landscapes
[35] 2019	Raspberry Pi	Domestic	Ensure water supply quality by detecting and preventing water losses, a significant global issue. Implements a network of low-cost, low-consumption wireless sensor nodes in water pipes managed by a Raspberry Pi-based central processing unit	Limited environmental validation and need for Real-time performance evaluation
[36] 2020	Raspberry Pi	Domestic	Enables real-time monitoring of pH, t emperature, and turbidity via IoT sensors, ensuring autonomous control within acceptable limits, accessible remotely for prompt adjustments, enhancing water quality and public health while simplifying user interaction through a user-friendly interface	Full autonomy is constrained due to varying environmental conditions and potential sensor inaccuracies
[37] 2021	Sensors, Arduino processors	Domestic	Efficiently collecting and utilizing rainwater through smart systems reduces dependency on conventional sources, promotes sustainability, and enables versatile applications	Initial setup complexity and energy consumption add to potential challenges in widespread adoption, while limited storage capacity and risks of overflow or contamination could impact its efficiency in managing rainwater
[38] 2022		Domestic	Advance water quality monitoring in agriculture and daily life by analyzing existing models	Grapples with precision in identifying relevant studies despite robust database sources
[39] 2023	IoT-SCADA	Domestic	Novel integration of Deep Belief Networks (DBNs) into an IoT-based water treatment system fortified with Supervisory Control And Data Acquisition (SCADA). optimize predictive maintenance, oversee sewer systems effectively, prevent failures, and manage resources efficiently	Challenges in identification despite using extensive and reliable databases, Time-specific studies may not wholly capture the subject's influence or application
[40] 2019		Industrial	WaterGrid-sense, a LoRa-based node within a smart water management system, emphasizing its application in harsh industrial environments	Limited Battery Lifespan, Environmental Dependency

(continued)

Table 2.1 (continued)

SWM System/year	Hardware/ sensors/software	Appli-cation	Functionalities	Limitations
[41] 2020		Industrial	Smart water meters use IoT, Cloud computing, and machine learning to differentiate and monitor water usage, aiming for efficient resource management.	Connectivity issues and potential vulnerability may disrupt data transmission and monitoring. Environmental dependency concerns for a large-scale implementation
[42] 2021		Industrial	Utilizes data analytics to analyze water consumption patterns and prevent water misuse by providing insights through data storage and analysis	Dependency on technology infrastructure. Implementation challenges and data Security and privacy concerns
[43] 2022		Industrial	IoT-SWM system collects, analyzes, and transmits water usage data for optimized distribution while autonomously detecting faults, monitoring quality, and issuing alerts for immediate action	Cost implications, uncertainties in IoT-based predictions
[44] 2023		Industrial	Combining IEEE 802.15.4g and NB-IoT standards to create an efficient wireless network for smart water metering, estimating over a decade of battery life for high-power nodes. It emphasizes low power consumption	Real-world deployment challenges and limited validation scenarios
[45] 2019	Blockchain	Industrial	Conceptual architecture utilizing blockchain for industrial waste water management. Identifies key requirements for incorporating blockchain in to wastewater management, focusing on aspects like securing edge nodes, consensus algorithm evaluation, security vulnerabilities analysis, machine learning analytics, and smart contracts	Theoretical nature of implementation, challenges or integration complexities during actual implementation
[46] 2020	Blockchain	Industrial	Wastewater management and blockchain integration, implement an incentive model using blockchain tokens to encourage industries to recycle wastewater based on quantity and quality metrics	Challenges adapting to fluctuating costs and encountering inefficiencies when storing extensive data on existing blockchain platforms
[47] 2021	Blockchain	Consumer	Blockchain-based predictive framework leveraging a peer-to-peer network incorporates an intelligent prediction algorithm and demonstrates improved performance in forecasting water consumption	Limited scope of factors considered and generalization of Results

(continued)

Table 2.1 (continued)

SWM System/year	Hardware/ sensors/software	Appli-cation	Functionalities	Limitations
[48] 2022	Blockchain	Environmental	Framework merges IoT, blockchain, and GIS to monitor irrigation water quality in real-time, tracing pollution sources using WASP simulations. It introduces backward pollution tracing for rapid identification of pollutants, leveraging immutable blockchain data to preserve pollution event integrity	Limited sensor coverage hinders broader environmental monitoring efforts.
[49] 2023	Blockchain	Domestic	Automated flow-sensor valve system to regulate water supply, mitigate water contamination from industries and improve water quality	Scaling challenges, integration issues and resource constraints

2.4 Future Research Directions

The intersection of IoT and Blockchain in the context of Smart Water Management presents a promising field for future research. Here are potential future research directions:

1. **Security and Privacy in Water IoT Networks**: In SWM, heterogeneous devices are deployed across different geographical locations to collect and process data for monitoring and controlling the different operations. All these devices communicate with each other, leading to vulnerability in maintaining confidentiality, availability, and Integrity. It mandates strong research to secure and protect IoT-enabled SWM systems, services, and applications. An innovative intrusion detection and defense system is required for the seamless function of SWM [50].
2. **Decentralized Data Logging and Validation**: Integrating IoT and blockchain in SMW promises benefits and requires huge effort. One significant issue is the complexity of data generated by IoT sensors, posing issues related to storage, processing, and real-time validation on a decentralized blockchain. Enabling diverse IoT device data into a unified blockchain network remains challenging. It requires standardized protocols to demand innovative solutions to handle the increasing volume of transactions and data points sustainably. Furthermore, energy consumption of IoT devices and processing blockchain data are also areas of concern. Mitigating these issues is essential to utilize potential decentralized data logging and validation fully, fostering trust and reliability in smart water systems amidst the complexities of IoT and blockchain integration [51].
3. **Smart Contracts for Water Governance**: smart contracts in water management could explore advanced AI integration for predictive analytics, enabling proactive

decision-making. Additionally, incorporating decentralized autonomous organizations may enhance community-driven governance in water resource allocation. Research could focus on interoperability standards, fostering compatibility among diverse smart contract platforms. Implementing secure oracles for real-time data integration into smart contracts could improve accuracy. Exploring eco-friendly consensus mechanisms to mitigate blockchain's environmental impact is another crucial avenue. Finally, investigating the socio-economic implications and ethical considerations of smart contract-based water governance is essential for comprehensive research in the future [26].

4. **Integration with Emerging Technologies**: Integrating emerging technologies in water management, such as IoT, AI, and blockchain, enables real-time monitoring, analysis, and secure transactions. AI algorithms enhance decision-making by processing data from IoT devices, optimizing resource allocation, and detecting anomalies. Blockchain ensures transparency and integrity in water-related transactions, fostering trust among stakeholders. Advanced sensor technologies and satellite imaging contribute to comprehensive water monitoring. Integrating 5G networks facilitates rapid communication among connected devices, enabling agile responses to dynamic water management challenges. This holistic approach holds promise for transforming water management, ensuring sustainable and efficient use of water resources [26].
5. **Scalability and Energy Efficiency**: Water management achieves scalability and energy efficiency by designing adaptable systems capable of handling growing demands. Optimizing sensor networks, employing low-power IoT devices, and leveraging edge computing are key strategies for enhancing energy efficiency. Incorporating renewable energy sources for powering monitoring devices further reduces the ecological footprint. Decentralized approaches can streamline operations, promoting scalability and resource efficiency. Overall, prioritizing these aspects in water management infrastructures is crucial for building resilient, environmentally sustainable systems that meet evolving demands while minimizing energy consumption [50].
6. Cross-Domain Interoperability: Cross-domain interoperability in water management involves creating seamless connections between diverse systems and stakeholders for effective collaboration. Different components like sensor networks and management platforms can exchange information efficiently by establishing standardized data formats and communication protocols. This interoperability facilitates a comprehensive monitoring approach to water resources, integrating meteorology, agriculture, and infrastructure data. Standardized communication protocols ensure compatibility among various technologies, enabling a cohesive water management system. Collaborative frameworks that bridge traditionally separate domains enhance decision-making and resource allocation. Achieving cross-domain interoperability empowers water management systems to operate cohesively, optimizing efficiency and enabling an integrated response to complex water challenges [50].
7. Community Engagement and Behavioral Studies: Incorporating IoT and blockchain technologies alongside community engagement and behavioral stud-

ies can revolutionize sustainable practices in water management. IoT devices can provide real-time data on individual water consumption, aiding in behavioral studies to understand usage patterns. Through transparent and secure data recording, blockchain can incentivize responsible water practices by offering tokens or rewards tied to community-wide conservation efforts. Community engagement can be facilitated through decentralized decision-making processes enabled by blockchain, ensuring that residents actively participate in water-related initiatives. This holistic approach, leveraging IoT for data insights and blockchain for secure and community-inclusive strategies, enhances the effectiveness of water management efforts while fostering collective responsibility for sustainable water use [26].

2.5 Conclusion

In conclusion, this book chapter thoroughly examines the transformative potential of IoT technologies in modern water management. By autonomously servicing requests and responses, IoT emerges as a crucial technology for ensuring sustainable and efficient water resource management. The chapter has extensively reviewed state-of-the-art IoT solutions, exploring various applications, identifying encountered challenges, and highlighting research gaps in water management. Additionally, the integration of blockchain technology has been proposed as a viable solution to enhance transparency and security in water services. Utilizing blockchain facilitates accurate water consumption tracking, empowers consumers with real-time billing information, and ensures the security of online transactions. The shared ledger functionality of blockchain fosters transparency, builds trust among diverse entities, and validates transactions effectively. In embracing IoT and blockchain technologies, this chapter emphasizes their combined potential to revolutionize smart water management practices. By shedding light on these transformative technologies, the chapter contributes to the discourse on achieving sustainable and efficient water resource management for the future.

References

1. Connor, R., Renata, A., Ortigara, C., Koncagül, E., Uhlenbrook, S., Lamizana-Diallo, B.M., Brdjanovic, D.: The United Nations World Water Development Report 2017: wastewater: the un-tapped resource. United Nations World Water Development Report (2017)
2. Saad, A., Gamatié, A.: Water management in agriculture: a survey on current challenges and technological solutions. IEEE Access **8**, 38082–38097 (2020)
3. Lin, J., Yu, W., Zhang, N., Yang, X., Zhang, H., Zhao, W.: A survey on internet of things: architecture, enabling technologies, security and privacy, and applications. IEEE Internet Things J. **4**(5), 1125–1142 (2017)
4. Hossain, E., Khan, I., Un-Noor, F., Sikander, S.S., Sunny, M.S.H.: Application of big data and machine learning in smart grid, and associated security concerns: a review. IEEE Access **7**, 13960–13988 (2019)
5. Hileman, G., Rauchs, M.: Global Blockchain Benchmarking Study. University of Cambridge, UK (2017). https://doi.org/10.2139/ssrn.3040224
6. Lalle, Y., Fourati, M., Fourati, L.C., Barraca, J.P.: Communication technologies for smart water grid applications: overview, opportunities, and research directions. Comput Netw **190**(107940) (2021)
7. Sheng, Z., Mahapatra, C., Zhu, C., Leung, V.C.M.: Recent advances in industrial wireless sensor networks toward efficient management in IoT. IEEE Access **3**, 622–637 (2015)
8. Clavin, J., Duan, S., Zhang, H., Janeja, V.P., Joshi, K.P., Yesha, Y., Erickson, L.C., Li, J.D.: Blockchains for government: use cases and challenges. Dig. Govern.: Res. Pract. **1**(3), 1–21 (2020)
9. Aggarwal, S., Kumar, N.: Blockchain components and concepts. Adv. Comput. **121**, 387–398 (2021)
10. Kumar, G., Tomar, P.: A survey of IPv6 addressing schemes for internet of things. IGI-Glob. IJHIoT **2**(2), Article 4 (2018)
11. Kumar, G., Tomar, P.: IPv6 addressing scheme with a secured duplicate address detection. IETE J. Res. **68**(5), 3371–3378 (2022). https://doi.org/10.1080/03772063.2020.1756938
12. Kumar, G., Tomar, P.: A stateless spatial IPv6 address configuration scheme for internet of things. IETE J. Res. **69**(9), 6039–6052 (2023). https://doi.org/10.1080/03772063.2021.1994037
13. Ismail, S., Dawoud, D.W., Ismail, N., Marsh, R., Alshami, A.S.: IoT-based water management systems: survey and future research direction. IEEE Access (2022). https://doi.org/10.1109/ACCESS.2022.3163742. 10, 35942-35952
14. Park, D., You, H.: A digital twin dam and watershed management platform. Water **15**(11), 2106 (2023). https://doi.org/10.3390/w15112106
15. Singh, S., Alotaibi, Y., Kumar, G., Rawat, S.S.: Intelligent adaptive optimisation method for enhancement of information security in IoT-enabled environments. Sustainability **14**, 13635 (2022). https://doi.org/10.3390/su142013635
16. Song, M., et al.: Spatiotemporal characteristics and influencing factors of China's urban water resource utilization efficiency from the perspective of sustainable development. J. Clean. Prod. **338**, 130649 (2022)
17. Zulkifli, C.Z., et al.: IoT-based water monitoring systems: a systematic review. Water **14**, 3621 (2022). https://doi.org/10.3390/w14223621
18. Thenmozhi, S., et al.: IoT based smart water leak detection system for a sustainable future. In: 2021 Sixth International Conference on Wireless Communications, Signal Processing and Net-working (WiSPNET), pp. 359–362, Chennai, India (2021). https://doi.org/10.1109/WiSPNET51692.2021.9419456
19. Obaideen, K., et al.: An overview of smart irrigation systems using IoT. Energy Nexus **7**, 100124 (2022)
20. Geetha, S., Gouthami, S.: Internet of things enabled real-time water quality monitoring system. Smart Water **2**(1) (2016). https://doi.org/10.1186/s40713-017-0005-y

21. Shankar, B.M., et al.: Internet of things based smart flood forecasting and early warning system. In: 2021 5th International Conference on Computing Methodologies and Communication (ICCMC), pp. 443–447, Erode, India (2021). https://doi.org/10.1109/ICCMC51019.2021.9418331
22. Ramos, H.M., et al.: Smart water Gr3ds and digital twin for the management of system efficiency in water distribution networks. Water **15**, 1129 (2023). https://doi.org/10.3390/w15061129
23. Rani, K.P., et al.: Rain water harvesting for smart water management using IoT. In: 2021 5th International Conference on Intelligent Computing and Control Systems (ICICCS), pp. 475–478, Madurai, India (2021)
24. Mahmoud, H.H.M., et al.: Secure data aggregation mechanism for water distribution system using blockchain. In: 2019 25th International Conference on Automation and Computing (ICAC), pp. 1–6, Lancaster, UK (2019). https://doi.org/10.23919/IConAC.2019.8895146
25. Asgari, M., Nemati, M.: Application of distributed ledger platforms in smart water systems-a literature review. Front. Water **4**, 848686 (2022). https://doi.org/10.3389/frwa.2022.848686
26. Xia, X., Chen, X., Song, C.: A framework of blockchain technology in intelligent water management. Front. Environ. Sci. **10**, 909606 (2022). https://doi.org/10.3389/fenvs.2022.909606
27. Thakur, T., et al.: Smart water conservation through a machine learning and blockchain-enabled decentralized edge computing network. Appl. Soft Comput. **106**, 107274 (2021)
28. Ali, S., et al.: Photovoltaic energy conversion smart irrigation system-Dubai case study (goodbye overwatering & waste energy, hello water & energy saving). In: 2018 IEEE 7th World Conference on Photovoltaic Energy Conversion (WCPEC), pp. 2395–2398 (2018)
29. Rivas-Sánchez, Y.A., et al.: Environment control with low-cost microcontrollers and microprocessors: application for green walls. Sustainability **11**(3), 782 (2019)
30. Roy, S.K., et al.: AgriSens: IoT-based dynamic irrigation scheduling system for water management of irrigated crops. IEEE Internet Things J. **8**(6), 5023–5030 (2020)
31. Angelopoulos, C.M., et al.: Keeping data at the edge of smart irrigation networks: a case study in strawberry greenhouses. Comput. Netw. **167**(107039) (2020)
32. Stolojescu-Crisan, C., Butunoi, B.-P., Crisan, C.: An IoT based smart irrigation system. IEEE Consum. Electron. Mag. **11**(3), 50–58 (2021). https://doi.org/10.1109/MCE.2021.3084123
33. Fathy, F., Ali, H.M.: A secure IoT-based irrigation system for precision agriculture using the expeditious cipher. Sensors **23**, 2091 (2023). https://doi.org/10.3390/s23042091
34. Sangeetha, S.B.P., et al.: IOT based smart irrigation management system for environmental sustainability in India. Sustain. Energy Technol. Assess. **52**, 101973 (2022)
35. Machado, M.R., et al.: Smart water management system using the microcontroller ZR16S08 as IoT solution. In: Proceedings of the Latin American Symposium Circuits Systems (LASCAS), pp. 169–172 (2019)
36. AlMetwally, S.A.H., Hassan, M.K., Mourad, M.H.: Real-time internet of things (IoT) based water quality management system. Proc. CIRP **91**, 478–485 (2020)
37. Rani, K.P., et al.: Rainwater harvesting for smart water management using IoT. In: Proceedings of the 5th International Conference on Intelligence and Intelligent Systems (ICICCS), pp. 475–478 (2021)
38. Zulkifli, C.Z., et al.: IoT-based water monitoring systems: a systematic review. Water **14**, 3621 (2022). https://doi.org/10.3390/w14223621
39. Dwarakanath, D.B., et al.: Smart IoT-based water treatment with a supervisory control and data acquisition (SCADA) system process. Water Reuse **13**(3), 411–431 (2023). https://doi.org/10.2166/wrd.2023.052
40. Khutsoane, O., et al.: WaterGrid-sense: a LoRa-based sensor node for industrial IoT applications. IEEE Sens. J. **20**(5), 2722–2729 (2020)
41. Ray, A., Goswami, S.: IoT and cloud computing based smart water metering system. In: Proceedings of the International Conference on Power Electronic and IoT Applications in Renewable Energy its Control (PARC), pp. 308–313 (2020)
42. Donbosco, I.S., Chakraborty, U.K.: An IoT-based water management system for smart cities. In: Water Security and Sustainability, pp. 247–259. Springer, Singapore (2021)

43. Al Ghamdi, R., Sharma, S.K.: IoT-based smart water management systems for residential buildings in Saudi Arabia. Processes **10**, 2462 (2022). https://doi.org/10.3390/pr10112462
44. García-Martín, J.P., et al.: IoT solution for smart water distribution networks based on a low-power wireless network, combined at the device-level: a case study. Internet Things **22**, 100746 (2023)
45. Hakak, S., et al.: Industrial wastewater management using blockchain technology: architecture, requirements, and future directions. IEEE Internet Things M. **3**(2), 38–43 (2020). https://doi.org/10.1109/IOTM.0001.1900092
46. Iyer, S., et al.: Blockchain and anomaly detection based monitoring system for enforcing wastewater reuse. In: 2019 10th International Conference on Computing, Communication and Networking Technologies (ICCCNT), pp. 1–7 (2019). https://doi.org/10.1109/ICCCNT45670.2019.8944586
47. Li, H., et al.: Data-driven peer-to-peer blockchain framework for water consumption management. Peer-to-Peer Netw. Appl. **14**(5), 2887–2900 (2021). https://doi.org/10.1007/s12083-021-01121-6
48. Lin, Y.-P., et al.: Real-time identification of irrigation water pollution sources and pathways with a wireless sensor network and blockchain framework. Sensors **20**(13), 3634 (2020). https://doi.org/10.3390/s20133634
49. Sundaresan, S., et al.: Blockchain architecture for intelligent water management system in smart cities. In: Saravanan, K. (ed.) Blockchain for Smart Cities, pp. 57–80. Elsevier publishing (2021). https://doi.org/10.1016/B978-0-12-824446-3.00006-5
50. Pacheco, J., et al.: IoT security framework for smart water system. In: 2017 IEEE/ACS 14th International Conference on Computer Systems and Applications (AICCSA), pp. 1285–1292 (2017). https://doi.org/10.1109/AICCSA.2017.85
51. Pahontu, B.-I., et al.: A blockchain approach for migrating a cyber-physical water monitoring solution to a decentralized architecture. Water 15:2874 (2023). https://doi.org/10.3390/w15162874

Chapter 3
An Integrated Water Management System for Smart Cities Using an IoT and Secure Blockchain Framework

B. C. Girish Kumar, S. Nagamani, G. Pushpa, C. A. Latha, K. M. Veeresh, and R. S. Chaithra

Abstract Less than 1% of the water covering two-thirds of the planet is suitable for human use. Water is a natural resource and a necessity for human survival. Water scarcity, which is becoming a global emergency, impacts domestic animal husbandry, drinking water supply for humans and other water-dependent activities, and crop yields in agriculture. Future water use is put at risk, and less rain makes the water issue worse. Studies have already been conducted utilizing Technologies including wireless sensor networks, cloud computing, machine learning techniques, and the Internet of Things to address these challenges. Through the use of this existing research, we have been able to identify various gaps, such as challenges related to the safe firmware updates of field-deployed sensors and physical attacks against sensor devices located in remote field locations. Other vulnerabilities that we have identified include device cloning, network hacking jamming, and eavesdropping. The centralized traditional design seen in water management systems has an issue that makes it impossible for equipment to communicate safely and reliably with one another. We have examined previous studies and created a blockchain technology as a remedy. A distributed, decentralized ledger technology called blockchain helps to handle India's water scarcity problem. With a suggested framework model known as the System of Integrated Water Management for Smart Cities Using an IoT and Secure Blockchain Framework, we will address the opportunities and difficulties in employing blockchain technology in water management systems in this research study. We will successfully apply the suggested framework model in further research projects.

Keywords IoT · Blockchain · Water management · Smart city · Decentralization

---

B. C. Girish Kumar (✉) · C. A. Latha
RV Institute of Technology and Management, Bengaluru, India
e-mail: girishshekar.89@gmail.com

S. Nagamani · K. M. Veeresh · R. S. Chaithra
SJB Institute of Technology, Bengaluru, India

G. Pushpa
R N S Institute of Technology, Bengaluru, India

S. S. Rawat et al. (eds.), *Unleashing the Power of Blockchain and IoT for Water Informatics*, Water Informatics for Water Resource Management,
https://doi.org/10.1007/978-981-96-3886-4_3

3.1 Introduction

Before undivided India attained its independence, the area used for irrigation was 2 million hectares (mha), and out of these 15.2 million ha [1] (mha) of canal-irrigated land, Even though according to current statistics of the total gross irrigated area of 135 million hectares, the canal-irrigated area is only about 54 million ha. War, conflicts, and biogeographic barriers have also affected this facility in the following ways: After the partition of the country into two regions; India and Pakistan, India lost the irrigation [3] land which belonged to Pakistan. An estimated 2 million tons of approximately 62 million tons of water have been irrigated between 1949 and 1950. India has to set self-food adequacy [4] pace and no longer depend on other countries to produce irrigation for which they made five-year plans. It can be seen from the figures that the expansion of the food-grain irrigation system, during the period 1964–1965, to 1970–1971, took place at a growth rate of 3.3%, thereby raising the irrigation area, with the support from Sarma and Roy.

Based on recent observations, India's growing water consumption is primarily caused by the country's population boom. The population of people migrating from rural to urban regions for a variety of reasons, including education, trade, and employment, is presumably growing at an exponential rate, which increases the requirement for drinking water as well as water for residential use and food production [4]. Water was required to produce final goods and to handle the substances that manufacturers were producing, even as institutions expanded to encompass industries across the nation. In many arid and semiarid regions, excessive groundwater use has resulted in a dramatic decline in water availability from both surface and groundwater sources, making it impossible to meet water demands [5]. In some basins, the virtually universal application of the surface water is realized. Industrial effluent disposal is a threat to surface and groundwater resources through polluting the water sources. The effect of dumping municipal waste primarily originating from industrial zones is that water is affected by pollution. Estimation at the time of India's independence showed that India per capital annually availed approximately 6008 m^3 of clean water.

India's water resources were confronted with two challenges: reduced availability of natural sources of freshwater that caused a scarcity and an increase in the need for water for different manufacturing processes, *reserved_special_token_*265, water supply, agriculture, and environmental regulation. The second issue is conflict regarding data sharing because it influences strictly the minimum data necessary for supply/demand.

A scientific database with data on water supply at the societal level is necessary for such a water management plan. Water-related problems and hardships are the source of this pressure that is endangering the world's population. To ensure that the board can support the weight of the water, an overview is therefore necessary. Thus, more powerful, effective frameworks that can be utilized for water measurement and that will encourage greater plant cultivation are required in this situation [5]. The projected security engineering for water management with good frameworks makes use of the systems security that has already been built [4]. A strategy for managing water that minimizes waste and duplication of water is necessary. The management of water resources in India is considered to be centralized now, but it has some disadvantages: Centralization means high costs, low performance, and, most importantly, dangerous storage of data. The researcher's study also has a restricted IOT-implemented representation of these water management queries.

3.1.1 IoT (Internet of Things)

This was seen in sectors such as the cloud computing sector, and data analytics, as well as Moore's law [6]; to be precise, the IP-based networking technologies that involved wireless communication between the sensor, and actuator-linked devices were in play. It includes people, machines, and information and causes a lot of sociological effects in various ways. As rightly pointed out in [7], IoT cannot be explained in its entirety due to the numerous takes and the possible scale of implementation it can be deployed.

Small-scale IoT deployment is the first technique; in this method, objects can be individualized, and they can also sense, act, and program. Gathered ubiquitously, the data is modifiable from any place in the world.

The second method includes the establishment of general communication standards on a large scale to shape objects or devices in complex networks. Objects do not require human interfaces, and rather than relying on a person's real- or virtual-world awareness of other objects, they can locate themselves in a physical or virtual business environment and respond according to the information programmed into them concerning their position, state, or other organizational parameters. It could also be available at any time and from any place due to the advanced interfaces. Using IoT in water management, leakage can be easily addressed, the quality of the water can be determined, security for monitoring water can be managed, transparency in the distribution of water can be achieved easily, and checking on the infrastructure that needs to be maintained can be predicted. Smart metering systems can play a role to contribute for the better management of water as the following [8].

There are also other issues such as security, regulations, and legal issues other than the Internet of Things.

Standards Security and Privacy Issues: Digital information generated and or exchanged is very sensitive; information should therefore be conveyed in a discreet form or manner. Information can also be susceptible to anonymous cyber-terrorism, dos attacks, hacking/data theft, and remote hijacking/holdup. Interoperability and Standardization: Developing an Internet of Things system requires technologies like Sensor technology, Wireless communication technology, embedded technology, cloud technology, and virtualization technology among others.

Regulatory, Legal, and Right Issues: This problem relates to the generation of data by Internet of Things (IoT) devices continuously, thereby posing threats of misusing information, violating the rights of the data users, and legal consequences if the information is stored and used in international countries. Developmental Concerns and the Developing Economy: Regarding the anticipated consequences for national development due to IoT, one can expect the overall elevation of such aspects as the population's social rank, political power, and, of course, economic well-being. To address the aforementioned problems, we have invented a technology referred to as Blockchain.

3.1.2 Water Quality Detection Using IoT

The work offers a cheap method of eliminating water contamination above the tanks in homes. Smart objects are employed for water quality measurement and prognoses about possible emissions in water are made using machine learning. Some of them are interfaced with Node McU in the proposed system to acquire the water properties as mentioned below. Before the water gets contaminated the user is alerted. The concrete approach enables the elaboration of cost-effective interventions and the cessation of water pollution. Other future directions of the project are to identify diseases that are due to various risks; and, to design the optimal schedule for cleaning the tanks [9].

3.1.3 Blockchain

The most recent technology is called the Blockchain, as explained in Nakamoto's article "Bitcoin: The two major documents are", "A Peer-to-Peer Electronic Cash System" (2008). Since blockchain is decentralized, the data may be distributed in all systems and is not required to be in any one system. Furthermore, it stands as unalterable because once the information has been entered into the system it cannot be altered by anybody. Therefore, although an account generated cannot be the subject of a closed ledger, new materials can continue to be added to it.

According to the e-time sequence, blockchain is composed of scattered and linked chains [10]. Blockchain uses encryption to guarantee fast data delivery. The blockchain provides impenetrable, secure, and reliable data storage and transmission. The block is made up of a head and a body. The block header contains metadata about the current block as well as address-based hashing information for the block content [11]. The header also contains the hash of the previous block [12], which makes it possible to retrieve historical transaction data with timestamps using the Merkle root hash. The body of the Blockchain contains information about the data that is recorded in the block. Some of the applications of blockchain are described in the papers [35, 36] (Table 3.1).

Table 3.1 Blockchain characteristics

SL.No.	Name	Description
1	Data decentralization [11]	A peer-to-peer network has numerous nodes connected to it. Chaining prevents data from being stored in a single location at a time because there are no centralized devices
2	No data falsification [12]	Blockchain technology disperses data throughout all nodes, making it impossible for outside parties to access or change the data. Attackers find it difficult to compromise the encrypted data in Blockchain as a result
3	Traceability [13]	A blockchain system creates time-stamped, easily traceable data storage blocks by cryptographically connecting several nodes. The fact that transaction data is precisely stored, searchable from any node, and query able to retrieve any block information from the Blockchain allows for transparent interaction. It is easy to verify the transaction records that are entered at each node because the data is open and available. With this kind of capability, nodes can talk to each other and build mutual trust
4	Programmability [11]	The Blockchain additionally enables on-chain scripting for the creation of application-layer services. This platform allows users of blockchain technology to develop smart contracts, which offer transaction and automated activity security. In a blockchain, smart contracts are a type of optimized and integrated algorithms that are identifiable to both parties involved. As a result, smart contract applications frequently leverage blockchain. Any exchange between a vendor and a buyer could be documented on nodes as an online transaction
5	Data decentralization [11]	A peer-to-peer network has numerous nodes connected to it. Chaining prevents data from being stored in a single location at a time because there are no centralized devices

3.2 Related Work

Regarding the preservation and management of water, there are numerous points of contention in the subject [14]. In addition to these disagreements, shortages continue to be a significant concern, necessitating effective management of the water distribution infrastructure [15]. The main economic sector in Iowa is agriculture, which depends entirely on the availability of water. Irrigation techniques such as farming, cultivation, and excessive irrigation can cause injury and overuse of agricultural land, increasing the area's susceptibility to drought. When there is not enough water available for irrigation, droughts lower crop yield, meaning that agricultural foods are the only source of sustenance for humans [16].

Everyone requires water, but some individuals within particular communities take advantage of it [17] to exchange it for cash and other advantages within the community.

Governments and other centrally organized institutions have control over the production and distribution of water. Users in the municipal corporation's jurisdiction must pay their water bills by the amount of water they use, which determines how the water is distributed. The buyer did not meet their demands, despite having paid the agreed-upon sum. The water quality [18] is inadequate. Stalinized water availability on Earth requires purification at the lowest feasible cost. To acquire pure water, the desalination process is required. The water may contain naturally occurring organic waste and lead micropollutants. Water supplies become contaminated as a result of factory waste emissions. Blockchain offers further benefits in addition to successfully doing away with centralized water trades and prohibiting excessive user data collection.

A distributed, open network that supplies water equitably over various geographical areas [19] can be established using blockchain technology. Indeed, it might be conceivable to eliminate any centralized agencies or middle-man distribution firms that handle nothing but the water supply. One strategy would be to develop a peer-to-peer communication network based on blockchain technology [13] that would facilitate simple interaction between participants and discussion on water management, conservation, and delivery. Stakeholders from corporations, government bodies, and end-users would all be involved on this platform. By doing away with the need for dubious third parties, the Blockchain makes it possible to create a more equal and transparent system for setting water prices [15, 20]. The Blockchain platform can be used to conduct exchanges involving water volume allocated, fees incurred, and excess amount of water.

3.3 Intelligent Water Management System Using IoT and Blockchain

Framework for a Water Resource Management System: As shown in Fig. 3.1, Blockchain-based integrated Water Management Systems (BBIWMS) will be able to solve the shortcomings of the existing conventional framework employed in water management systems [13, 21]. The Confluence layer [17, 22], the application layer, the Blockchain network tier, and the data aggregation and transmission tier in the Blockchain framework are the four components that collectively oversee water resources. Blockchain technology [23] is used in both the Blockchain network layer and the application layer to provide distributed data storage and sharing between nodes and to prevent data manipulation. The code for the smart contract [14] is used to automatically detect problems and provide users rewards or penalties. Layer for Data Collection [24, 25] This layer provides several services for acquiring and transporting live data concerning water resources and integrating it with existing databases. It is dependent on the monitoring system.

Blockchain Network Layer [26, 27] Everyone in the community-water providers, utilities, water users, and wastewater treatment facilities evaluates the results [21].

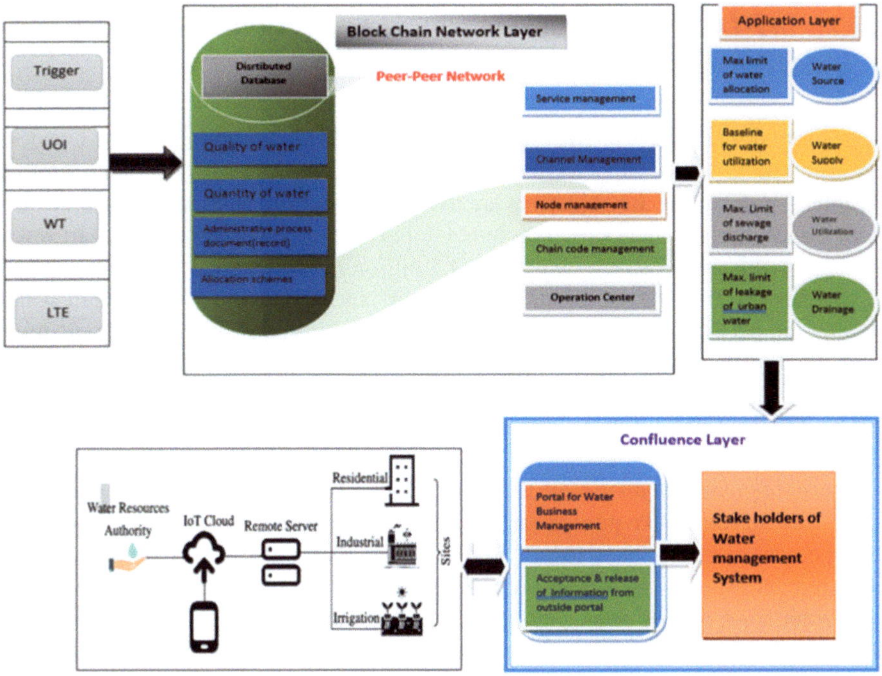

Fig. 3.1 Blockchain and IOT-powered integrated water management system

Every node also has information about water resources. Time stamps are used to build Blockchain successions and create a peer-to-peer network among the nodes. Documenting commercial operations [13] related to managing water resources is another use for this block. Index criteria and planning frameworks are retained in the block as essential data. The Blockchain network layer also manages data queries, uploads and transfers between nodes, and the development of smart contract rules. The operation and maintenance of the Blockchain are done in collaboration with internet service providers to implement the Blockchain service functionalities and streamline the management of the water sector.

In the application layer, four modules are set up (as per the application layer [28]) to oversee water resources, water provisioning, water usage, and water disposal, addressing needs for information services, operational management, accountability, traceability, scheduling, setup, crisis management, and other functionalities [14].

This strategy backs the three red-line management systems: the upper limit of sewage discharge, the baseline of water resource utilization efficiency, and the top limit of water resource allocation [29]. This strategy backs the three red-line management systems: the upper limit of sewage discharge, the baseline of water resource utilization efficiency, and the top limit of water resource allocation.

3.3.1 IoT-Driven Water Management System: Advantages & Remedies

Is it possible that by 2025, two-thirds of the world's population won't have access to clean water? An obvious answer to this problem is water management through the Internet of Things. Its objectives are to lessen pollution, encourage resource efficiency, and improve water infrastructure. Global corporate investment in smart water management is expected to rise from $14.3 billion in 2021 to $53.6 billion in 2031. Businesses use Internet of Things (IoT) sensors and gadgets to monitor their water distribution networks in an effort to conserve resources. Today, Webby Lab will delve more into the advantages of a smart water management system driven by the Internet of Things. We will demonstrate the potential applications of these technologies with real-world examples from our projects, such as the 2Smart Standalone automation platform [30].

In order to manage, distribute, and track water resources as well as maintain associated infrastructure like pumps and pipes, an Internet of Things (IoT)-based water management system makes use of IoT hardware and software. IoT-enabled water management systems use sensors, controllers, meters, and other devices connected to internet apps, mobile apps, and tools for data processing and analysis. All of this lays the groundwork for efficient management of the water supply, including tracking freshwater quality, spotting pollution, and other tasks [31]. How does a smart water management system work? IoT devices and sensors attached to the pipes and pumps continuously gather data on the temperature, level, velocity, and other aspects of the water. After that, they use the Internet to transfer this data to a cloud server for further processing and analysis. Acquiring knowledge contributes to the maintenance of equipment and the efficient management of water resources.

3.3.2 Key Advantages of Water Management Systems Via IoT

Among the parties for whom the Internet of Things in smart water management works well are businesses, governments, and consumers. In addition to providing useful information about water resources and associated equipment, it facilitates efficiency and sustainability. Additional benefits of IoT-powered smart water management systems for agriculture include the following:

Real-Time Analysis of Water Consumption: IoT water management systems use a variety of sensors to collect data on resource consumption in real time. These devices supply the user's web application with the gathered data. This information encourages more prudent water use and makes it easier to examine consumption patterns.

Decreased Equipment Upkeep Costs: Numerous pieces of gear and equipment used in the water sector need upkeep. Businesses can save maintenance costs by attaching

Internet of Things (IoT) devices to storage tanks, pipelines, pumps, treatment plants, and other assets through continuous monitoring and automation initiatives.

Openness and Improved Correspondence Between Stakeholders: IoT in the water supply chain will make all processes visible by gathering real-time data. All stakeholders have access to the data, which lowers misunderstandings, improves productivity, and helps make more informed business decisions [32].

Remote Monitoring: Establishing connections between industrial IoT monitoring devices and the water supply chain allows stakeholders to remotely manage their water networks and equipment. The 2Smart Standalone and 2Smart Cloud systems from Webby Lab enable water system monitoring from any place with an Internet connection.

3.3.3 IoT-Based Water Management System Solutions

There are several uses for IoT water management technologies. Let's concentrate on the main ones.

Astute Watering: These Internet of Things-based solutions enable on-demand irrigation. They employ sensors to take readings of the temperature and humidity of the soil, analyze weather trends, plan the frequency of watering, and, with the data acquired, suggest the best irrigation strategy. Our 2Smart Standalone platform offers smart irrigation features for the best possible plant health and production.

Intelligent Water Tracking: Smart water monitoring systems integrate the irrigation functions and water system integrity previously discussed. They also have sensors to measure water quality, telemetry systems, and devices to track rainfall. Because of all of this, it is feasible to keep an eye on the water and utilize the information obtained to make informed judgments. Our 2Smart Standalone solution is one such system, whose architecture allows several water monitoring sensors to be connected via any protocol. Water management systems driven by the Internet of Things are being employed in many sectors, including agricultural and urban planning. Let's look at some real-world uses for these technologies.

Management of Rain and Storm water

Water flow and quality are monitored by smart IoT sensors that are installed in stormwater and sewer drains. With the data collected, it is possible to optimize drainage systems and prevent floods following significant rainfall.

However, stormwater management systems can control the quantity of storm water released and protect watersheds from pollution. The smart pond technology in Baltimore serves that purpose. This system uses data from the pond and current weather projections to adjust water release as needed. It uses cloud-based technologies from AWS to control rainfall.

Water treatment facilities use the Internet of Things to streamline their purification processes. By utilizing sensors that assess water quality factors including turbidity, pH, and pollutant concentrations, plant managers can ensure that discharge complies with requirements. Companies like Veolia offer water treatment systems powered by the Internet of Things.

Flood Control: Water level sensors can be used to identify floods in rivers, drainage systems, and flood-prone areas. When combined with machine learning algorithms that analyze historical sensor and meteorological data.

Agriculture and Greenhouses: By arranging smart watering of plants in greenhouses or agricultural facilities based on data from soil quality sensors, it is possible to improve crop cultivation and save water resources. By figuring out the water's composition and providing the soil and plants with the nutrients they require, this technology also makes timely fertilization easy. Even more is provided by a smart greenhouse that Webby Lab installed, which is based on the 2Smart Standalone automation system. It keeps an eye on the lighting, ventilation, and heating systems.

3.3.4 Blockchain Technology's Application in Water Management and the Economic Development of New Energy

Social modernization has pushed resource management and economic development to the forefront of social construction. Water is the most vital resource for human survival and development. The increasing issues and inconsistencies around water management pose serious challenges to the sustainable development of local resources and the environment. The growth of land resources and urban construction are the causes of these problems. Apart from conventional energy throughout its first phases of creation and application, new energy is an alternative form of energy. It is the main route for future energy production and has great market potential. Grain production and agriculture may effectively meet their irrigation water requirements through effective management of water resources (Fig. 3.2).

Module for Water Source Management [33]. This module's goal is to guarantee a sufficient supply of water, both in terms of quantity and quality. The quantity of water in reservoirs affects the water supply to various towns because they are sources of drinking water. The water distribution node's block receives real time, time-oriented data on reservoir water levels from the sensors. Information on reservoir water level [15, 33] is compared with control indices, such as the drought limit water level, using an integrated data analysis tool. The results are then uploaded to the Blockchain for

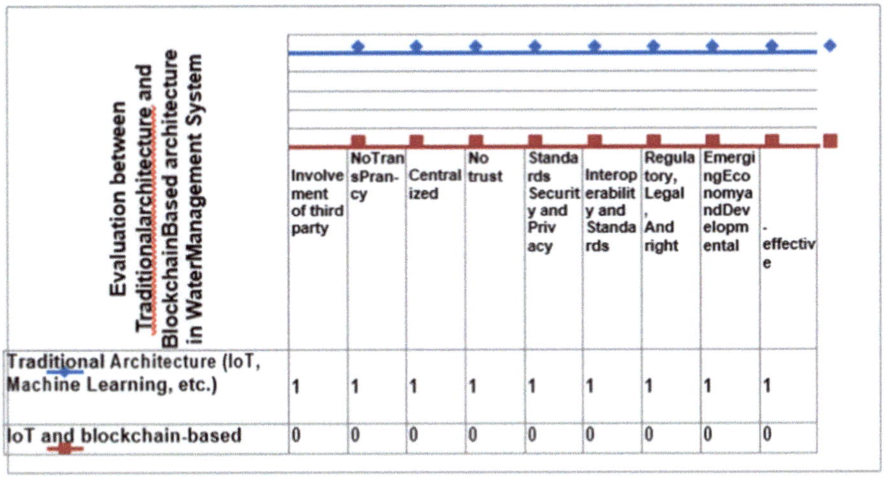

Fig. 3.2 Assessment of conventional and IoT-blockchain architectures in water management systems

storage. Making decisions is another component of the module for managing water resources.

Based on the results of the evaluation, the water supply strategy is improved through the use of knowledge reasoning, optimization algorithms, and other technologies. Additionally, sensors on the node's block provide data for storing regarding the water quality of the water sources. Smart contracts are used to compare the measured data to the water quality targets before uploading the evaluation results to the blockchain. Making decisions is another task that this module performs [16, 34]. The water quality is monitored, and the results are disseminated instantly, to promptly detect any cases of water contamination.

Scheduling changes for water supplies can be made quickly and scientifically thanks to the incorporation of real-time monitoring data for reservoir water quality and quantity. Blockchain technology [17, 34] is used to handle digital licenses to enhance the security of electronic licenses, offer storage and verification services, and preserve the uniformity and reliability of water abstraction permits. To prevent manipulation, blockchain technology also makes sure that data and electronic licenses are permanently stored on the chain. It is practical and efficient to verify certificates using this method. Furthermore, the Blockchain ensures data tracking and prevents theft by keeping a complete record of every license authorization. The public's concerns over security have nearly entirely been allayed by the capacity to track every action. In this paper, LSTM has been implemented for forecasting of electric load [37]. The same can be implemented for water forecasting.

3.4 Conclusion

To address problems including poor management techniques, a lack of trust, and the high risk involved in storing data in conventional centralized water management systems, this study investigated how blockchain technology may be applied to improve water management. Furthermore, there was a suggestion for an Integrated Water Management System for Smart Cities Using an IoT and Secure Blockchain Framework. High levels of trust, safe data storage, and administrative effectiveness characterize this suggested solution. To regulate water sources, water supply, water consumption, and water discharge, it has four useful modules. The advantages of this suggested system include high information transmission efficiency, dependable and secure data storage on water sources, and improved traceability of water purity issues. In the following research project, we will address the difficulties listed below to implement the suggested framework model (an Integrated Water Management System for Smart Cities Using an IoT and Secure Blockchain Framework). Data sharing across departments, legal issues with blockchain technology, and the absence of a defined framework are a few of the difficulties in integrating blockchain technology into water governance systems. It is essential to challenge conventional wisdom and modify corporate procedures for the Blockchain. To achieve the required changes, it's also imperative to interact with current information systems and promote the use of blockchain technology.

References

1. Dogo, E.M., Salami, A.F., Nwulu, N.I., Aigbavboa, C.O.: Blockchain and internet of things-based technologies for intelligent water management system, pp. 129–150 (2019). https://doi.org/10.1007/978-3-030-04110-6_7
2. Paramathma, M.K., Pravin, A.C., Rajarajan, R., Velmurugan, S.P.: Development and implementation of efficient water and energy management system for Indian villages. In: IEEE International Conference on Intelligent Techniques in Control, Optimization and Signal Processing, INCOS2019, pp. 1–4 (2019). https://doi.org/10.1109/INCOS45849.2019.8951362
3. Bordel, B., Martin, D., Alcarria, R., Robles, T.: A blockchain-based water control system for the automatic management of irrigation communities. In: 2019 IEEE International Conference on Consumer Electronics ICCE 2019, no. 1, pp. 1–2 (2019). https://doi.org/10.1109/ICCE.2019.8661940
4. Saad, A., Benyamina, A.E.H., Gamatie, A.: Water management in agriculture: a survey on current challenges and technological solutions. IEEE Access **8**, 38082–38097 (2020). https://doi.org/10.1109/ACCESS.2020.2974977
5. Narendran, S., Pradeep, P., Ramesh, M.V.: An internet of things (IoT) based sustainable water management. GHTC2017-IEEE Global Humanitarian Technology Conference Proceedings, pp. 1–6 (2017). https://doi.org/10.1109/GHTC.2017.8239320
6. Fatima, M., Jain, S., Chikara, A., Luthra, M.: Review on implementing smart water grid for smart cities in-India: challenges and solutions. In: 2019 5th International Conference on Advanced Computing Communication Systems, ICACCS, pp. 216–219 (2019). https://doi.org/10.1109/ICACCS.2019.8728485
7. Anjana, S., Sahana, M.N., Ankith, S., Natarajan, K., Shobha, K.R., Paventhan, A.: An IoT based 6LoWPANenabled experiment for water management. In: International Symposium on

Advanced Networks and Telecommunication Systems ANTS, pp. 1–6. https://doi.org/10.1109/ANTS.2015.7413654
8. Treiblmaier, H.: Blockchain and tourism. In: Handbook e-Tourism, pp. 1–21 (2020). https://doi.org/10.1007/978-3-030-05324-6_28-2
9. Tasatanattakool, P., Techapanupreeda, C.: Blockchain: challenges and applications. In: International Conference on Information Network, pp. 473–475. https://doi.org/10.1109/ICOIN.2018.8343163
10. Feng, Q., He, D., Zeadally, S., Khan, M.K., Kumar, N.: A survey on privacy protection in blockchain system. J Netw Comput Appl **126**, 45–58 (2019). https://doi.org/10.1016/j.jnca.2018.10.020
11. Velliangiri, S., Karthikeyan Karunya, P.: Blockchain technology: challenges and security issues in consensus algorithm. In: 2020International Conference on Computer Communications and Informatics, ICCCI2020 (2020). https://doi.org/10.1109/ICCCI48352.2020.9104132
12. Ozdemir, A.I., Ar, I.M., Erol, I.: Assessment of blockchain applications in travel and tourism industry. Qual. Quant. **54**(5–6), 1549–1563 (2020). https://doi.org/10.1007/s11135-019-00901-w
13. Xia, W., Chen, X., Song, C.: A framework of blockchain technology in intelligent water management. Front. Environ. Sci. **10**(June), 1–12 (2022). https://doi.org/10.3389/fenvs.2022.909606
14. Kassou, M., Bourekkadi, S., Khoulji, S., Slimani, K., Chikri, H., Kerkeb, M.L.: Blockchain-based medical and water waste management conception. In: E3S Web Conference, vol. 234, pp. 1–6 (2021). https://doi.org/10.1051/e3sconf/202123400070
15. Gurudas Vernekar, A.: Blockchain based water management system. Int. Res. J. Eng. Technol. (May), pp. 7505–7507 (2020). www.irjet.net
16. Mahmoud, H.H.M., Wu, W., Wang, Y.: Secure data aggregation mechanism for water distribution system using blockchain. In: ICAC 2019—2019 25th IEEE International Conference on Automation and Computing, (September), 1–6 (2019). https://doi.org/10.23919/IConAC.2019.8895146
17. Tiwari, S., Gautam, J., Gupta, V., Malsa, N.: Smart contract for decentralized water management system using blockchain technology. Int. J. Innov. Technol. Explor. Eng. **9**(5), 2046–2050 (2020). https://doi.org/10.35940/ijitee.e3202.039520
18. Abu-Amara, F., et al.: a blockchain solution for water and electricity management. Mater. Today Proc. **63**, 731–736 (2022). https://doi.org/10.1016/j.matpr.2022.05.106
19. Satiya, N., Varu, V., Gadagkar, A., Shaha, D.: Optimization of water consumption using dynamic quota based smart water management system. In: TENSYMP 2017—IEEE International Symposium on Technology Smart Cities (2017). https://doi.org/10.1109/TENCONSpring.2017.8070075
20. Hakak, S., Khan, W.Z., Gilkar, G.A., Haider, N., Imran, M., Alkatheiri, M.S.: Industrial wastewater management using blockchain technology: architecture, requirements , and future directions (June), 38–43 (2020)
21. Pincheira, M., Vecchio, M., Giaffreda, R., Kanhere, S.S.: Exploiting constrained IoT devices in a trustless blockchain-based water management system. IEEE International Conference on Blockchain Cryptocurrency, ICBC 2020 (2020). https://doi.org/10.1109/ICBC48266.2020.9169404
22. Ismail, S., Dawoud, D.W., Ismail, N., Marsh, R., Alshami, A.S.: IoT-based water management systems: survey and future research direction. IEEE Access **10**, 35942–35952 (2022). https://doi.org/10.1109/ACCESS.2022.3163742
23. Shah, J.: An internet of things based model for smart water distribution with quality monitoring. Int. J. Innov. Res. Sci. **6**(3), 3446–3451 (2017). https://doi.org/10.15680/IJIRSET.2017.0603074
24. Kaur, P., Parashar, A.: A systematic literature review of blockchain technology for smart villages, vol. 29, no. 4. Springer Netherlands (2022). https://doi.org/10.1007/s11831-021-09659-7
25. Kakkar, M., Gupta, V., Garg, J., Dr. Dhiman, S.: Detection of water quality using machine learning and IoT. IJERT **10**(11) (2021). ISSN:2278-0181. https://doi.org/10.17577/IJERTV10IS110022

26. Kumar, B.C.G., Garg, M., Saini, J., Chauhan, K., Malsa, N., Malsa, K.: Accurate rating system using blockchain. In: Shaw, R.N., Paprzycki, M., Ghosh, A. (eds.) Advanced Communication and Intelligent Systems. ICACIS 2022. Communications in Computer and Information Science, vol. 1749. Springer, Cham (2023). https://doi.org/10.1007/978-3-031-25088-0_44
27. Girish Kumar, B.C., Nand, P., Bali, V.: Opportunities and challenges of blockchain technology for tourism industry in future smart society. In: 2022 Fifth International Conference on Computational Intelligence and Communication Technologies (CCICT), pp. 318–323 (2022). https://doi.org/10.1109/CCiCT56684.2022.00065
28. Girish Kumar, B.C., Nand, P., Bali, V.: Review on opportunities and challenges of blockchain technology for tourism industry in future smart society. In: Bali, V., Bhatnagar, V., Lu, J., Banerjee, K. (eds.) Decision Analytics for Sustainable Development in Smart Society 5.0. Asset Analytics. Springer, Singapore (2022). https://doi.org/10.1007/978-981-19-1689-2_16
29. Singh, A.N., Arya, A., Sharma, A., Girish Kumar, B.C.: Contact tracing for communicable diseases using blockchain. Int. J. Emerg. Technol. Innov. Res. **9**(5), j528–j532. ISSN:2349-5162 (2022)
30. Girish Kumar, B.C., Gupta, A.K., Verma, A., Chaudhary, D., Pandey, R.: An encrypted automatic multiple-choice question generator for self-assessment using natural language processing. Int. J. Emerg. Technol. Innov. Res. **9**(5), j337–j343 (2022). ISSN:2349-5162 (ww.jetir.org)
31. Girish Kumar, B.C., Nand, P., Bali, V.: BBACTFM (Blockchain Based Accurate Contact Tracing Framework Model) for tourism industry. In: Shaw, R.N., Paprzycki, M., Ghosh, A. (eds.) Advanced Communication and Intelligent Systems. ICACIS 2022. Communications in Computer and Information Science, vol. 1749. Springer, Cham (2023). https://doi.org/10.1007/978-3-031-25088-0_46
32. Kumar, B.C.G., Harsha, K.G., Mahesh, G., Shukla, V., Talari, S.: BBIWMS: a secure blockchain-based framework for integrated water management system for smart city. In: Roy, B.K., Chaturvedi, A., Tsaban, B., Hasan, S.U. (eds.) Cryptology and Network Security with Machine Learning. ICCNSML 2022. Algorithms for Intelligent Systems. Springer, Singapore (2024). https://doi.org/10.1007/978-981-99-2229-1_15
33. Mahesh, G., Kumar, B.G., Pathak, S., Surekha, M., Harsha, K.G., Raj, M., (eds.).: "E-policing and information management system using blockchain technology. In: Artificial Intelligence, Blockchain, Computing and Security Volume 1: Proceedings of the International Conference on Artificial Intelligence, Blockchain, Computing and Security (ICABCS 2023), 1st edn. CRC Press, Gr. Noida, UP, India (2023). https://doi.org/10.1201/9781003393580
34. Agrawal, A., Teotia, A., Gupta, D., Srivastava, A., Mahesh, G., Kumar, B.G., (eds.).: Land transaction and registration system using blockchain. In: Artificial Intelligence, Blockchain, Computing and Security Volume 1: Proceedings of the International Conference on Artificial Intelligence, Blockchain, Computing and Security (ICABCS 2023), 1st edn. CRC Press, Gr. Noida, UP, India (2023). https://doi.org/10.1201/9781003393580
35. Malsa, N., Srivastave, T., Sahni, U., Garg, S., Ghosh, A., Shaw, R.N.: SMART CITIES: P2P energy trading using blockchain. In: International Conference on Advanced Communication and Intelligent Systems, pp. 682–694. Springer Nature Switzerland, Cham (2022)
36. Sahni, U., Garg, S., Srivastava, T., Sharma, T., Malsa, N., Ghosh, A., et al.: Framework for land registry system using Ethereum blockchain. In: International Conference on Advanced Communication and Intelligent Systems, pp. 431–440. Springer Nature Switzerland, Cham (2022)
37. Gupta, P., Malsa, N., Saxena, N., Agarwal, S., Singh, S.P.: Short-term load forecasting using parametric and non-parametric approaches. In: Soft Computing: theories and Applications: proceedings of SoCTA 2018, pp. 747–755. Springer Singapore (2020)

Chapter 4
Transfer Learning and Transformer for Multi-parameter Water Quality Assessment: A Novel Framework

Sunil Kumar, Prabal Pratap Singh, Vishal Awasthi, Alok Kumar, and Ritesh Agarwal

Abstract The inspection and assessment of water quality hold significant significance in guaranteeing the safety and integrity of our water resources for diverse applications, such as potable consumption, agricultural practices, and industrial utilization. The utilization of machine learning (ML) methods, including transfer learning and the use of transformers, has led to significant progress in the automation of evaluating water quality criteria. This article explores the field of water quality evaluation through the utilization of transfer learning and transformers. It specifically concentrates on significant metrics such as pH value, Hardness, Total Dissolved Solids (TDS), Chloramines, Sulfate, and Organic Carbon. The combination of transfer learning and transformer models may greatly increase the process of water quality evaluation by using the abundant data obtained from Internet of Things (IoT) sensors. Furthermore, we will investigate the potential utilization of well-known transfer learning models, including ResNet-50, DenseNet-121, EfficientNet-B0, Darknet, and VGG16, for this particular objective. Tab-Transformer has a phenomenal accuracy of 94.5%, demonstrating its exceptional capacity to foresee events properly. The

S. Kumar (✉)
Department of Information Technology, School of Engineering and Technology (UIET), CSJM University, Kanpur, UP, India
e-mail: sunilymca24@gmail.com

P. P. Singh
Department of Physics, School of Basic Science (UIET), CSJM University, Kanpur, UP, India

V. Awasthi
Department of Electronics and Communication Engineering, School of Engineering and Technology (UIET), CSJM University, Kanpur, UP, India
e-mail: vishalawasthi@csjmu.ac.in

A. Kumar
Department of Computer Science and Engineering, School of Engineering and Technology (UIET), CSJM University, Kanpur, UP, India
e-mail: alok@csjmu.ac.in

R. Agarwal
Department of Computer Application, School of Engineering and Technology (UIET), CSJM University, Kanpur, UP, India
e-mail: riteshagarwal@csjmu.ac.in

S. S. Rawat et al. (eds.), *Unleashing the Power of Blockchain and IoT for Water Informatics*, Water Informatics for Water Resource Management,
https://doi.org/10.1007/978-981-96-3886-4_4

excellent capacity of the system is confirmed by the Precision, Recall, and F1 Score values, which are 93.2%, 94.8%, and 94.0%, respectively.

Keywords Convolutional Neural Network (CNN) · Deep learning · Machine learning · Transformer · Water quality

4.1 Introduction

Water usage plans, pollution prevention, and resource efficiency may be improved via water quality prediction. The assessment of water quality is essential for safeguarding the security and long-term viability of the water we use. Traditional water quality evaluation depends mainly on practitioners' expertise and visual observations, which introduces subjectivity and observability variations. Utilizing the capabilities of transfer learning and transformer-based models has become a very promising method in this field, especially when examining data obtained from Internet of Things (IoT) devices [1]. Transfer learning enables the model to use pre-existing knowledge from a source domain, such as a varied collection of water quality datasets, and customize it for a particular target domain, hence enhancing performance even with a limited amount of labeled data. Transformers, equipped with attention mechanisms, have exceptional proficiency in collecting intricate connections and patterns within sequences, making them highly suitable for time-series data produced by IoT devices [2]. Through the use of a transformer model trained on an extensive dataset including many water quality factors, the model may acquire the ability to accurately forecast and assess water quality measures. This methodology not only simplifies the procedure of evaluating water quality but also allows the model to adjust to various environmental circumstances, hence enhancing the resilience and dependability of water quality monitoring systems [3, 4].

Transfer learning is an ML technique that entails leveraging the knowledge acquired by a pre-trained model to address a distinct yet related problem. Transfer learning can be a highly effective method in the realm of water quality evaluation. Transfer learning offers a viable alternative to the arduous process of training a model from the ground up, which necessitates substantial amounts of data and processing power. It enables us to leverage the acquired knowledge and representations of pre-existing models as a foundation for further development [5]. The utilization of this approach holds notable benefits in the context of water quality evaluation since it enables the attainment of precise outcomes despite the presence of restricted data [6]. Prominent architectural models, like ResNet-50 [7], DenseNet-121 [8], EfficientNet-B0 [9], Darknet [10], and VGG16 [11], have exhibited remarkable performance when trained on extensive datasets like ImageNet.

The present study examines the utilization of transfer learning techniques in the context of water quality assessment. Specifically, the focus is on evaluating the many factors associated with water quality, such as pH value, hardness, TDS, chloramines, sulfate, and organic carbon. A dataset of water samples can be gathered and linked to their corresponding quality values, which are referred to as features. For example, water with distinct characteristics can be identified by its associated pH value, TDS level, and similar parameters [1–4].

Once the employed dataset has been fed, transfer learning can be utilized to refine the aforementioned pre-trained models for the purpose of water quality evaluation. During the process of fine-tuning, the model acquires the ability to adjust its features in order to better align with the particular patterns and correlations present within the water quality data. The model's output will not alone reveal the existence of specific parameters, but will also offer a quantification of their magnitudes [4, 5]. Figure 4.1 presents the approach employed for water quality assessment and illustrates the employed methodology in the investigation, in it we employed the transfer learning and transformer on the water quality potability dataset and done assessment.

The transformers architecture has garnered significant attention in the field of natural language processing (NLP) owing to its remarkable capacity to capture extensive dependencies and contextual information. Although transformers were originally developed for sequential data, they have demonstrated excellent applications in several domains. The fundamental principle underlying transformers is rooted in the utilization of self-attention processes. These processes enable the model to assess the significance of various components of the input throughout the generation of output, thereby successfully capturing intricate interactions [12]. In the realm of water quality evaluation, transformers have the potential to be employed for the processing of spatial and spectral data [13].

The utilization of Transformers in the evaluation of water quality involves the application of data processing techniques that involve the division of data into smaller segments known as patches. These patches are then subjected to a self-attention mechanism, allowing the model to learn the interdependencies and relationships within the data. This feature allows the model to effectively capture both local and global interdependence, which is of utmost importance in comprehending the intricate relationships among various water quality metrics. The integration of transformers has the

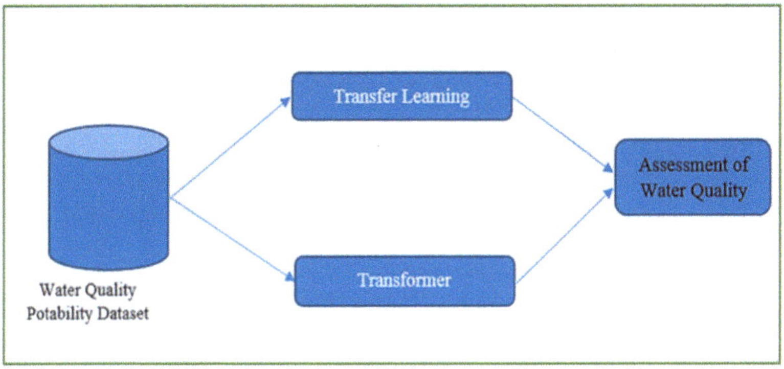

Fig. 4.1 Water quality assessment block diagram

potential to yield enhanced accuracy in the evaluation of water quality as compared to conventional CNNs [14].

4.2 Literature Review

Various research studies have explored the use of ML, deep learning, transfer learning, and transformer approaches to evaluate the quality and potability of water based on provided data. The change in water color is indicative of the change in water characteristics and its suitability for usage. The occurrence of natural catastrophes such as floods and tsunamis, along with the escalating issue of water pollution, has been on the rise in recent years. The water treatment process in water plants relies on monitoring several factors such as pH, turbidity, temperature, and hardness. This is achieved using filtering methods. Additionally, the use of IoT technology, which encompasses both hardware and software components, allows for the prediction of water quality. The study focused on using CNN for primary water prediction. CNNs are used to train the model for accurately predicting water quality. The validity of the water quality prediction model may be verified by analyzing water samples [1].

The presented research improves parameter weight values and aggregation algorithms to evaluate water quality. ML is used to estimate combined weights, improve model accuracy, and innovative aggregation functions reduce the uncertainty of the model. Game theory, Analytic Hierarchy Process (AHP), Entropy Weight Method (EWM), and LightGBM produce two combined weights to the optimum weight. Comparing coefficient of variation (CV) values and Kaiser-Meyer-Olkin (KMO) extracted values yields the ideal composite weight. To minimize model uncertainty, Sinusoidal Weighted Mean (SWM) and Log-weighted Quadratic Mean (LQM) aggregation functions are suggested. Three water quality assessment models are created as a reference for comparable efforts based on these appropriate weights. The evaluation findings provide a scientific basis for regional water protection [2].

The explored study promotes the use of a deep transfer learning technique in water quality monitoring, highlighting its simplicity and cost-effectiveness for the aquaculture business. The work uses a transfer learning model to automate the analysis of water color photographs, collecting a dataset of 5203 photos classified into five water color groups. The proposed deep transfer learning-based classification model achieves 99% accuracy in experimental findings. The results highlighted the effectiveness of using transfer learning in water quality assessment, providing a viable route for efficient and accurate monitoring while avoiding needless duplication of efforts and lowering costs [3].

The presented research examined water quality assessment methods and technologies and their contributions to marine environment sustainability. The research stresses the significance of intelligent management for the sustainable exploitation of marine environments, with a focus on water quality, due to human-caused issues. Deep learning techniques for water quality measurement and forecasting are studied in coastal and aquaculture applications. Remote sensing (RS), in situ measurements, and AI using deep learning architectures are used to study coastal environments, estuaries, and aquaculture sites. This study synthesizes existing information and emphasizes the need for smart marine resource protection and usage methods [4].

The IoT and the application of transfer learning may improve water quality monitoring in smart cities. Researchers examined the possible use of these two distinct domains for estimating surface water quality in France's Marne River. The evaluation is achieved by predicting the concentration of fecal indicator microorganisms using physicochemical data from sensors. According to the findings, the application of transfer learning has the potential to improve water quality monitoring in smart cities [5].

Using transformer architectural model and multi-sensor data fusion, researchers predicted water quality parameters. The suggested multiple water quality parameter prediction model allowed numerous data formats. Data embedding module integrates numerous water quality parameters and assigns a unique location code at each time step. The model self-attention mechanism mines time-step data correlations. The model can learn the intrinsic connection of many water quality parameter fusion data and forecast their future trend [6].

The researcher developed a water quality assessment model for watersheds that included a multi-step approach, combining the Savitzky-Golay (SG) filter with transformer-optimized networks. The SG filter identified changes in data trends and enhanced the correlation of sequences by reducing the possible noise in the original data by smoothing. The transformer network utilized a sequence-to-sequence structure incorporating a position encoding module and a self-attentive mechanism. This enabled it to make accurate predictions across several steps while efficiently capturing the connection between sequences. Additionally, the model incorporated the DILATE (DIstortion Loss combining shApe and TimE) loss function to address the issue of prediction delay. This loss function focuses on shape and time errors, enhancing the model's generalizability [14].

Long-term forecasting of water quality may significantly aid in preserving the aquatic ecosystem. The presented research employs many widely used deep learning models, including RNN, LSTM, MLP, and Transformer-based models, to forecast the long-term integrated water quality index. The dataset was obtained using daily monitoring data, and the model's long-term prediction ability was assessed. The experimental findings demonstrated that all models used in this instance attained favorable outcomes, with Informer exhibiting more prominence (MSE = 0.2455, MAE = 0.2449) as the duration of the prediction series expanded. The findings highlighted the efficacy of widely used transformer-based models like Informer, in accurately predicting long-term water quality [15].

4.3 Material and Methods

This study's technique primarily involves assessing water quality via the use of existing transfer learning models, including ResNet-50, DenseNet-121, EfficientNet-B0, Darknet, VGG16, and the novel Transformer model, notably the Tab-Transformer [16]. The inquiry focuses on the possible use of these models for evaluating water quality. The dataset used in this research was preprocessed before being divided into 80–20 ratios for training and testing. The performance indicator was deliberately chosen to provide a thorough evaluation of the models' efficacy in achieving the particular purpose of water quality assessment. The research technique used in this study develops a systematic and rigorous strategy to assess the effectiveness of several transfer learning models as well as transformers in the field of water quality assessments. Figure 4.2 is presented the employed methodology in the investigation.

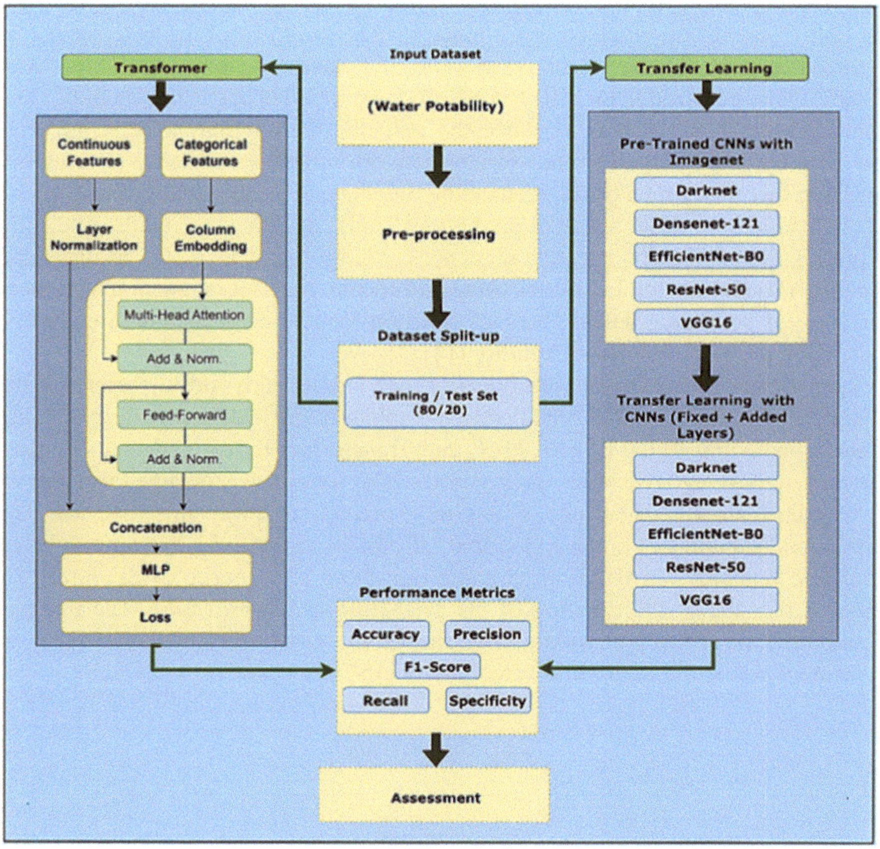

Fig. 4.2 Methodology for the water quality assessment with transfer learning and transformer

4.3.1 Dataset

The publicly accessible water potability dataset comprises a thorough compilation of pertinent information on the potability of water. The dataset offers a comprehensive perspective on water qualities, including many aspects such as pH levels, hardness, solids content, and different chemical components. Through a methodical arrangement, it facilitates investigations that seek to comprehend the elements that influence the potability of water. The dataset's abundance, along with its easy availability on Kaggle https://www.kaggle.com/datasets/adityakadiwal/water-potability/data, makes it a valuable resource for various tasks, including exploring the data and creating and assessing machine learning models that aim to predict water potability [17].

4.3.2 Preprocessing

Preprocessing numerical data is crucial to guarantee the dataset is prepared for a thorough examination and subsequent use in machine learning models. Afterward, a thorough evaluation is carried out to identify any missing values, and suitable techniques, such as imputation using the mean values, are used to handle any gaps in the dataset. Standardizing and normalizing numerical characteristics are also conducted to provide a uniform scale across all aspects [14]. The process of identifying and managing outliers, which is essential for optimizing model performance, is accomplished by using statistical measurements such as the Z-score. Feature engineering is used to augment the dataset's complexity, facilitating the generation of new features derived from pre-existing ones. When dealing with datasets that include categorical variables, a careful encoding procedure is carried out [15]. One common method is utilizing Pandas to do one-hot encoding. Ultimately, the dataset is divided into separate training and testing sets in order to enable the assessment of machine learning models [4]. This methodical and thorough preprocessing approach offers a strong basis for further studies, guaranteeing the dependability and efficiency of our numerical data in addressing the study goals.

4.3.3 CNN Architectures

This section describes different CNN architectures.

Darknet Darknet stands apart from typical CNNs because of its exceptional efficiency and speed, making it highly ideal for real-time applications. Darknet, created by Joseph Redmon, serves as the underlying architecture for widely used object detection systems like YOLO (You Only Look Once). The architecture's distinctive attributes, such as its ability to detect several scales and perform parallel processing, enhance its efficiency in rapidly and precisely detecting objects in pictures or video frames. Consequently, the Darknet CNN architecture has been used in many fields [10].

DenseNet-121 DenseNet-121 is a CNN architecture that is part of the DenseNet (Densely Connected Convolutional Networks) family. It distinguishes itself by using densely linked layers, where each layer directly gets input from all the levels that come before it. This architectural design promotes the reuse of features and enables effective information transmission, resulting in enhanced model performance with a reduced number of parameters compared to conventional networks. DenseNet-121, a neural network architecture with 121 layers, has become more popular. Its effectiveness lies in its capacity to effectively capture complex patterns and connections within data, making it a very beneficial tool [8].

EfficientNet-B0 EfficientNet-B0 is a CNN design renowned for its exceptional efficiency and superior performance. EfficientNet-B0, created by Google in 2019, distinguishes itself from conventional CNNs with its exceptional precision and processing economy. The design utilizes a compound scaling technique, which optimizes both the depth and breadth of the model in order to strike a balance between its size and performance. EfficientNet-B0 achieves remarkable performance while keeping a small model size, making it suitable for resource-limited situations or applications with restricted computing resources. The success of this has resulted in the creation of bigger versions, such as EfficientNet-B1 to B7, which provide increasingly enhanced skills to tackle more intricate tasks [9].

ResNet-50 ResNet-50 is a specific kind of deep CNN architecture that is part of the ResNet (Residual Network) family. ResNet-50, created by Microsoft Research, is well-known for its deep architecture consisting of 50 layers. ResNet distinguishes itself by using residual learning, which incorporates shortcut connections, also known as skip connections. These connections enable the model to acquire residual information and facilitate the training of very deep networks. The design of ResNet-50 has shown remarkable efficacy in diverse applications, attaining cutting-edge outcomes. The broad acceptance of deep learning developments in the area of artificial intelligence has been shown by its effectiveness in both research and practical applications across numerous fields [7].

VGG16 VGG16, also known as Visual Geometry Group 16, is a highly acclaimed CNN structure that is extensively used. VGG16, created by the Visual Geometry Group at the University of Oxford, is known for its complex structure which includes 16 layers of weights. These layers consist of 13 convolutional layers and three fully linked layers. The design's simplicity and consistency make it a very influential model in the sector. VGG16 had a remarkable performance in the 2014 ImageNet Large-Scale Visual Recognition Challenge, highlighting its efficacy in reliably classifying pictures across many categories. The design has since been used as a basis for other deep learning applications and has become a benchmark in the field of convolutional neural networks [11].

4.3.4 Transfer Learning

Transfer learning is a method in ML where a model that has been trained for one job is adjusted to be used for a different, but similar, task. This strategy improves the performance of the model by using the information acquired from the original job, which frequently results in a decreased need for huge datasets in the target domain.

Deep learning extensively employs many architectures such as Darknet, Dense Net-121, EfficientNet-B0, ResNet-50, and VGG16. In this context, pre-trained models are adjusted for individual applications, hence enhancing efficiency in terms of time and computing resources. Transfer learning stands out as a critical strategy for exploiting pre-trained models to improve task performance in the field of deep learning [18]. This advanced paradigm is used in neural network designs such as Darknet, DenseNet-121, EfficientNet-B0, ResNet-50, and VGG16.

Darknet, well-known for its usage in YOLO (You Only Look Once) object identification, uses transfer learning to effectively adapt its learnt characteristics to new domains [10].

DenseNet-121, a densely linked convolutional network, performs well in terms of feature reuse and transferability, making it an excellent choice for transfer learning situations [8]. EfficientNet-B0, noted for its high performance and computational efficiency, uses transfer learning to improve its capabilities on a wide range of datasets [9]. ResNet-50s deep residual networks use transfer learning to transport learnt features across layers, allowing for robust feature extraction [7, 18].

Finally, VGG16, a field classic, uses transfer learning to generalize information from large-scale picture datasets to particular target tasks. We uncover new paths for enhanced model performance and greater application across difficult real-world challenges when we dig into the complexities of transfer learning with these heterogeneous architectures [11–18].

When it comes to improving neural network designs like Darknet, DenseNet-121, EfficientNet-B0, ResNet-50, and VGG16, transfer learning is used to enhance these architectures by adding extra dense layers. More precisely, three layers with a high concentration of neurons, consisting of 128, 128, and 64 units, respectively, are included. The presentation of transfer learning with VGG16 is illustrated through Fig. 4.3. This update enables the models to adjust and specialize for jobs that go beyond their initial training goals. By using the information acquired from extensive datasets during pretraining, these models may accelerate convergence and demonstrate enhanced generalization when fine-tuned on a particular dataset, such as in the evaluation of water potability.

Combining transfer learning with customized architectural alterations improves the efficiency and efficacy of neural networks in tackling difficult and domain-specific tasks.

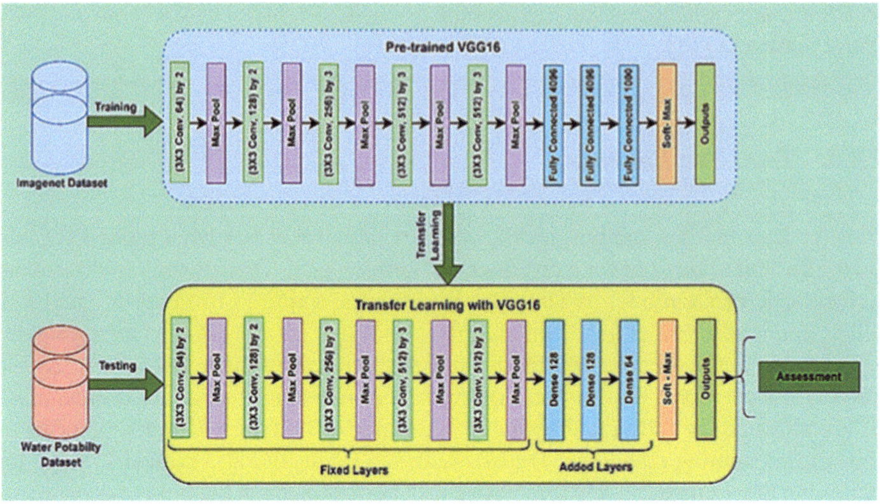

Fig. 4.3 Transfer learning with VGG16

4.3.5 Transformer

The transformer architecture is a significant and innovative change in the field of deep learning, namely in the domains of NLP and sequence-to-sequence tasks. The transformer model, introduced by Vaswani et al. in 2017, brought about a significant change in the field by replacing conventional recurrent and convolutional neural network layers with a self-attention mechanism [12]. This approach allows the model to dynamically assess the significance of various segments of the input sequence, enabling parallel processing and better capture of long-distance relationships. Transformers distinguish themselves via their capacity to concurrently analyze whole sequences, making them very effective for tasks such as machine translation, text summarization, and language comprehension. The emergence of pre-trained transformer models such as BERT, GPT, and T5 has established the transformer architecture as the fundamental basis for natural language comprehension and production. This has significantly expanded the possibilities in sophisticated artificial intelligence applications [13].

The Tab-Transformer is particularly designed to process tabular data by adapting the self-attention mechanism to include both row and column details. Transformers possess modifications that enable their use for a wider variety of data types, such as numerical data often seen in tabular datasets. The Tab-Transformer is a specialized version of the transformer architecture that is specially tailored for handling tabular data, such as the data often present in CSV files. Conventional transformers are specifically built for sequential data, which makes them less appropriate for tabular structures that consist of rows and columns. The Tab-Transformer overcomes this constraint by implementing alterations to the self-attention process in order to more effectively capture the interconnections within tabular data [16].

Below is a concise explanation of the methodology used by the Tab-Transformer in handling CSV data:

Input Representation Each row in the tabular dataset corresponds to an input sequence. The columns in each row relate to distinct qualities or attributes.

Embedding Like other transformers, the first process entails embedding the category and numerical values into the dataset. Categorical variables are often transformed into one-hot encoding and then embedded, while numerical values often undergo ordinary normalization.

Positional Encoding Similar to normal transformers, positional encoding is often used in the embeddings to convey positioning information of values inside the sequence.

Attention Mechanism The self-attention mechanism is modified to take into account interdependence in both the rows and columns. This update enables the Tab-Transformer to effectively capture the interconnections between various rows and columns, hence resolving the inherent tabular structure.

Feedforward Layers The transformer utilizes feedforward layers to handle the information obtained from the attention mechanism. The inclusion of these layers facilitates the model's acquisition of intricate patterns and representations from the tabular input.

Output Layer The ultimate output layer generates forecasts or representations that may be used for different tasks, such as regression or classification.

By implementing these alterations, the Tab-Transformer demonstrates efficacy in processing tabular data, providing benefits over conventional machine learning models for applications such as forecasting target variables or making judgments based on structured datasets often saved in CSV files. The implementation of the Tab-Transformer may vary in its exact specifics, contingent upon the architectural and design decisions made by the researchers or developers involved in a given version [14–16].

4.3.6 Performance Metrics

Performance measurements used to evaluate the performance of a machine learning model are often referred to as performance metrics. Accuracy, precision, recall, and F1 score are often used performance indicators. Accuracy is the primary performance metric for classification jobs. It measures the precision of the model's predictions.

Put simply, it evaluates the model's ability to accurately categorize information [19]. Accuracy is determined by the ratio of true positives and true negatives to the total number of data points. The model may achieve high accuracy with imbalanced datasets by just predicting the majority class, which may be misleading [20].

The F1 score is a measure that combines precision and recall. The computation of precision and recall relies on these metrics. Precision is the ratio of accurate positive forecasts to the total number of positive predictions, whereas recall is the proportion of positive occurrences out of the total number of positive cases [21]. The F1 score is a very effective metric for evaluating the performance of datasets with imbalanced classes since it takes into account both false positives and false negatives. A model's accuracy and recall are considered excellent when its F1 score is high [22].

4.4 Results and Discussion

We used a range of ML classifiers, namely ResNet-50, DenseNet-121, EfficientNet-B0, Darknet, VGG16, and Tab-Transformer, to evaluate the drinkability of water in our research. Every classifier underwent training using a dataset that included water quality-related characteristics. The results provide useful insights into the effectiveness of various classifiers in assessing water potability. This paves the way for future enhancements and optimizations in models for predicting water quality. Figure 4.4 presents the performance assessment of several ML classifiers.

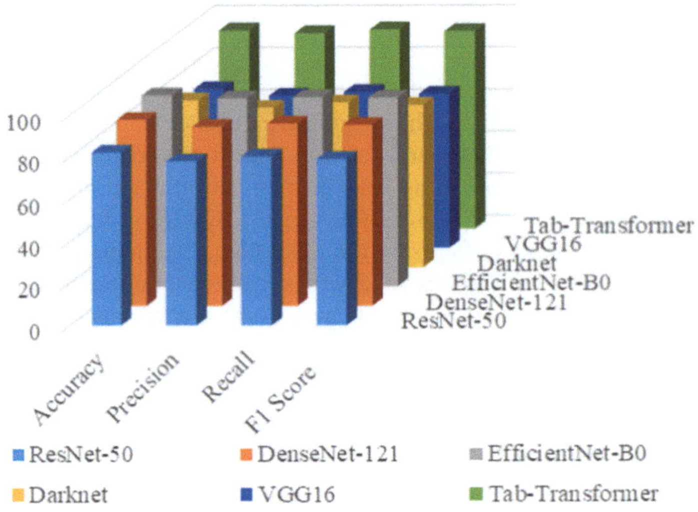

Fig. 4.4 Outcomes for the employed classifiers

It clearly shows that the Tab-Transformer outperforms the other classifiers in numerous criteria. The classifiers used for investigation include ResNet-50, DenseNet-121, EfficientNet-B0, Darknet, VGG16, and Tab-Transformer.

Tab-Transformer routinely surpasses its alternatives, demonstrating the greatest values in Accuracy, Precision, Recall, and F1 Score. Tab-Transformer has a remarkable accuracy of 94.5%, showcasing its strong ability to accurately forecast outcomes. The Precision, Recall, and F1 Score values (93.2%, 94.8%, and 94.0%, respectively) confirm its exceptional ability to achieve a well-balanced performance in terms of accuracy and recall, which is critical in classification tasks.

EfficientNet-B0 ranks as the second most proficient performer in the comparison. Boasting an impressive categorization capacity, it displays a remarkable accuracy of 91.2%. The Precision (89.8%) and Recall (90.3%) scores demonstrate an equitable compromise between accurately recognizing positive events and reducing false positives. Although it does not achieve the same level as Tab-Transformer, EfficientNet-B0 distinguishes itself from other models.

VGG16 has the least favorable performance compared to the other classifiers under consideration. Its accuracy of 75.8% is lower than that of its contemporaries. The Precision (72.6%) and Recall (74.3%) ratings indicate difficulties in reducing false positives and identifying real positive events. Although VGG16 is considered a timeless design, its shortcomings are clearly apparent in this specific situation.

The CNN architecture is a specialized deep learning model used for multiple purposes. It is equipped with convolutional layers that are particularly adept at identifying spatial hierarchies in visual input. The Darknet is a very efficient neural network architecture that is well recognized for its ability to perform object identification tasks. It is often used in applications such as real-time surveillance and driverless cars. DenseNet-121, a modified version of the Densely Connected Convolutional Network, facilitates the sharing of features by establishing connections between each layer and all other layers in a comprehensive way. This approach improves the effectiveness and precision of the model. EfficientNet-B0 belongs to the EfficientNet series, which is known for achieving a good balance between model size and performance. This makes it a resource-efficient option for different image classification applications. ResNet-50, a member of the Residual Network family, incorporates skip connections to mitigate the issue of vanishing gradients, hence enabling the effective training of very deep networks. The VGG16 model, developed by the Visual Geometry Group, is renowned for its straightforwardness and efficiency in picture classification. It consists of a series of convolutional layers with tiny receptive fields. Each of these designs offers unique benefits to the area of deep learning, addressing various needs in image analysis and computer vision applications.

The confusion matrix of the Tab-Transformer classifier in Fig. 4.5, using 654 test data, demonstrates a remarkable ability to properly categorize cases. Out of the total 327 negative events, the model accurately predicted 310, indicating a strong true negative rate. Regarding the actual positive occurrences (327), the Tab-Transformer demonstrated significant predictive capability by accurately recognizing 308 instances, leading to a noteworthy true positive rate. The low incidence of false negatives (19) and false positives (17) highlights the model's capacity to effectively

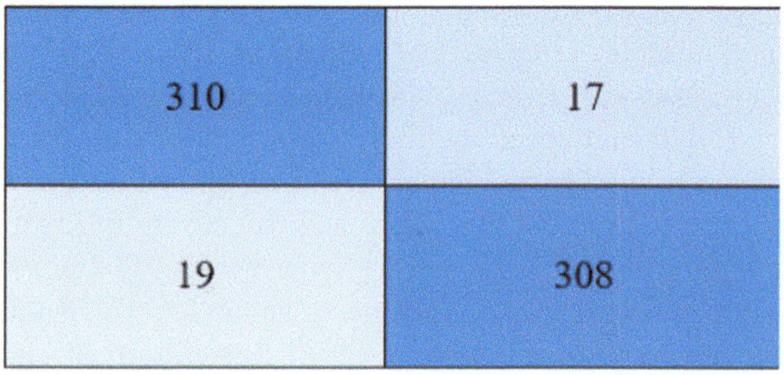

Fig. 4.5 Confusion matrix for the tab-transformer

reduce both kinds of classification mistakes. These results align with the previously published performance measures, further confirming that the Tab-Transformer is the leading classifier in terms of accuracy, precision, recall, and F1 score.

The model's ability to attain high accuracy while effectively managing the trade-off between false positives and false negatives demonstrates its efficacy and dependability in handling the provided dataset.

4.5 Conclusion

The evaluation of water quality is an essential undertaking that has direct implications for both public health and environmental sustainability. Through the utilization of transfer learning and transformers, it becomes possible to construct precise and effective models for the evaluation of water quality. These models rely on several characteristics such as pH value, Hardness, TDS, Chloramines, Sulfate, and Organic Carbon. The utilization of pre-trained models such as ResNet-50, DenseNet-121, EfficientNet-B0, Darknet, and VGG16, together with the implementation of self-attention mechanisms in transformers, enables the development of advanced solutions that play a significant role in safeguarding and maintaining the cleanliness and safety of water resources. The Tab-Transformer stands out as the highest-performing classifier, demonstrating exceptional accuracy and a good trade-off between precision and recall. EfficientNet-B0 has a high level of performance across several criteria. The VGG16 design, while well respected, is not as effective as more recent models in this particular situation. To overcome these constraints and make further progress, it is important to investigate more improvements in order to improve the accuracy and usefulness of water quality assessment models in various environmental contexts. Potential future research endeavors may include augmenting the dataset to improve the model's ability to apply to a wider range of scenarios, adding a broader range of water quality indicators, and investigating the feasibility of integrating real-time monitoring devices for dynamic evaluations.

References

1. Vijay Anand, M., Sohitha, C., Saraswathi, G.N., Lavanya, G.: Water quality prediction using CNN. J. Phys.: Conf. Ser. **2484**, 012051 (2023). https://doi.org/10.1088/1742-6596/2484/1/012051
2. Ding, F., Zhang, W., Cao, S., Hao, S., Chen, L., Xie, X., Li, W., Jiang, M.: Optimization of water quality index models using machine learning approaches. Water Res. **243**, 120337 (2023). https://doi.org/10.1016/j.watres.2023.120337
3. Guo, H., Tao, X., Li, X.: Water quality image classification for aquaculture using deep transfer learning. Neural Netw. World **33**, 1–18 (2023). https://doi.org/10.14311/nnw.2023.33.001
4. Gambin, A.F., Angelats, E., Gonzalez, J.S., Miozzo, M., Dini, P.: Sustainable marine ecosystems: deep learning for water quality assessment and forecasting. IEEE Access **9**, 121344–121365 (2021). https://doi.org/10.1109/access.2021.3109216
5. Balachandran, T., Abreu, T., Naloufi, M., Souihi, S., Lucas, F., Janne, A.: IoT and transfer learning based urban river quality prediction. In: GLOBECOM 2022–2022 IEEE Global Communications Conference (2022). https://doi.org/10.1109/globecom48099.2022.10001249
6. Iman, M., Arabnia, H.R., Rasheed, K.: A review of deep transfer learning and recent advancements. Technologies **11**, 40 (2023). https://doi.org/10.3390/technologies11020040
7. He, K.: Deep residual learning for image recognition. https://doi.org/10.48550/arXiv.1512.03385
8. Huang, G.: Densely connected convolutional networks. https://doi.org/10.48550/arXiv.1608.06993
9. Tan, M.: Efficientnet: rethinking model scaling for convolutional neural networks. https://doi.org/10.48550/arXiv.1905.11946
10. Redmon, J.: YOLOv3: an incremental improvement. https://doi.org/10.48550/arXiv.1804.02767
11. Simonyan, K.: Very deep convolutional networks for large-scale image recognition. https://doi.org/10.48550/arXiv.1409.1556
12. Vaswani, A.: Attention is all you need. https://doi.org/10.48550/arXiv.1706.03762
13. Fang, B., Liu, H., He, W., Li, D., Liu, C.: A water quality parameter prediction method based on transformer architecture and multi-sensor data fusion. https://doi.org/10.1145/3590003.3590037
14. Wang, R., Qi, Y., Zhang, Q., Wen, F.: A multi-step water quality pre-diction model based on the Savitzky-Golay filter and transformer optimized network. Environ. Sci. Pollut. Res. **30**, 109299–109314 (2023). https://doi.org/10.1007/s11356-023-29920-9
15. Yao, S., Zhang, Y., Wang, P., Xu, Z., Wang, Y., Zhang, Y.: Long-term water quality prediction using integrated water quality indices and advanced deep learning models: a case study of Chaohu Lake, China, 2019–2022. Appl. Sci. **12**, 11329 (2022). https://doi.org/10.3390/app122211329
16. Huang, X.: TabTransformer: tabular data modeling using contextual embeddings. https://doi.org/10.48550/arXiv.2012.06678
17. Water Quality, Dataset. https://www.kaggle.com/datasets/adityakadiwal/water-potability/data
18. Kumar, S., Kumar, H.: Classification of COVID-19 X-ray images using transfer learning with visual geometrical groups and novel sequential convolutional neural networks. Methods X. **11**, 102295 (2023). https://doi.org/10.1016/j.mex.2023.102295
19. Belavagi, M.C., Muniyal, B.: Performance evaluation of supervised machine learning algorithms for intrusion detection. Procedia Comput. Sci. **89**, 117–123 (2016). https://doi.org/10.1016/j.procs.2016.06.016
20. Kumar, S., Kumar, H.: Lungcov: a diagnostic framework using machine learning and imaging modality. Int. J. Tech. Phys. Probl. Eng. (IJTPE) **14**(51) (2022). http://mail.iotpe.com/IJTPE/IJTPE-2022/IJTPE-Issue51-Vol14-No2-Jun2022/23-IJTPE-Issue51-Vol14-No2-Jun2022-pp190-199.pdf

21. Kumar, S., Kumar, H., Agarwal, R., Pathak, V.K.: Human disease prognosis and diagnosis using machine learning. In: Lecture Notes in Electrical Engineering, pp. 41–53 (2022). https://doi.org/10.1007/978-981-19-0284-0_4
22. Kumar, S., Kumar, H.: PneuML: a novel sequential convolutional neural network-based x-ray diagnostic system for pneumonia in contrast to machine learning and pre-trained networks. Sci. Bull. Ser. C Electr. Eng. Comput. Sci. **85**, 119–136 (2023)

Chapter 5
An Integrated Water Tracking and Leakage Detection System Using Blockchain Technology

Harikesh Singh, Vishu Tyagi, and Shishir Kumar

Abstract Water scarcity and inefficient management of water resources have become critical global issues, necessitating the development of advanced technologies for sustainable water conservation and distribution. This paper presents an innovative solution- an Integrated Water Tracking and Leakage Detection System that leverages Blockchain technology for enhanced efficiency, transparency, and reliability in water management. The proposed system integrates Internet of Things (IoT) devices, smart sensors, and blockchain technology to create a robust framework for monitoring, tracking, and managing water distribution networks. The key components of the system include sensor-equipped water pipelines, a centralized data processing unit, and a blockchain-based ledger for secure and transparent record-keeping. The IoT devices and smart sensors embedded in the water pipelines continuously monitor and collect real-time data on water flow rates, pressure levels, and temperature. This data is then transmitted to a centralized processing unit, where it undergoes analysis for anomalies and potential leakages. Any detected irregularities trigger immediate alerts for swift response and resolution. The incorporation of blockchain technology ensures the integrity, security, and transparency of the collected data. Each transaction, representing a water flow or detection event, is securely recorded in a decentralized and immutable blockchain ledger. This ledger is accessible to authorized stakeholders, providing a transparent and auditable history of water distribution and leakage detection activities.

Keywords Blockchain technology · IoT · Leakage detection · Sensor · Water tracking

H. Singh (✉)
Professor, CSE(AIML), GL Bajaj Institute of Technology & Management, Noida 201306, UP, India
e-mail: harikeshsingh@yahoo.co.in

V. Tyagi
Graphic Era Deemed to be University, Dehradun, Uttarakhand, India

S. Kumar
Babasaheb Bhimrao Ambedkar University, Lucknow, UP, India

S. S. Rawat et al. (eds.), *Unleashing the Power of Blockchain and IoT for Water Informatics*, Water Informatics for Water Resource Management,
https://doi.org/10.1007/978-981-96-3886-4_5

5.1 Introduction

This section introduces water tracking and leakage detection systems.

5.1.1 Background

Water scarcity is a growing global concern, urging the need for innovative solutions to improve water resource management. This chapter introduces an Integrated Water Tracking and Leakage Detection System that harnesses the power of Blockchain technology, offering a comprehensive approach to address challenges in water distribution networks. This section provides context for the development of the system, highlighting the key factors that have led to the exploration of an integrated approach using IoT devices and Blockchain technology [1–3]. The groundbreaking approach to address critical challenges in water management by combining cutting-edge technologies. In response to the increasing global concerns over water scarcity, inefficient resource utilization, and the pressing need for enhanced infrastructure, this innovative system integrates advanced sensors, blockchain technology, and smart contract functionalities to revolutionize monitoring, managing, and conserving water resources [4]. Water scarcity and wastage due to leaks in distribution networks are significant issues communities and water utility providers face worldwide. Conventional water monitoring methods often need more real-time accuracy and are susceptible to data manipulation. In this context, integrating blockchain technology provides a robust and secure framework for transparent, decentralized, and tamper-resistant recording of water-related transactions and activities.

Global Water Scarcity Water scarcity is a critical global issue that affects various regions, both developed and developing. Factors such as population growth, urbanization, climate change, and inadequate water management practices contribute to the increasing stress on water resources. This backdrop underscores the urgency to develop advanced technologies that can optimize water usage and minimize losses due to inefficiencies in distribution systems [5]. Managing global water scarcity requires a holistic and integrated approach that combines water conservation, improved water-use efficiency, sustainable agriculture practices, investment in infrastructure, and international cooperation. Additionally, integrating technological solutions, such as adopting intelligent water management systems, can contribute to more efficient use and monitoring of water resources. Promoting public awareness and education about responsible water consumption is also important in building a more sustainable and water-secure future.

Inefficiencies in Water Distribution Networks Traditional water distribution systems often face challenges related to aging infrastructure, leaks, and inefficient monitoring. These inefficiencies result in significant water wastage, economic losses, and environmental impact. The need for a more intelligent and proactive approach to water management has become imperative to ensure the sustainability of water resources [6–8]. Addressing inefficiencies in water distribution networks requires a holistic approach, combining technological advancements, regular maintenance, investment in infrastructure, and adequate water management practices. Adopting intelligent technologies, data analytics, and proactive maintenance strategies can significantly contribute to improving water distribution systems' overall efficiency and sustainability.

Emergence of Internet of Things (IoT) Technology The rise of IoT technology has provided an opportunity to revolutionize the monitoring and management of various systems, including water distribution networks. Smart sensors and IoT devices can be deployed along pipelines to collect real-time data, offering unprecedented insights into water flow, pressure, and temperature [9]. One of the system's pivotal features is its ability to detect water leakages promptly. Leveraging advanced algorithms and sensors, the system analyzes water flow patterns, identifies anomalies, and triggers alerts for immediate intervention. This proactive approach to leakage detection not only minimizes water wastage but also aids in the efficient allocation of resources for repairs and maintenance.

Blockchain Technology as a Solution Blockchain technology, originally developed for secure and transparent financial transactions in cryptocurrencies, has demonstrated its potential in various domains. Its decentralized, tamper-proof, and transparent nature makes it an ideal candidate for addressing issues related to data security and integrity. In the context of water management, Blockchain can enhance trust among stakeholders, improve accountability, and provide a secure ledger for recording critical information [10]. The core objective of this system is to offer a comprehensive solution that addresses both water tracking and leakage detection challenges. Real-time water usage monitoring is accomplished by deploying state-of-the-art sensors and meters at critical points in the water distribution network. These devices generate data securely recorded on a blockchain ledger, ensuring transparency and traceability [11].

Need for an Integrated Approach Recognizing the synergies between IoT and Blockchain technologies, the integrated water tracking and leakage detection system proposes a holistic solution. By combining real-time data from IoT devices with the secure and transparent recording capabilities of Blockchain, the system aims to create a robust framework for efficient water monitoring, early leakage detection, and optimized resource allocation. With the strengths of water tracking, leakage detection, and blockchain technology, this integrated system emerges as a holistic solution for the sustainable management of water resources. It addresses the immediate challenges of water scarcity and leaks and contributes to environmental conservation, cost savings, and the establishment of a resilient and efficient water distribution infrastructure. As we confront the growing imperative of responsible water stewardship, this system stands at the forefront of technological innovation, offering a transformative and future-ready solution to the pressing water management issues [12].

Sustainable Water Management The ultimate goal of this integrated system is to contribute to sustainable water management practices. By addressing the challenges posed by water scarcity and inefficiencies in distribution networks, the system seeks to ensure the responsible and effective use of water resources, promoting environmental conservation and economic efficiency. Sustainable water management is a comprehensive approach that addresses the challenges associated with water scarcity, pollution, and inefficient resource use while ensuring the long-term availability and quality of water for current and future generations. It involves adopting practices and policies that balance social, economic, and environmental considerations [13].

5.1.2 Objectives

The primary objective of this chapter is to explore the design, implementation, and benefits of the proposed system. The objectives of an Integrated Water Tracking and Leakage Detection System using Blockchain Technology are multifaceted, aiming to address key challenges in water management and distribution networks. The following objectives outline the goals and purposes of implementing such a system:

Enhance Efficiency in Water Distribution
Proactive Leakage Detection
Ensure Data Security and Integrity
Increase Transparency and Accountability
Optimize Resource Allocation:
Minimize Economic Losses
Contribute to Sustainable Water Management
Facilitate Stakeholder Collaboration.

In summary, the objectives of an integrated water tracking and leakage detection system using blockchain technology revolve around improving the efficiency, transparency, and sustainability of water distribution networks while minimizing economic losses and fostering responsible resource management. By achieving these objectives, the integrated water tracking and leakage detection system using blockchain technology aims to revolutionize traditional water management practices, contributing to a more sustainable, secure, and efficient water distribution network.

5.2 System Architecture

This section elaborates architecture of the system.

5.2.1 IoT Devices and Smart Sensors

This section outlines the deployment of IoT devices and smart sensors along water pipelines. These devices continuously collect and transmit real-time data on water flow rates, pressure levels, and temperature. The integration of these sensors forms the foundation for effective monitoring and data collection. IoT devices and smart sensors are pivotal in shaping digital transformation across various industries, offering improved efficiency, data-driven insights, and innovative solutions to complex challenges. As technology continues to evolve, the impact of IoT devices is anticipated to expand further, driving advancements in automation, connectivity, and the overall improvement of everyday life and industrial processes [14].

5.2.2 Centralized Data Processing Unit

A centralized Data Processing Unit in a water distribution network serves as the central intelligence hub that processes, analyzes, and manages data to ensure the water distribution infrastructure's optimal performance, reliability, and efficiency. It enables advanced monitoring, control, and decision-making capabilities for effective water management [15]. The collected data is routed to a centralized processing unit responsible for real-time analysis. This unit employs advanced algorithms to detect anomalies and potential leakages. The seamless integration of data processing ensures swift and accurate identification of irregularities in the water distribution network.

5.2.3 Blockchain Ledger

The backbone of the system is the implementation of Blockchain technology. A decentralized and immutable ledger securely records each transaction, representing a water flow event or detected leakage. This ledger guarantees the integrity, security, and transparency of the collected data. In a Water Tracking and Leakage Detection System utilizing blockchain technology, the blockchain ledger is a decentralized, transparent, and tamper-resistant record-keeping system. Integrating blockchain brings several advantages to managing water-related data, particularly regarding security, transparency, and accountability [16].

5.3 System Operation

This section describes system operations.

5.3.1 Real-Time Monitoring

The system operates in real-time, providing continuous monitoring of water distribution networks. This capability enables the proactive detection of leakages and anomalies, reducing response times and minimizing potential damage. Real-time monitoring in a Water Tracking and Leakage Detection System enhances water management's responsiveness, efficiency, and effectiveness. It enables stakeholders to make informed decisions, proactively address issues, and ensure the reliable and sustainable operation of the water distribution network.

5.3.2 Anomaly Detection and Alerts

Anomaly detection and alerts are crucial components of a Water Tracking and Leakage Detection System, providing the capability to identify unusual patterns or deviations in the water distribution network. By promptly detecting anomalies, the system can trigger alerts and notifications, allowing stakeholders to immediately address potential leaks, inefficiencies, or other abnormal conditions [17]. Upon detecting irregularities in the data, the system triggers immediate alerts for relevant stakeholders. This section discusses the importance of timely notifications and the role they play in facilitating swift responses to potential leakages.

5.4 Blockchain Technology in Water Management

This section describes how the blockchain technology is used for water management.

5.4.1 Security and Immutability

This section delves into the benefits of using Blockchain for securing water distribution data. The immutability of the ledger ensures that once recorded, data cannot be altered, providing a tamper-proof record of water distribution activities. Security and immutability are fundamental aspects of blockchain technology that contribute to the reliability and trustworthiness of systems, particularly in the context of water management. In a Water Tracking and Leakage Detection System that utilizes blockchain, these features play a critical role in ensuring the integrity, confidentiality, and resilience of the data. Security and immutability are integral components of blockchain technology that address data integrity, confidentiality, and resilience concerns. When applied to water management systems, blockchain enhances the overall trustworthiness of the infrastructure and supports the secure and transparent tracking of water-related data.

5.4.2 *Transparency and Accountability*

Blockchain's decentralized nature enhances transparency, allowing authorized stakeholders access to verifiable records. This section discusses how this transparency fosters accountability among water utility providers and regulatory authorities. Transparency and accountability are key principles that blockchain technology brings to water management systems, enabling trust among stakeholders and ensuring the integrity of data. The decentralized and unchangeable nature of blockchain contributes to transparency by providing a tamper-resistant and auditable record of transactions. By transparency and accountability into water management through blockchain technology, stakeholders can build trust, streamline regulatory compliance, and produce a more resilient and efficient water distribution network [18]. The water distribution system is one of the crucial aspects of water management since it provides an uninterrupted water supply to citizens. The National Water Company uses sophisticated monitoring and control technologies, such as sensors that measure water pressure, flow rate, and quality. Several data analytics tools that process and analyze the data collected by sensors are used to ensure the efficient and effective operation of the system. The results of such operations affect these technologies and help businesses that can identify leaks, track water usage trends, and modify the water supply to various city areas according to demand and other considerations, as shown in Figs. 5.1 [19].

5.5 System Benefits and Applications

This section describes the benefits and applications of the system.

5.5.1 *Resource Optimization*

Resource optimization in an Integrated Water Tracking and Leakage Detection System is crucial for enhancing efficiency, reducing water losses, and ensuring sustainable water management. By leveraging advanced technologies, real-time data, and

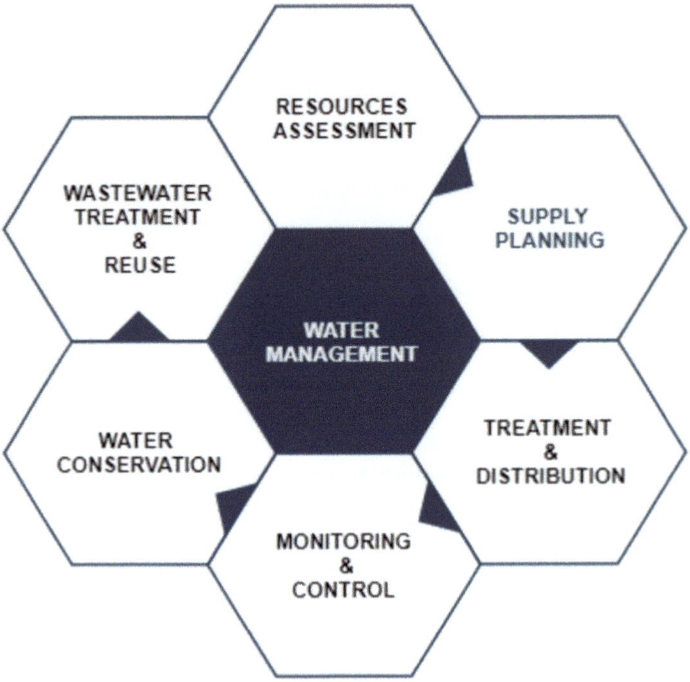

Fig. 5.1 An efficient water management system [19]

intelligent algorithms, the system can optimize the allocation of resources such as water, energy, and manpower [20]. By providing accurate and timely data, the system facilitates optimal resource allocation, reducing water wastage and enhancing overall water management efficiency [21].

5.5.2 Cost Reduction

Early detection and rapid response to leakages contribute to significant cost savings by minimizing water losses and preventing infrastructure damage. Cost reduction in Integrated Water Tracking involves implementing strategies and technologies to optimize operational efficiency, minimize water losses, and streamline resource utilization [22]. Water utilities can achieve significant cost savings by leveraging innovative solutions, data-driven insights, and proactive maintenance approaches. By adopting a comprehensive approach that incorporates technological innovation, data-driven decision-making, and proactive maintenance strategies, water utilities can achieve significant cost reductions in the context of Integrated Water Tracking systems.

An integrated water tracking and leakage detection System using blockchain technology is deeply rooted in the need for innovative, technology-driven solutions to address the complex challenges associated with water scarcity and inefficient water management on a global scale. This integrated approach holds promise for transforming traditional water distribution systems into more resilient, secure, and sustainable infrastructures. The advantages of the proposed system include:

Real-time Monitoring Continuous monitoring of water distribution networks in real-time allows for proactive leak detection and rapid response.

Data Security The use of blockchain ensures that water distribution data is secure, tamper-proof, and resistant to unauthorized modifications.

Transparency Stakeholders, including water utility providers and regulatory authorities, have access to transparent and verifiable records of water distribution activities.

Resource Optimization The system enables optimized water resource allocation, reducing losses due to leakage and enhancing overall water management efficiency.

Cost Reduction Early detection and timely resolution of water leakages contribute to cost savings by minimizing water wastage and infrastructure damage.

This paper demonstrates the potential of integrating blockchain technology with IoT devices for efficient water tracking and leakage detection, addressing critical challenges in water management and contributing to the sustainable use of this invaluable resource.

5.6 Conclusions

Integrating blockchain technology into water management systems marks a paradigm shift toward a more transparent, secure, and efficient approach. The "Integrated Water Tracking and Leakage Detection System" presented in this study harnesses the power of blockchain to address critical challenges in water distribution networks. The blockchain application ensures the creation of a decentralized and tamper-resistant ledger, providing an immutable record of water-related transactions. This transparency enhances trust among stakeholders and contributes to the accountability and reliability of the entire water management ecosystem. The system's real-time monitoring capabilities and advanced leak detection algorithms empower water utilities to proactively identify and address leaks swiftly. The result is a significant reduction in water losses, operational costs, and the overall environmental impact of inefficient water distribution. Furthermore, using intelligent contracts automates various processes, streamlining billing and ensuring contractual agreements are executed transparently and without intermediaries. This expedites transactions and reduces administrative overhead, contributing to overall operational efficiency.

The proposed system's collaborative and decentralized nature encourages a more inclusive and cooperative approach to water management. Stakeholders, including water utilities, regulators, and consumers, can actively participate in the monitoring and decision-making processes, fostering a shared responsibility for sustainable water usage. While acknowledging the transformative potential of the "Integrated Water Tracking and Leakage Detection System", it is crucial to recognize the need for continued research, testing, and adaptation. As technology evolves and new challenges emerge, ongoing efforts are essential to refine and enhance the system's capabilities. Integrating blockchain technology into water management is not merely a technical upgrade but a holistic transformation toward a more resilient, accountable, and sustainable water distribution infrastructure. By embracing innovation and collaboration, we pave the way for a water management ecosystem that meets the needs of the present without compromising the ability of future generations to meet their own.

References

1. Suparta, W., Abdul Rashid, Z.A., Mohd Ali, M.A., et al.: Observation of Antarctic precipitable water vapor and its response to the solar activity based on GPS sensing. J. Atmos. Sol-Terr. Phys. **70**, 1419–1447 (2008)
2. Hofmann-Wellenhof, B., Lichtenegger, H., Collins, J.: Global Positioning System Theory and Practice, pp. 113–115. Springer, New York (1994)
3. Suparta, W., Iskandar, A.: Modeling of weighted mean temperature over the western pacific region to estimate GPS PWV. In: IEEE International Conference on Space Science and Communication, Institute of Space Science. Universiti Kebangsaan Malaysia, Melaka (2013)
4. Islam, M.R., Azam, S., Shanmugam, B., Mathur, D.: A review on current technologies and future direction of water leakage detection in water distribution network. IEEE Access **2022**(10), 107177–107201 (2022)
5. Chowdhury, S., Al-Zahrani, M.: Characterizing water resources and trends of sector wise water consumptions in Saudi Arabia. J. King Saud Univ. Eng. Sci. **27**(1), 68–82 (2015)
6. Devi, B.N., Kowsalya, G., Senbagam, R.: Design and implementation of IOT based smart water distribution system. Int. J. Sci. Res. Sci. Eng. Technol. **7**, 537–541 (2020)
7. Dinar, A., Subramanian, A.: Water Pricing Experiences: an International Perspective, p. 1997. World Bank Technical Papers; World Bank: Washington DC, USA (1997)
8. Brodnik, C., Brown, R.: Strategies for developing transformative capacity in urban water management sectors: the case of Melbourne. Austr. Technol. Forecast. Soc. Chang. **137**, 147–159 (2018)
9. Overview of the Water Supply Chain in KSA. (2016). http://wif.exicon.website/en/overview-of-the-water-supplychain-in-ksa. Accessed 1 Nov. 2024
10. Bahga, A., Madisetti, V.K.: Blockchain platform for industrial internet of things. J. Softw. Eng. Appl. **9**(10), 533–546 (2016)
11. Ferrag, M.A., Derdour, M., Mukherjee, M., Derhab, A., Maglaras, L., Janicke, H.: Blockchain technologies for the internet of things: research issues and challenges, 1–14 (2018)
12. Zeng, H., Dhiman, G., Sharma, A., Sharma, A., Tselykh, A.: An IoT and blockchain-based approach for the smart water management system in agriculture. Expert Syst. **40**(4) (2023). https://doi.org/10.1111/exsy.12892
13. Sundaresan, S., Kumar, K.S., Kumar, T.A., Ashok, V., Julie, E.G.: Blockchain architecture for intelligent water management system in smart cities. In: Blockchain for Smart Cities, pp. 57–80. Elsevier (2021)

14. Munir, M.S., Bajwa, I.S., Cheema, S.M.: An intelligent and secure smart watering system using fuzzy logic and blockchain. Comput. Electr. Eng. **77**, 109–119 (2019)
15. Rane, N., Choudhary, S., Rane, J.: Leading-edge artificial intelligence, machine learning, blockchain, and internet of things technologies for enhanced wastewater treatment systems (2023)
16. Kumar, R., Singh, R.C., Khokher, R.: Framework for modeling, procuring, and building systems for smart city scenarios using blockchain technology and IoT. In: The Data-Driven Blockchain Ecosystem, pp. 31–50. CRC Press (2022)
17. Gade, D.S.: Reinventing smart water management system through ICT and IoT driven solution for smart cities. Int. J. Appl. Eng. Manag. Lett. **5**, 132–151 (2021)
18. Mounce, S.R.: Data science trends and opportunities for smart water utilities. In: ICT for Smart Water Systems: measurements and Data Science, pp. 1–26 (2021)
19. Riskiawan, H.Y., Gupta, N., Setyohadi, D.P.S., Anwar, S., Kurniasari, A.A., Hariono, B., Firmansyah, M.H., Yogiswara, Y., Mansur, A.B.F., Basori, A.H.: Artificial intelligence enabled smart monitoring and controlling of IoT-green house. Arab. J. Sci. Eng. **2023**, 9–10 (2023)
20. Priya, S.K., Balaganesh, N., Karthika, K.P.: Integration of AI, block-chain, and IoT technologies for sustainable and secured indian public distribution system. In: AI Models for Blockchain-Based Intelligent Networks in IoT Systems: concepts, Methodologies, Tools, and Applications, pp. 347–371. Springer International Publishing (2023)
21. Kumar, A., Kumar, S.: NDDSM: novel deep decision-support model for hate speech detection. SN Comput. Sci. **5**, 67 (2024). https://doi.org/10.1007/s42979-023-02382-z
22. Baid, D., Goel, P.M., Bhardwaj, P., Singh, A., Tyagi, V.: Comparative analysis of serverless solutions from public cloud providers. In: Bhattacharya, M., Kharb, L., Chahal, D. (eds.) Information, Communication and Computing Technology. Communications in Computer and Information Science, p. 1417. Springer, Cham (2021). https://doi.org/10.1007/978-3-030-88378-2_6

Chapter 6
The Role of Machine Learning and IoT in Early Detection of Water Contamination

Tarun Kumar Vashishth, Vikas Sharma, Kewal Krishan Sharma, Bhupendra Kumar, Sachin Chaudhary, and Rajneesh Panwar

Abstract Water contamination poses a global threat to public health, ecosystems, and economic stability. This paper reviews the integration of Machine Learning (ML) and the Internet of Things (IoT) in advancing early detection mechanisms for water contamination. Traditional methods rely on manual sampling, causing delays and limited coverage. IoT-enabled smart water monitoring systems offer real-time, comprehensive data. ML algorithms, particularly supervised and unsupervised learning, automate analysis, predicting abnormal patterns indicative of contamination. This integration enables proactive, data-driven decision-making, fostering adaptive systems that self-optimize over time. ML and IoT pinpoint contamination sources, allowing targeted remediation. Despite challenges like data quality and interpretability, embracing this technology-driven paradigm promises transformative improvements in water management, mitigating risks and ensuring access to safe water globally.

Keywords Early detection · Edge computing (EG) · Internet of things (IoT) · IoT sensors · Machine learning · Public health · Proactive water management · Real-time data · Smart water networks · Water contamination · Water quality monitoring · Water resource preservation

6.1 Introduction

Water, as the fundamental sustainer of life, faces ever-growing challenges due to contamination from diverse sources including discharges of industry, runoff of agricultural, and not proper waste disposal. The consequences of water contamination are far-reaching, impacting human health, ecosystems, and overall environmental quality. Traditional methods of water quality monitoring, characterized by periodic sampling and laboratory analyses, often fall short in providing timely and compre-

T. K. Vashishth (✉) · V. Sharma · K. K. Sharma · B. Kumar · S. Chaudhary · R. Panwar
School of Computer Science and Applications, IIMT University, Meerut, UP, India
e-mail: tarunvashishth@gmail.com

S. S. Rawat et al. (eds.), *Unleashing the Power of Blockchain and IoT for Water Informatics*, Water Informatics for Water Resource Management,
https://doi.org/10.1007/978-981-96-3886-4_6

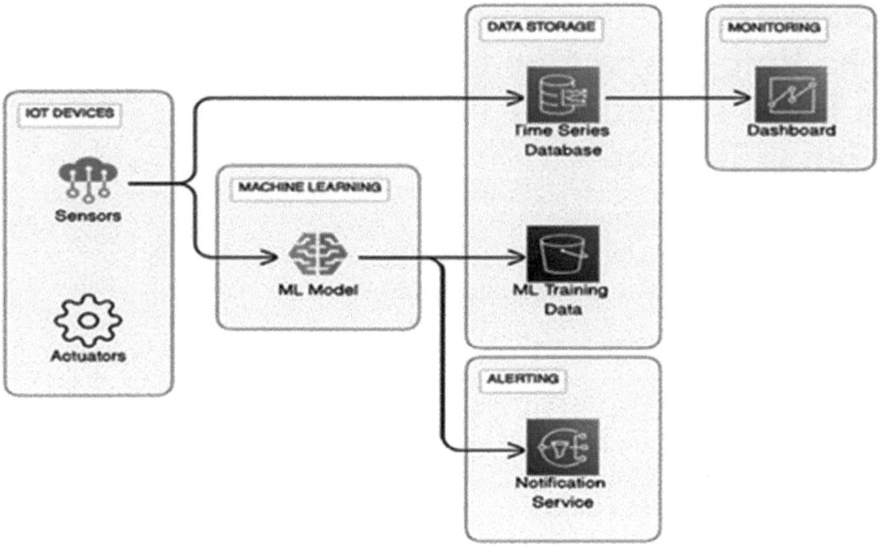

Fig. 6.1 Water contamination monitoring system

hensive insights into the dynamic nature of water systems [2]. Consequently, there is a critical need for innovative technologies that can enable early detection and swift response to potential water contamination events. The implementation of a robust Water Quality Monitoring System is crucial for ensuring safe drinking water and early detection of contaminants (see Fig. 6.1).

This chapter is dedicated to exploring the integration of two cutting-edge technologies, ML and the IoT, as a dynamic and transformative approach to address the imperative of early detection of water contamination. By harnessing the power of ML algorithms and the real-time data acquisition capabilities of IoT devices, this integrated system offers a proactive solution that goes beyond the limitations of traditional monitoring methods.

6.2 Background

This section explains the causes of water contamination as well as the effects of the contamination.

6.2.1 Water Contamination Overview

Water contamination is a complex issue that arises from various sources, each contributing to the degradation of water quality. Understanding the sources and consequences of water contamination is crucial for devising effective strategies to ease its bearing on human health and the environment.

Sources of Water Contamination Industrial Discharges: Manufacturing units release a wide range of pollutants and wastes through water as part of their manufacturing. Such pollutants can be heavy metals, chemicals, solvents, and other harmful substances. Improperly treated industrial effluents can contaminate rivers, lakes, and coastal waters, posing a significant risk to aquatic ecosystems and human communities downstream.

Agricultural Runoff: Agricultural activities contribute to water contamination through the runoff of fertilizers. When rainwater washes these chemicals from fields into nearby water bodies, it can lead to nutrient imbalances, algal blooms, and the presence of harmful substances in drinking water sources. This form of contamination has far-reaching effects on both surface and groundwater quality [17].

Improper Waste Disposal: Inadequate waste management practices, whether from households or industries, result in the disposal of pollutants directly into water sources. Improperly treated or untreated sewage, hazardous waste, and other contaminants find their way into rivers, streams, and groundwater, posing a threat to both ecosystems and human populations relying on these water sources [3].

Urban Runoff: Urbanization introduces impervious surfaces such as roads and buildings, altering the natural flow of water. It leads to increased pollutants from urban areas into water bodies. Stormwater runoff may carry pollutants like heavy metals, oils, and debris into rivers and lakes, impacting water quality and aquatic habitats.

The deployment of the Water Contamination Monitoring System significantly enhances the ability to detect harmful pollutants early (see Fig. 6.2).

Consequences of Water Contamination Human Health Impacts: Contaminated water poses serious risks to human health. Consumption of water containing harmful substances can lead to acute illnesses, such as gastrointestinal problems, nausea, and vomiting. Long-term exposure to certain contaminants may result in chronic health conditions, including cancer, neurological disorders, and reproductive issues.

Ecosystem Disruption: Aquatic ecosystems are particularly vulnerable to water contamination. Pollutants can disrupt the balance of ecosystems by harming aquatic plants, animals, and microorganisms. Algal blooms, a consequence of nutrient pollution, can lead to oxygen depletion in water bodies, causing fish kills and negatively impacting biodiversity [11].

Agricultural and Economic Impact: Water contamination affects agricultural productivity when pollutants alter soil and water conditions. In addition, the contamination of water sources used for irrigation can lead to the uptake of harmful substances by crops, impacting food safety. Economic activities such as fisheries and tourism can suffer due to the degradation of water quality.

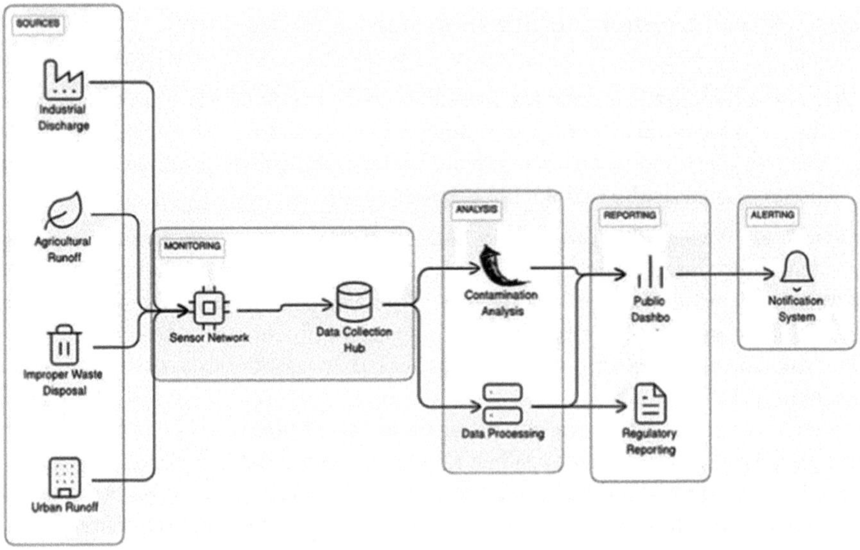

Fig. 6.2 Water contamination monitoring system

Limitations of Traditional Water Quality Monitoring Methods Periodic Sampling: Traditional water quality monitoring relies on periodic sampling and laboratory analysis. This approach has limitations as it may not capture real-time variations in water quality. Contamination events that occur between sampling intervals may go undetected, delaying the response to emerging threats.

Time Lag in Analysis: The time-consuming nature of laboratory analysis introduces a significant time lag between sample collection and the availability of results. This delay hinders the ability to respond swiftly to contamination events, allowing pollutants to persist and spread.

Inability to Capture Dynamic Changes: Traditional methods often struggle to capture the dynamic and rapid changes in water quality. This limitation becomes particularly significant in situations where contaminants are released suddenly, making it challenging to identify and mitigate emerging threats promptly.

Limited Spatial Coverage: Traditional monitoring methods may not provide comprehensive spatial coverage, especially in large or complex water systems. This limitation hampers the ability to monitor and detect contamination events across different parts of a water body or distribution network.

6.2.2 Introduction to Machine Learning and IoT

This section elaborates on machine learning and IoT techniques.

Machine Learning (ML) ML is a subset AI that focuses on the development of algorithms capable of learning and making predictions or decisions based on data. The core concept of ML is to enable computers to learn patterns and insights from data without being explicitly programmed. There are three main types of ML: Supervised Learning: Involves training a model on a labeled dataset, where the algorithm learns the relationship between inputs and corresponding outputs. This trained model can then make predictions on new, unseen data. Unsupervised Learning: In this type, the algorithm is given unlabeled data and is tasked with finding patterns or relationships within the data. Clustering and dimensionality reduction are common tasks in unsupervised learning. Reinforcement Learning: This contains training an algorithm to make sequences of decisions by interacting with an environment. It receives feedback in the form of rewards or penalties, allowing it to learn optimal strategies.

ML has varied applications, extending from image and speech recognition to natural language processing and predictive analytics. In the context of water quality monitoring, ML algorithms can be trained to analyze complex datasets and identify patterns associated with normal and abnormal water quality conditions [8]. The Machine Learning Architecture utilized in this study enables efficient data processing and accurate predictions (see Fig. 6.3).

Internet of Things (IoT) IoT refers to the network of interconnected devices, sensors, and systems that transfer data. Such devices can be embedded with sensors and actuators, permitting them to collect and transmit data to other devices or centralized structures. Key components of IoT include: Sensors: Devices equipped with sensors to measure various physical parameters such as temperature, pH, turbidity, dissolved oxygen, and chemical quantity.

Connectivity: IoT devices are connected to networks, allowing to transfer data in real time to centralized systems for analysis.

Data Processing: The collected data is processed either locally or in the cloud, providing valuable insights for decision-making.

Actuators: In addition to sensing, IoT devices can also have actuators that enable them to perform actions based on the data received.

IoT has found applications in various fields, including smart cities, healthcare, agriculture, and environmental monitoring. In context of water quality monitoring, IoT devices can be strategically deployed in water bodies, treatment plants, and distribution systems to continuously collect real-time data [19].

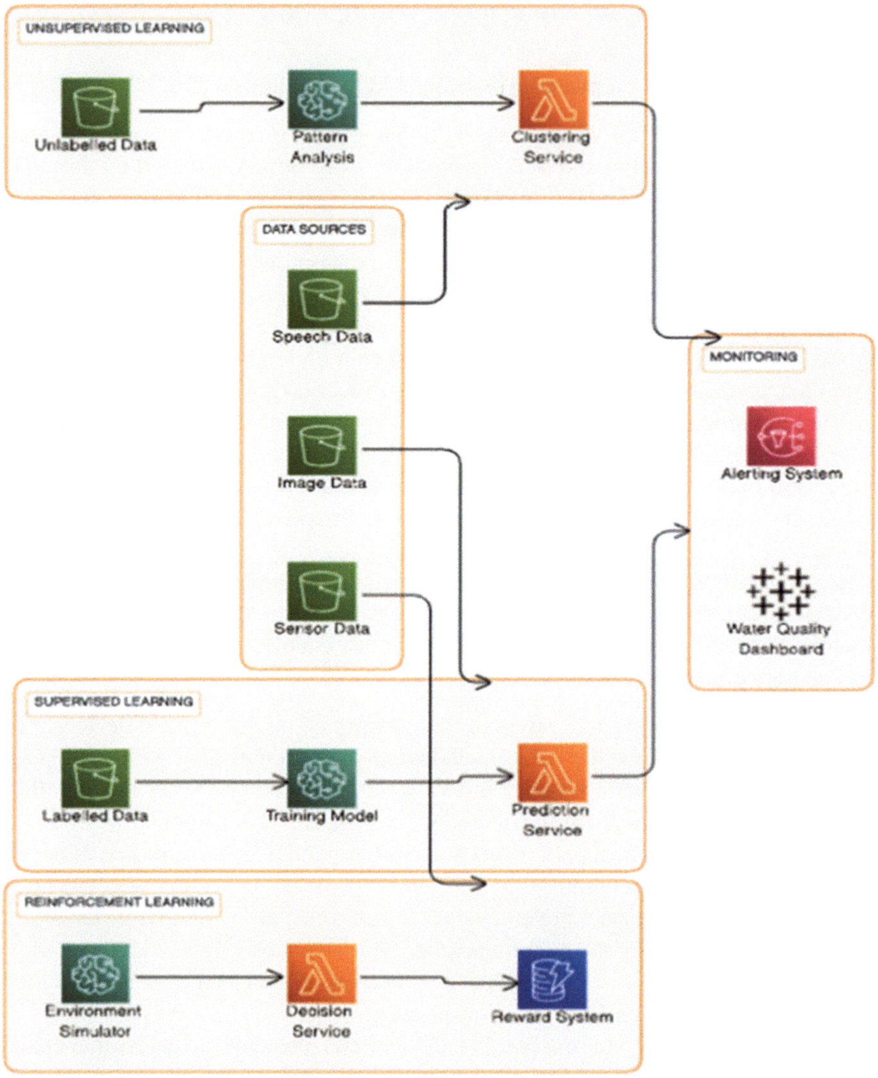

Fig. 6.3 Machine learning architecture

6.3 Emphasizing Potential Applications in Water Quality Monitoring

Water quality monitoring is a critical aspect of environmental management, and the combination of ML and the IoT introduces transformative applications in this domain. By harnessing the strengths of both technologies, various potential applications emerge, enhancing the accuracy, efficiency, and scope of water quality monitoring.

6.3.1 Machine Learning in Water Quality Monitoring

Pattern Recognition: ML algorithms can analyze historical water quality data to recognize patterns associated with normal conditions. When presented with new data, the algorithms can identify deviations from these patterns, signaling potential contamination events.

Anomaly Detection: ML can be used for anomaly detection by establishing baseline water quality parameters and flagging unusual deviations. This is crucial for early detection of contaminants or changes in water quality that might go unnoticed by traditional monitoring methods [5].

Predictive Modeling: ML trained to forecast water quality trends based on various environmental factors. This predictive modeling enables authorities to anticipate changes and take preventive measures.

6.3.2 IoT in Water Quality Monitoring

Continuous Data Collection: IoT devices facilitate continuous data collection, allowing for a more comprehensive understanding of water quality dynamics. This real-time data transmission is essential for early detection and timely response to contamination events.

Remote Monitoring: The interconnected nature of IoT devices enables remote monitoring of water quality in various locations. This is especially valuable in large water distribution networks or bodies where manual monitoring may be challenging [10].

Integration with ML: The data collected by IoT devices serves as input for ML algorithms. By integrating IoT and ML, the system can leverage the strengths of both technologies, providing a powerful tool for accurate and timely water quality analysis [1].

The integration of Machine Learning and the Internet of Things in water quality monitoring holds immense potential for transforming traditional approaches. ML algorithms can analyze vast datasets, identify patterns, and detect anomalies, while IoT devices enable continuous data collection and real-time monitoring. Together, these technologies offer a proactive and dynamic solution for early detection and management of water contamination, contributing to the safeguarding of water resources and public health [15].

6.4 The Role of IoT in Water Monitoring

This section focuses on IoT uses for water monitoring.

6.4.1 IoT Devices in Water Systems

The deployment of IoT instruments in water systems represents a technological leap forward in the monitoring, management, and conservation of water resources. Such instruments, with sensors and communicating capacities, offer a dynamic and real-time approach to understanding and ensuring the quality of water in various contexts, including natural water bodies, treatment plants, and distribution systems [12].

Deployment of Sensors in Water Bodies, Treatment Plants, and Distribution Systems are as follows.

Water Bodies: IoT devices, in the form of sensors, can be strategically deployed in natural water bodies such as rivers, lakes, and reservoirs. The sensors are considered to measure various water quality parameters in real time. For instance, temperature sensors can track variations in water temperature, which is crucial for understanding the thermal characteristics of water bodies. pH sensors can measure the acidity or alkalinity of the water, providing insights into its chemical composition.

Treatment Plants: In water treatment plants, IoT devices play a pivotal role in monitoring and optimizing the water treatment processes. Sensors can be installed at different stages of water treatment to measure parameters like turbidity, chlorine levels, and dissolved oxygen [4]. Turbidity sensors help assess the cloudiness or haziness of water, indicating the presence of suspended particles. Monitoring chlorine levels is essential for ensuring effective disinfection while measuring dissolved oxygen is critical for understanding the oxygen content in the treated water.

Distribution Systems: Within water distribution systems, IoT sensors can be integrated into pipelines and storage tanks. These sensors continuously collect data on factors such as pressure, flow rates, and water quality. Pressure sensors aid in identifying potential leaks or bursts in the distribution network. Flow rate sensors help monitor the movement of water through pipelines, ensuring an efficient and consistent supply. Water quality sensors can detect changes in parameters that might indicate contamination during the distribution process [16].

The Continuous Data Collection Capabilities of IoT Devices are as follows: Real-time Monitoring: IoT devices offer real-time monitoring capabilities, allowing for instantaneous collection and transmission of data. This is a fundamental advantage over traditional monitoring methods that involve intermittent sampling and delayed laboratory analyses [6].

The continuous nature of data collection ensures that any changes or anomalies in water quality are promptly detected, providing an early warning system for potential contamination events.

Remote Sensing: IoT devices are often equipped with communication capabilities, enabling remote data transmission to centralized systems. This remote sensing capability is particularly valuable in large or geographically dispersed water systems. Remote monitoring allows authorities to access and analyze water quality data from various locations, providing a comprehensive view of the entire water network without the need for physical presence.

Data Integration: IoT devices produce vast amounts of data, encompassing multiple parameters and locations. This data can be integrated into a centralized system, creating a holistic understanding of water quality dynamics. Integration of information from dissimilar sources allows for more analysis, enabling a proactive approach to water quality management and facilitating quick responses to emerging issues.

6.4.2 *Data Transmission and Centralized Monitoring*

IoT devices transmit real-time data to centralized systems using communication protocols, cloud-based infrastructure and sometimes incorporating edge computing. Constant surveillance through centralized monitoring is essential for early contamination detection, with benefits ranging from preventive actions to improving public health outcomes. The integration of data analytics and machine learning enhances the system's capability to process and analyze large datasets, contributing to more effective monitoring and detection. Safety and confidentiality considerations are serious to maintaining the integrity of the transmitted data.

Introduction to IoT and Data Transmission: IoT refers to the network of interconnected devices embedded with sensors, s/w, and other technologies to exchange data with other devices and systems over the Internet. IoT devices are designed to gather and communicate data in real time, creating a seamless flow of information.

Sensors and Data Collection: IoT devices are armed with various sensors, such as temperature sensors, humidity sensors, cameras, and more, depending on their specific purpose. Sensors continuously collect information from the environment or the device itself.

Communication Protocols: IoT devices use different communication protocols to transmit data. Common protocols include MQTT (Message Queuing Telemetry Transport), CoAP (Constrained Application Protocol), and HTTP. MQTT is widely used for its lightweight nature and efficiency in low-bandwidth, high-latency, or unreliable networks.

Edge Computing: Some IoT devices leverage EC, so information processing happens closer to the information source instead of relying solely on a centralized server. Edge computing helps reduce latency, optimize bandwidth, and enhance real-time data processing capabilities.

Cloud-Based Centralized Systems: Real-time data from IoT devices is transmitted to centralized systems, often hosted in the cloud. Cloud-based systems provide scalability, flexibility, and accessibility, allowing users to monitor and manage data from anywhere with an internet connection.

Importance of Centralized Monitoring: Centralized monitoring is crucial for several applications, including environmental nursing, industry processes, and healthcare. Early contamination detection is a significant advantage of centralized monitoring systems.

Constant Surveillance for Early Contamination Detection: Constant surveillance involves continuous monitoring of data streams in real time to identify abnormal patterns or deviations. In scenarios like water quality monitoring, air quality monitoring, or food processing, early contamination detection is vital to prevent widespread issues.

Benefits of Early Contamination Detection: Preventive Actions: Early detection allows for prompt preventive actions, reducing the impact of contamination on the environment or products.

Public Health: In healthcare applications, early detection of anomalies can lead to faster response times, potentially saving lives.

Data Analytics and Machine Learning: Centralized monitoring systems often employ data analytics and ML algorithms to analyze large datasets. These technologies enhance the system's ability to classify patterns, anomalies, and trends, contributing to more precise and timely detection of contamination.

Security and Privacy Considerations: As data is transmitted from IoT devices to centralized systems, ensuring the security and privacy of the transmitted data is paramount. Encryption, safe communication protocols, and admission controls are implemented to protect sensitive information.

6.5 Machine Learning Algorithms for Water Quality Analysis

This section elaborates on machine learning algorithms for water quality analysis.

6.5.1 ML Algorithms in Data Analysis

ML algorithms are powerful tools for data analysis, capable of processing large datasets, identifying patterns, and detecting deviations from baseline data. Their ability to learn from data and make predictions or classifications makes them invaluable in various domains, from finance to healthcare. However, careful consideration of data quality and model interpretability is essential for successful implementation.

Introduction to ML Algorithms in Data Analysis: ML algorithms are computational models that better their performance on a task over time through experience, without being explicitly programmed. In data analysis, ML algorithms play a crucial role in processing and extracting meaningful in side from large datasets.

Power of ML Algorithms in Processing Large Datasets: ML algorithms are particularly powerful in handling large datasets that may be too complex or voluminous for traditional analytical methods. These algorithms can efficiently process and analyze vast amounts of data, extracting patterns.

Types of ML Algorithms in Data Analysis: Supervised Learning: Algorithms learn from labeled training data to make forecasts or classify new, hidden information.

Unsupervised Learning: Algorithms work with unlabeled data, discovering patterns, relationships, or groupings dataset.

Semi-Supervised Learning: A combination of supervised and unsupervised learning, where the algorithm is trained on a mix of labeled and unlabeled data.

Reinforcement Learning: Agents learn by trial and error, feedback in the form of prizes or penalties based on their activities.

Identifying Patterns in Data: ML algorithms excel at recognizing outlines within datasets. This can include recognizing correlations, dependencies, and trends that may not be apparent through traditional analysis. Pattern recognition allows the algorithm to make predictions or classifications based on similarities to previously seen patterns in the data.

Deviation Detection: ML algorithms are active in detecting deviations or anomalies in datasets. Anomaly detection is crucial for identifying unusual patterns or outliers that may signify errors, fraud, or significant changes in the underlying data distribution.

Baseline Data and Anomaly Detection: ML algorithms often establish a baseline from historical or normal data patterns. When new data deviates significantly from this baseline, the algorithm can flag it as an anomaly, indicating a potential issue or interesting event that requires further investigation.

Common ML Algorithms for Data Analysis: Common algorithms are as follows.

Regression Algorithms: Predict a continuous output based on input features.

Decision Trees: Hierarchical structures that make decisions based on input features.

Clustering Algorithms: Group similar data points together based on certain criteria.

Neural Networks: Mimics structure and function of the human mind, used for complex pattern recognition tasks.

Support Vector Machines (SVM): Categorize information points by finding the optimal hyperplane that separates diverse classes.

Applications of ML in Data Analysis: Financial Fraud Detection: ML algorithms can identify unusual patterns in financial transactions to detect potential fraud.

Healthcare Diagnostics: ML algorithms analyze medical data to assist in disease analysis and conduct planning [13].

Predictive Maintenance: ML algorithms predict when equipment is likely to fail based on historical data, enabling proactive maintenance.

Challenges and Considerations: ML algorithms require careful consideration of data quality, feature engineering, and model interpretability. Overfitting and underfitting are common challenges that need to be addressed through appropriate model tuning.

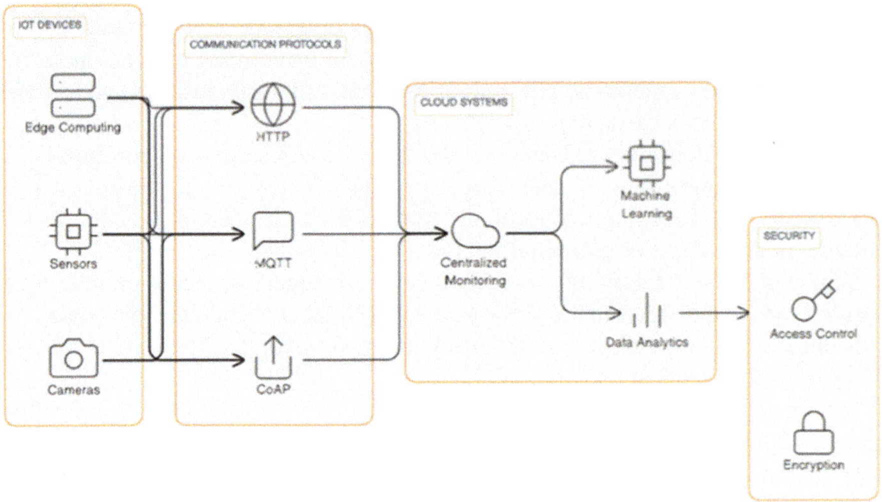

Fig. 6.4 IoT centralized monitoring architecture

The IoT Centralized Monitoring Architecture provides a comprehensive framework for real-time data collection and analysis (see Fig. 6.4).

6.5.2 Training Models for Water Quality Recognition

This section discusses different training models for Water Quality Recognition.

Discuss the training of ML models to recognize abnormal patterns indicating potential contamination Training ML models to recognize abnormal patterns indicating potential contamination in various domains, such as water quality monitoring, involves a systematic process. The goal is to develop models that can effectively distinguish between normal and abnormal conditions based on input data. The detailed discussion on training for ML models for recognizing abnormal patterns in the context of water quality.

Data Collection: The first step is to collect a comprehensive dataset that includes historical records of water quality measurements. This dataset should cover a range of scenarios, including both normal and contaminated conditions. Parameters such as pH levels, turbidity, dissolved oxygen, and concentrations of pollutants are essential features in the dataset.

Data Preprocessing: Raw data often requires preprocessing to handle missing values, outliers, or inconsistencies. This step ensures the dataset's quality and reliability. Data normalization or standardization may be applied to ensure that different features are on a similar scale. Feature Selection and Engineering: Relevant features that contribute to distinguishing between normal and abnormal patterns are selected.

Feature engineering may involve transforming or combining features to progress model's capability to capture patterns.

Labeling Data: Data instances in the dataset are labeled to indicate whether they represent normal or contaminated water. The labeling process is crucial for supervised learning, where the model learns from labeled examples.

Model Selection: Option choice of ML algorithm hinges on the features of data and the complexity of the problem. Common algorithms for anomaly detection include Isolation Forests, One-Class SVM, and autoencoders in neural networks.

Training Process: The model is trained using the labeled dataset, where it learns to recognize patterns associated with normal water conditions. During training, the model regulates its internal parameters to minimize the variance between its forecasts and the true labels.

Anomaly Detection: ML models, once trained, can identify abnormal patterns in new, unseen data. Anomalies are instances that deviate significantly from what the model has learned as normal. Different algorithms may use diverse approaches, such as proximity-based methods or reconstruction errors in autoencoders, to detect anomalies.

Hyperparameters Tuning: Hyperparameters, which are parameters external to the model that affect its learning process, may need to be tuned to optimize the model's performance. This is often done through techniques like cross-validation.

Model Evaluation: The trained model needs to be evaluated using a separate dataset that it has not seen before. Metrics such as precision, recall, F1 score, and receiver operating characteristic curve can be used to assess the model's performance in identifying abnormal patterns.

Validation and Testing: The model should be validated on diverse datasets to ensure its generalizability. Testing with real-world data and simulated contamination events helps assess the model's robustness.

Continuous Monitoring and Updating: ML models for water quality recognition should be integrated into a continuous monitoring system. Regular updates and retraining are necessary to adapt to evolving water quality conditions.

Interpretability: Understanding the basis of the model's predictions is crucial for trust and decision-making. Ensuring model interpretability can be achieved through techniques like feature importance analysis.

Incorporation with IoT and Sensor Networks: Incorporation with IoT devices and sensor networks allows for real-time data input, enhancing the model's ability to detect and respond to abnormal patterns promptly.

Consideration of False Positives and False Negatives: Balancing the trade-off between false positives and false negatives is important. Depending on the application, minimizing one type of error may be more critical than the other.

Explore the adaptability of ML algorithms to changing environmental conditions The adaptability of ML algorithms to changing environmental conditions is a result of their ability to learn, generalize, and adjust based on new information. Techniques such as continuous training, transfer learning, ensemble methods, and reinforcement learning contribute to the flexibility of ML models in handling dynamic and evolving scenarios. The integration of adaptive algorithms with real-time data streams and monitoring systems further enhances their applicability in diverse and changing environments. Here are several ways in which ML algorithms demonstrate adaptability to changing environmental conditions.

Dynamic Learning: ML models can dynamically adjust their parameters and learning strategies based on changes in input data. This adaptability allows them to accommodate variations in environmental conditions over time.

Continuous Training: ML models can be designed to undergo continuous training. As new data becomes available, the model can be updated to adapt to shifts in environmental patterns and conditions.

Online Learning: Some ML algorithms support online learning, where the model is updated in actual time as new data streams in. Capability is mainly beneficial in environments where conditions change rapidly.

Transfer Learning: Transfer learning allows a model trained on one task or dataset to be fine-tuned for a related task or a dataset representing a different time period. This approach is beneficial when adapting to changes while leveraging knowledge gained from previous training.

Ensemble Learning: Ensemble approaches, e.g., Random Forests or Gradient Boosting, mixing multiple copies to improve overall performance. The diversity of the ensemble can enhance adaptability by allowing the model to capture different aspects of changing conditions.

Reinforcement Learning: In environments with dynamic conditions, reinforcement learning can be employed. Agents learn by interacting with the environment and getting feedback, adapting their strategies based on the changing circumstances.

Feature Adaptation: ML models can be designed to adapt to changes in feature distributions. Feature adaptation techniques ensure that the model remains effective even when statistical properties of input features change over time.

Temporal Models: Time-series models, like as recurrent neural networks or Long Short-Term Memory networks, are well-suited for tasks where the input data varies over time. These models can capture temporal dependencies and adapt to changing patterns.

Robustness Testing: ML models can be tested for robustness against variations and perturbations in input data. Robust models are better equipped to handle unexpected changes and anomalies in the environment.

Adaptive Algorithms: Some ML algorithms are inherently designed to be adaptive. For example, adaptive learning rate techniques in optimization algorithms help models adjust their learning rates based on the local properties of the data.

Self-monitoring Systems: ML models integrated into self-monitoring systems can continuously assess their own performance and trigger retraining processes when degradation is detected. This self-awareness contributes to adaptability.

IoT Integration: ML algorithms integrated with IoT components and sensor can receive real-time updates from the environment. This mixing enhances the model's ability to adapt to changing conditions by providing continuous, up-to-date information.

Data Augmentation: Data augmentation techniques, such as introducing synthetic variations into the training data, can improve a model's ability to generalize to changing conditions and unseen scenarios.

Domain Adaptation: In cases where the source and target domains differ, domain adaptation techniques help ML models adapt to changes in the underlying distribution of data, ensuring better performance in the target environment.

6.6 Early Warning Systems

This section explains Ml and IoT integration for early detection of water contamination.

6.6.1 Integration of ML and IoT for Early Detection

The integration of ML and IoT for early detection combines the real-time data capabilities of IoT with the analytical power of ML models. This synergy enables proactive decision-making, timely responses to emerging events, and the optimization of various processes across different industries. The continuous monitoring and adaptability of the integrated system contribute to its effectiveness in providing early detection capabilities.

Introduction to ML and IoT Integration: Machine Learning (ML): ML involves the growth of algorithms and models that can learn from data to make predictions or decisions without programming.

Internet of Things (IoT): IoT refers to the network of interconnected devices that communicate and share data with each other through the Internet.

Data Collection through IoT Devices: IoT devices are equipped with sensors and actuators that collect data from the physical world. These devices can monitor various parameters such as temperature, humidity, pressure, motion, and more, depending on their application. The data collected by IoT devices is given to a centralized server or cloud for processing.

Real-Time Data Streams: One of the assets of IoT is to provide real-time information streams. This continuous flow of information allows for immediate analysis and response to changing conditions or events.

ML Algorithms for Early Detection: ML algorithms are employed to analyze the information collected by IoT devices. Algorithms can be trained to recognize patterns, anomalies, or deviations from normal behavior. Supervised learning can be used when labeled data is available, while unsupervised learning can be applied in scenarios where normal behavior is not explicitly defined.

Types of ML Models for Early Detection: Anomaly Detection Models: ML models can be trained to detect anomalies or deviations from expected behavior, signaling potential issues or events that require attention.

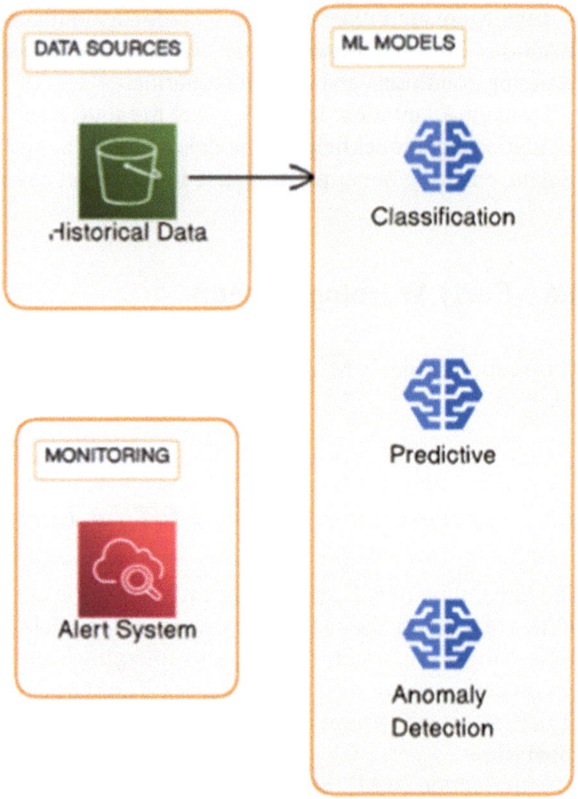

Fig. 6.5 Types of ML models for water anomaly detection

Predictive Models: ML models can predict future trends or conditions based on historical data, enabling early detection of emerging patterns.

Classification Models: ML models can classify data into different categories, allowing for the identification of specific events or conditions. The types of ML models used for water anomaly detection offer various approaches to identifying and addressing water quality issues (see Fig. 6.5).

Continuous Monitoring and Adaptability: ML models integrated with IoT enable continuous monitoring of the environment. As new data is collected, the models can adapt and update their predictions or classifications, ensuring responsiveness to changing conditions.

Edge Computing for Real-Time Processing: EC involves processing data closer to the source (on edge devices) rather than relying solely on centralized servers. It is particularly beneficial for real-time applications, as it reduces latency and bandwidth requirements. ML models can be deployed on edge devices for quick analysis and decision-making, complementing centralized processing.

Feedback Loop and Model Improvement: The addition of ML and IoT allows for a feedback loop where the performance of ML models is continuously evaluated. If the model identifies false positives or misses certain events, it can be retrained with additional data to improve its accuracy.

Use Cases for Early Detection: Healthcare Monitoring: IoT devices such as wearables can collect health data, and ML models can detect early signs of health issues.

Environmental Monitoring: IoT sensors can monitor air or water quality, and ML models can identify anomalies that indicate pollution or contamination [7].

Predictive Maintenance: In industrial settings, IoT sensors on machinery can collect data, and ML models can predict maintenance needs before equipment failure.

Security and Privacy Considerations: Safety actions, including encryption and secure communication protocols, are crucial to protect the data transmitted between IoT devices and the ML models. Privacy concerns should be addressed to ensure the ethical and responsible use of data collected by IoT devices.

Scalability and Flexibility: The integration of ML and IoT should be scalable to handle different devices and flexible enough to adapt to different applications and use cases.

6.6.2 Real-World Applications

Chicago: "Smart Chicago River" Project

Overview: The city of Chicago implemented the "Smart Chicago River" project to monitor and improve water quality in the Chicago River.

Implementation: IoT sensors were deployed throughout the river to collect data on various water quality parameters, including temperature, pH levels, and nutrient concentrations. ML algorithms were employed to analyze the data and detect anomalies or patterns indicative of contamination events.

Outcomes: Early Detection: ML algorithms demonstrated the capability to identify abnormal patterns in water quality data, enabling early detection of pollution incidents [14]. Improved Response Times: The integration of IoT and ML significantly reduced the response times for addressing contamination, allowing for quicker remediation efforts.

Singapore: "Smart Water Grid"

Overview: Singapore implemented a comprehensive "Smart Water Grid" system to monitor and manage water quality across its water distribution network.

Implementation: IoT sensors were embedded in water treatment plants, reservoirs, and distribution pipelines to continuously monitor parameters like chlorine levels, turbidity, and flow rates. ML algorithms were applied to analyze historical and real-time data to predict water quality changes and potential contamination events.

Outcomes: Predictive Maintenance: ML models helped predict equipment failures and maintenance needs in water treatment plants, improving the overall efficiency of the water distribution system [9]. Enhanced Water Quality: The early detection capabilities of ML algorithms contributed to maintaining high water quality standards and reducing the risk of waterborne diseases.

Stockholm, Sweden: "Smart Cities - Smart Water"

Overview: Stockholm's "Smart Cities - Smart Water" initiative focused on using IoT and ML to monitor water quality in both natural bodies of water and the city's water supply.

Implementation: Wireless sensors were deployed in lakes and rivers to collect data on parameters such as oxygen levels, temperature, and nutrient concentrations. ML algorithms were employed to analyze the collected data for abnormal patterns and trends.

Outcomes: Ecosystem Monitoring: The integration of ML and IoT facilitated comprehensive monitoring of aquatic ecosystems, helping researchers and authorities understand the impact of urbanization on water quality.

Proactive Environmental Management: ML-driven insights allowed for proactive environmental management, with interventions initiated before significant water quality degradation occurred.

Milwaukee, USA: "Smart Waters Project"

Overview: Milwaukee's "Smart Waters Project" aimed to enhance water quality monitoring in Lake Michigan and the Milwaukee River.

Implementation: IoT sensors were deployed to collect data on parameters such as nutrient levels, bacteria counts, and temperature. ML algorithms were applied to identify abnormal patterns in the data, with a focus on early detection of pollution events.

Outcomes: Public Health Improvement: The early detection capabilities of the ML algorithms contributed to better protection of public health by minimizing exposure to contaminated water. Regulatory Compliance: The city achieved better compliance with water quality regulations through more efficient monitoring and reporting enabled by IoT and ML technologies.

Melbourne, Australia: "Water Quality Monitoring in Smart Cities"

Overview: Melbourne initiated a "Water Quality Monitoring in Smart Cities" project to leverage IoT and ML for monitoring water quality in urban areas.

Implementation: IoT sensors were placed in stormwater drains, rivers, and lakes to collect data on water quality parameters. ML models were used to predict pollution events and assess the impact of urban activities on water quality.

Outcomes: Urban Planning: The insights derived from ML analyses influenced urban planning decisions, helping design infrastructure that minimizes the impact on water quality.

Community Engagement: The project engaged the community by providing real-time water quality data, fostering awareness and responsible water use.

6.7 Challenges and Future Directions

This section describes the challenges and future directions of the work.

6.7.1 Challenges in the Role of ML and IoT in Early Detection of Water Contamination

The integration of Machine Learning (ML) and the Internet of Things (IoT) in the early detection of water infection provides numerous promising possibilities, but it also comes with a set of large challenges. These demanding situations want to be addressed to recognize the total ability of those technology in safeguarding water first-class.

Data Quality and Quantity: One of the number one challenges is making sure of the exceptional quantity of statistics collected by IoT sensors. Accurate and reliable records are essential for powerful ML version education and prediction. However, sensors can be prone to mistakes, glides, and environmental interference, which could bring about noisy or misguided records. Additionally, the need for huge datasets to teach ML fashions may be elaborate, in particular in areas with sparse monitoring infrastructure.

Sensor Limitations: While improvements in the sensor era are ongoing, cutting-edge sensors might also nevertheless have barriers in phrases of sensitivity, selectivity, and sturdiness. Many sensors can locate the most effective particular contaminants and might not be capable of degree all applicable water nice parameters. Furthermore, sensors deployed in harsh environmental situations might also suffer from put on and tear, main to common maintenance and substitutes.

Energy Consumption: IoT gadgets, consisting of sensors, regularly depend upon battery strength, making power efficiency a crucial challenge. High strength consumption can restrict the deployment of IoT sensors in far-off or resource-limited regions. Ensuring a lengthy time period, and sustainable operation of these gadgets requires advancements in low-strength sensor technology and energy-harvesting methods.

Data Processing and Storage: The tremendous amount of information generated by using IoT sensors necessitates sturdy facts processing and garage answers. Edge computing can help reduce latency and bandwidth requirements by processing facts domestically, however, it additionally introduces demanding situations related to computational electricity and useful resource control at the threshold. Moreover, stable and green data garage solutions are needed to handle the continuous circulation of records and ensure their availability for evaluation [18].

Privacy and Security: Protecting the privacy and security of the data amassed via IoT gadgets is paramount. Water exceptional facts may be touchy, particularly if it relates to public health and safety. Ensuring facts integrity, stopping unauthorized access, and protecting in opposition to cyber-assaults are important demanding situations that must be addressed through strong cybersecurity measures and statistics encryption strategies.

Scalability and Interoperability: Deploying a massive-scale community of IoT sensors for water monitoring requires scalable solutions that can handle the integration and control of numerous gadgets. Ensuring interoperability between gadgets from special producers and standards is crucial to creating a cohesive and green tracking device. This project includes growing standardized protocols and verbal exchange frameworks.

Cost and Accessibility: The price of deploying and retaining IoT sensors and ML systems can be prohibitive, particularly for low-profit or resource-confined regions. Making these technologies handy and inexpensive is crucial for massive adoption.

This involves now not simply lowering the fee of sensors and gadgets but additionally imparting financial and technical guidance to communities and organizations.

Regulatory and Ethical Considerations: Implementing ML and IoT for water infection detection calls for navigating complicated regulatory and ethical landscapes. Ensuring compliance with local and worldwide rules, addressing moral issues associated with statistics collection and utilization, and gaining public trust are vital elements that have an impact on the success of these technologies.

In summary, at the same time as the integration of ML and IoT holds fantastic promise for early detection of water contamination, addressing those demanding situations is crucial for powerful implementation. By focusing on enhancing information first-rate, sensor technology, strength efficiency, information processing, protection, scalability, price, and regulatory compliance, we can harness the whole capacity of those technologies to protect water high-quality and public fitness.

6.7.2 Future Directions for ML and IoT in Early Detection of Water Contamination

The integration of Machine Learning (ML) and the Internet of Things (IoT) in the early detection of water contamination is a burgeoning field with significant ability. Looking ahead, numerous promising guidelines could considerably enhance the effectiveness and attainment of these technologies.

Advanced Sensor Development: Future improvements in sensor generation will play a critical position. Developing more sensitive, long-lasting, and multi-parameter sensors will permit more comprehensive and specific monitoring of water excellent. These sensors ought to stumble on a broader variety of contaminants at lower concentrations, imparting in advance warnings and more particular facts.

Enhanced ML Algorithms: As the quantity and complexity of statistics gathered with the aid of IoT gadgets grow, there might be a want for greater state-of-the-art ML algorithms. Future studies ought to recognition on developing algorithms that can manage large datasets with high dimensionality and improve anomaly detection accuracy. Techniques including deep getting-to-know and reinforcement studying will be in particular beneficial, presenting more nuanced insights and predictive skills.

Integration with Other Technologies: Combining ML and IoT with other emerging technologies could in addition decorate water infection detection. For instance, blockchain generation can be used to secure and confirm statistics integrity, ensuring that the statistics from sensors is dependable and tamper-proof.

Additionally, integrating Geographic Information Systems (GIS) may assist in visualizing infection patterns and expect the spread of pollutants.

Real-Time Data Processing and Decision-Making: Future systems should comprise side computing to manner data domestically on the sensor level. This could reduce latency and permit real-time selection-making, which is important for fast response to infection occasions. Coupled with cloud computing, these systems could offer scalable solutions that integrate local processing electricity with the tremendous computational resources of the cloud.

Predictive and Preventive Maintenance: ML algorithms may be employed not handiest for infection detection but also for predictive protection of the sensors and IoT infrastructure. This guarantees that the system stays operational and correct over long periods, reducing downtime and upkeep fees.

Public Engagement and Education: Future initiatives ought to be conscious of making water-pleasant information greater reachable to the public. Mobile packages and online structures may want to offer actual-time updates and indicators to groups, empowering them to take proactive measures to ensure their water protection. Educational programs could also be developed to elevate attention to water infection troubles and the position of an era in addressing them.

Policy and Regulatory Support: Collaboration with policymakers and regulatory bodies may be critical to make sure that those technological advancements are efficaciously carried out. Developing standards and hints for the deployment and use of ML and IoT in water first-rate tracking will ensure consistency, reliability, and public belief in those systems.

In the end, the destiny of ML and IoT in the early detection of water contamination is vibrant, with numerous possibilities for technological innovation and societal effects. By continuing to enhance sensor technology, refine ML algorithms, integrate with different technologies, and engage with the general public and policymakers, we can create robust, responsive, and scalable systems that appreciably enhance water satisfaction monitoring and safeguard public fitness.

6.8 Conclusion

The integration of Machine Learning (ML) and the Internet of Things (IoT) in the early detection of water infection represents a transformative technique for environmental monitoring and public health protection. By leveraging the talents of IoT, a community of sensors can be deployed throughout numerous water sources to continuously gather data on multiple parameters together with pH, turbidity, temperature, and precise contaminants. These actual-time records are then processed and analyzed with the usage of advanced ML algorithms, which are capable of detecting anomalies and patterns indicative of contamination with excessive accuracy and velocity. The synergistic mixture of ML and IoT no longer most effectively complements the sensitivity and specificity of infection detection but also allows for predictive analytics, permitting proactive measures to be taken before contamination levels attain important thresholds. Moreover, the continuous monitoring facilitated by way of IoT guarantees that even transient infection activities are detected, which is probably ignored through traditional periodic sampling strategies. The application of those technologies additionally gives scalability and fee effectiveness, making it viable to reveal massive and far-flung areas that are otherwise difficult to oversee. In conclusion, the role of ML and IoT in early water contamination detection is pivotal in advancing our capacity to guard water first-rate, supplying a robust solution that supports environmental sustainability and public health via providing well timed, accurate, and actionable records. As those technologies continue to adapt, their integration will possibly come to be increasingly vital in addressing the developing challenges of water contamination in a swiftly changing international.

References

1. Adeleke, I.A., Nwulu, N.I., Ogbolumani, O.A.: A hybrid machine learning and embedded IoT-based water quality monitoring system. Internet Things **22**, 100774 (2023). https://doi.org/10.1016/j.iot.2023.100774
2. Bhardwaj, A., Dagar, V., Khan, M. O., Aggarwal, A., Alvarado, R., Kumar, M., et al.: Smart IoT and machine learning-based framework for water quality assessment and device component monitoring. Environ. Sci. Pollut. Res. **29**(30), 46018–46036 (2022). https://doi.org/10.1007/s11356-022-19014-3
3. Bria, A., Cerro, G., Ferdinandi, M., Marrocco, C., Molinara, M.: An IoT-ready solution for automated recognition of water contaminants. Pattern Recogn. Lett. **135**, 188–195 (2020). https://doi.org/10.1016/j.patrec.2020.04.019
4. Chinnappan, C.V., John William, A.D., Nidamanuri, S.K.C., Jayalakshmi, S., Bogani, R., Thanapal, P., et al.: IoT-enabled chlorine level assessment and prediction in water monitoring system using machine learning. Electronics **12**(6), 1458 (2023). https://doi.org/10.3390/electronics12061458
5. Dogo, E.M., Nwulu, N.I., Twala, B., Aigbavboa, C.: A survey of machine learning methods applied to anomaly detection on drinking-water quality data. Urban Water J. **16**(3), 235–248 (2019). https://doi.org/10.1080/1573062X.2019.1637002
6. El-Shafeiy, E., Alsabaan, M., Ibrahem, M.I., Elwahsh, H.: Real-time anomaly detection for water quality sensor monitoring based on multivariate deep learning technique. Sensors **23**(20), 8613 (2023). https://doi.org/10.3390/s23208613
7. Jha, B.K., Sivasankari, G.G., Venugopal, K.R.: Cloud-based smart water quality monitoring system using IoT sensors and machine learning. Int. J. Adv. Trends Comput. Sci. Eng. **9**(3) (2020). https://doi.org/10.30534/ijatcse/2020/141932020
8. Koditala, N.K., Pandey, P.S.: Water quality monitoring system using IoT and machine learning. In: 2018 International Conference on Research in Intelligent and Computing in Engineering (RICE), pp. 1–5. IEEE. https://doi.org/10.1109/RICE.2018.8509050
9. Lowe, M., Qin, R., Mao, X.: A review on machine learning, artificial intelligence, and smart technology in water treatment and monitoring. Water **14**(9), 1384 (2022). https://doi.org/10.3390/w14091384
10. Narayanan, L.K., Sankaranarayanan, S., Rodrigues, J.J., Kozlov, S.: Water demand forecasting using deep learning in IoT enabled water distribution network: DL-water demand forecasting for water distribution design. Int. J. Comput. Commun. Control **15**(6) (2020)
11. Nayan, A.A., Mozumder, A.N., Saha, J., Mahmud, K.R., Azad, A.K.A., Kibria, M.G.: A machine learning approach for early detection of fish diseases by analyzing water quality (2021). arXiv:2102.09390. https://doi.org/10.48550/arXiv.2102.09390

12. Omambia, A., Maake, B., Wambua, A.: Water quality monitoring using IoT & machine learning. In: 2022 IST-Africa Conference (IST-Africa), pp. 1–8. IEEE (2021). https://doi.org/10.23919/IST-Africa56635.2022.9845590
13. Patil, S.S., Thorat, S.A.: Early detection of grapes diseases using machine learning and IoT. In: 2016 Second International Conference on Cognitive Computing and Information Processing (CCIP), pp. 1–5. IEEE (2016). https://doi.org/10.1109/CCIP.2016.7802887
14. Shafi, U., Mumtaz, R., Anwar, H., Qamar, A.M., Khurshid, H.: Surface water pollution detection using internet of things. In: 2018 15th International Conference on Smart Cities: improving Quality of Life Using ICT & IoT (HONET-ICT), pp. 92–96. IEEE (2018). https://doi.org/10.1109/HONET.2018.8551341
15. Singh, M., Ahmed, S.: IoT based smart water management systems: a systematic review. Mater. Today: Proc. **46**, 5211–5218 (2021). https://doi.org/10.1016/j.matpr.2020.08.588
16. Thai-Nghe, N., Thanh-Hai, N., Chi Ngon, N.: Deep learning approach for forecasting water quality in IoT systems. Int. J. Adv. Comput. Sci. Appl. **11**(8), 686–693 (2020)
17. Vashishth, T.K., Sharma, V., Chaudhary, S., Panwar, R., Sharma, S., Kumar, P.: Advanced Technologies and AI-enabled IoT applications in high-tech agriculture. In: Handbook of Research on AI-Equipped IoT Applications in High-Tech Agriculture, pp. 155–166. IGI Global (2023). https://doi.org/10.4018/978-1-6684-9231-4.ch008
18. Vashishth, T.K., Sharma, V., Sharma, K.K., Kumar, B., Chaudhary, S., Panwar, R.: Waste-to-energy solutions harnessing iot and ml for sustainable power generation in smart cities. In: Methodologies, Frameworks, and Applications of Machine Learning, pp. 125–146. IGI Global (2024). https://doi.org/10.4018/979-8-3693-1062-5.ch007
19. Zhu, M., Wang, J., Yang, X., Zhang, Y., Zhang, L., Ren, H., et al.: A review of the application of machine learning in water quality evaluation. Eco-Environ. Health (2022). https://doi.org/10.1016/j.eehl.2022.06.001

Chapter 7
Arduino IoT Platform with Bayes Theorem-Based Water Contamination Detection System

Gyanendra Kumar, Pragya, and Sur Singh Rawat

Abstract Water contamination is a growing concern that poses significant risks to public health and the environment. Developing precise and efficient water quality monitoring systems are crucial to address this issue. This paper introduces an automated real-time monitoring, alarming, and information-sharing system based on the Arduino Internet of Things (IoT) platform and the Bayes Theorem for detecting water contamination. The proposed system utilizes the Arduino IoT platform, cloud server, and data analytics to monitor key water parameters, including pH levels, turbidity, Hardness, Humidity, Temperature, and total dissolved solids (TDS), in real time. By employing the Bayes Theorem, the system can detect, predict, and monitor water contamination accurately and promptly. In the event of potential contamination, the system generates alerts and shares critical information with relevant authorities to take immediate preventive measures. The system has been rigorously tested in various scenarios, demonstrating high accuracy, sensitivity, and reliable prediction of water contaminants. This innovative approach shows great promise in revolutionizing water quality monitoring, ensuring safer water resources, and safeguarding public health.

Keywords Arduino · pH sensor · Turbidity sensors · Total dissolved solid sensors · Water treatment technology

G. Kumar
Department of IoT and Intelligent Systems, Manipal University Jaipur, Jaipur, Rajasthan, India
e-mail: maurya.gyanendra@gmail.com; gyanendra.kumar@jaipur.manipal.edu

Pragya (✉)
Department of Computer Science & Engineering, SCSE, Galgotias University, Greater Noida, UP, India
e-mail: agrawal.pragya11@gmail.com

S. S. Rawat
Department of Computer Science and Engineering, JSS Academy of Technical Education, Noida, India
e-mail: sur.rawat@jssaten.ac.in

S. S. Rawat et al. (eds.), *Unleashing the Power of Blockchain and IoT for Water Informatics*, Water Informatics for Water Resource Management,
https://doi.org/10.1007/978-981-96-3886-4_7

7.1 Introduction

The Internet of Things, often called IoT, connects physical devices, machines, software, and objects to the Internet [1, 2]. It constitutes a dynamic and extensive network infrastructure where intelligent entities and objects are integrated with sensors, actuators, software, and connectivity to facilitate seamless communication, data collection, and exchange [3]. Within this network, numerous nodes interact with the environment, share data, and respond to events, enabling control and manipulation of the physical world. An IoT system gains greater capabilities through collaborative data sharing and utilization among individual components than its parts [4, 5]. Each network node is deemed intelligent, consuming minimal data processing, storage, and energy resources.

The term "Internet of Things" was first introduced by Kevin Ashton, a digital innovation expert, in 1999 [6]. Since then, the IoT industry has experienced substantial growth and advancement, as it offers a platform that enables people to connect and control devices using big data technology [7]. The affected industries include Manufacturing, Agriculture, Public Service, Health, Electronics, Energy, and Mining [8].

In public services, installing and monitoring sensor devices enable intelligent transportation systems, efficient traffic management, and optimal water and electricity management. For instance, deploying a water flow-driven sensor network in urban water distribution systems can be cost-effective and reduce the time required to detect leakage or contamination [9]. Governments have strongly emphasized the integration of IoT into manufacturing operations, and the term "Industrial IoT" (IIoT) is used to create fully intelligent, connected, and autonomous manufacturing plants. Agriculture also reaps the benefits of IoT's real-time capabilities, optimizing productivity while reducing costs. Cipolla et al. [10] conducted a study showcasing how an IoT system can monitor soil moisture, electrical conductivity, and surface and groundwater electrical conductivity, leading to improved management of irrigation and drainage systems [10]. These examples highlight how IoT technology enhances various sectors by enabling data-driven decision-making and resource optimization.

Simultaneously, ensuring the health and consumability of water resources becomes paramount, especially in light of the ever-increasing industrial and agricultural activities that significantly contribute to water pollution through waste generation and chemical leakage [11]. The continuous monitoring and protection of water quality are vital to safeguarding public health and preserving the environment from the adverse effects of contamination. Implementing a smart meter controller, capable of accurately displaying the precise amount of water used and seamlessly communicating this data to the water city network, will effectively eliminate human errors associated with manual reading of consumptions. Additionally, this system will reduce the reliance on human labor for this task, leading to more efficient water usage. By adopting such technology, uncertainties in consumption patterns that could lead to resource shortages can be mitigated, ensuring a more sustainable and reliable water management system [7, 12].

By harnessing the capabilities of IoT technologies, the integration of various environmental factors, including water quality indicators, can be efficiently gathered and exchanged remotely. This enables early detection and management of potential water-related disasters, ensuring effective disaster response measures. Moreover, through continuous monitoring and control facilitated by IoT, water sustainability can be enhanced, contributing to better management and conservation of this valuable resource [13].

The structure of this work is as follows: Section 7.2 presents a related IoT-based water contamination detection system, Sect. 7.3 introduces the proposed system and then presents a prototype model and its deployment. The outcomes of experimental results and analyses are discussed in Sect. 7.4. Finally, Sect. 7.5 provides the conclusion of the proposed research.

7.2 Related IoT-Based Water Contamination Detection System

A smart water quality management system leveraging the power of the IoT offers a comprehensive and efficient solution for monitoring and controlling water quality. Integrating IoT technologies into the system allows real-time data on various water quality parameters to be collected and transmitted remotely. This enables timely detection of deviations or anomalies, allowing swift and proactive actions to maintain water quality standards. The IoT-driven approach enhances the overall effectiveness of water quality management, ensuring the sustainability and safety of our water resources.

Creating an IoT-driven Smart Water Quality Monitoring System requires seamless integration of diverse components capable of real-time monitoring and control of water quality [14]. In some cases, particularly in developing nations, the water supplied to tanks might not meet drinking water standards, emphasizing the need for real-time monitoring to prevent building and community health issues [15]. Understanding the parameters to be monitored is vital for effective drinking water quality control, with enhanced history logging sensors offering a feasible approach [16]. Other proposed systems employing minimal energy consumption and mobile networks to send SMS notifications offer real-time water level monitoring [17]. Additionally, low-power IoT models collect water quality data and issue alerts if values deviate from predetermined standards [18]. Furthermore, an IoT-based water monitoring system measures instantaneous water levels to prevent flooding in disaster-prone regions [19]. Another system evaluates water tank factors to determine suitability for consumption based on measured water quality parameters [20]. A continuous wireless sensor-based river water monitoring system sends data to a central base for simulation and quality evaluation [21]. The prevailing monitoring strategy focuses on the source water, involving the conveyance of river water to a treatment facility, where samples are gathered through a sampling tap within the treatment plant's laboratory. Additionally, the outcomes of water quality monitoring can be aggregated into a database, contributing to enhanced decision-making processes [22].

Examining the literature, several shortcomings have been recognized within existing water monitoring systems.

1. Despite its low power and user-friendly capabilities, the existing technology incurs higher costs.
2. While advanced water management systems can gather substantial data, precise parameter monitoring is restricted to using costly and inflexible hardware and software.
3. The realm of water anomaly detection systems still harbors numerous challenges, demanding the creation of an optimized, integrated, comprehensive, and efficient system that encompasses efficient monitoring, information sharing, and management.

To overcome the shortcomings, this paper proposed a system to monitor water contamination, pH levels, turbidity, conductivity, CO_2, humidity, and total dissolved solids (TDS). The objective is to enhance the water contamination detection system through IoT-based, cloud-enabled, cost-effective, and efficient mine monitoring and intelligent control systems. This research endeavor's pivotal contributions include:

1. This paper introduces an innovative water contamination monitoring, analysis, prediction, and information-sharing system based on the Arduino IoT platform.
2. Utilization of the ThingSpeak IoT analytics platform is implemented for storing sensor data and facilitating analysis, management, and information sharing while ensuring system implementation remains convenient and cost-effective.
3. The system employs a probability-based mathematical model that leverages historical and real-time monitored data to predict prealerts for anomalies.
4. A comprehensive experimental analysis is conducted to assess the performance of the proposed system.

7.3 Proposed Arduino IoT-Based Water Contamination Detection System

Given the progress and versatility of IoT technology, creating IoT-based application systems is both necessary and inevitable. Such systems possess the following distinct characteristics:

1. The IoT constitutes an interconnected network of intelligent entities like sensors, actuators, smart routers, servers, and communication devices. This network is characterized by its self-adaptive, dynamic, and self-configuring nature, interoperable protocols, distinct identities, and integration with information network capabilities.

2. Assigning a distinct digital label, such as IPv4, IPv6, and 6LoWPAN identifiers, allows for the individual recognition of each intelligent entity. This digital relationship can be upheld in the virtual realm without necessitating any physical connection between these entities [23].
3. With a dynamic and self-adapting nature facilitated by interoperable protocols and distinct identities, devices can exchange information among each other and with servers, enabling subsequent processing and application support.

Furthermore, an IoT-based water contamination detection system can effectively meet essential requirements, including the early anticipation of events through intelligent water analysis, precise monitoring, timely alerts, predictive insights, and remote data sharing. As a result, this system holds the potential to ensure safety, mitigate illnesses, and curtail system development expenses. In conclusion, it will automate the entire process, eliminating the need for human intervention in detecting water anomalies.

7.3.1 System Architecture

The intended goal of the presented model is to integrate water quality sensors (measuring pH, temperature, conductivity, Hardness, humidity, TDS, and turbidity) alongside water distribution sensors (ultrasonic water level and flow sensors) with a microcontroller (Arduino Uno). This arrangement is designed to collect data, process it, and initiate commands to other system components.

This section introduces a novel IoT-oriented platform that monitors water content data analysis and information dissemination for water contamination detection systems. The operational aspects of IoT-based platforms are delineated by a 5-layer architecture [24, 25], comprising the Application, Service, Support, Network, and Link Layers, as illustrated in Fig. 7.1. After this, an elaborate examination of the roles fulfilled by each layer is presented.

Sensors

pH Sensor The pH sensor is responsible for overseeing water's acidic and alkaline properties, producing a value ranging from 0 to 14 based on the concentration of hydrogen ions, employing a negative logarithmic scale. In this context, the water's pH level is regulated within the range of 6–8.5, which aligns with the permissible limits for human consumption [26]. The visual representation of the sensor is portrayed in Fig. 7.2.

Temperature Sensor The temperature sensor plays a pivotal role in gauging the water's temperature, measured in degrees Celsius, with a refined accuracy of 0.1° increments, surpassing the precision of a mercury thermistor. Its functional capacity encompasses a temperature span of –55 to 150 °C. In this context, the water's temperature is upheld within 25–30 °C, a range deemed optimal for human usage [27]. A visual depiction of the sensor is featured in Fig. 7.3.

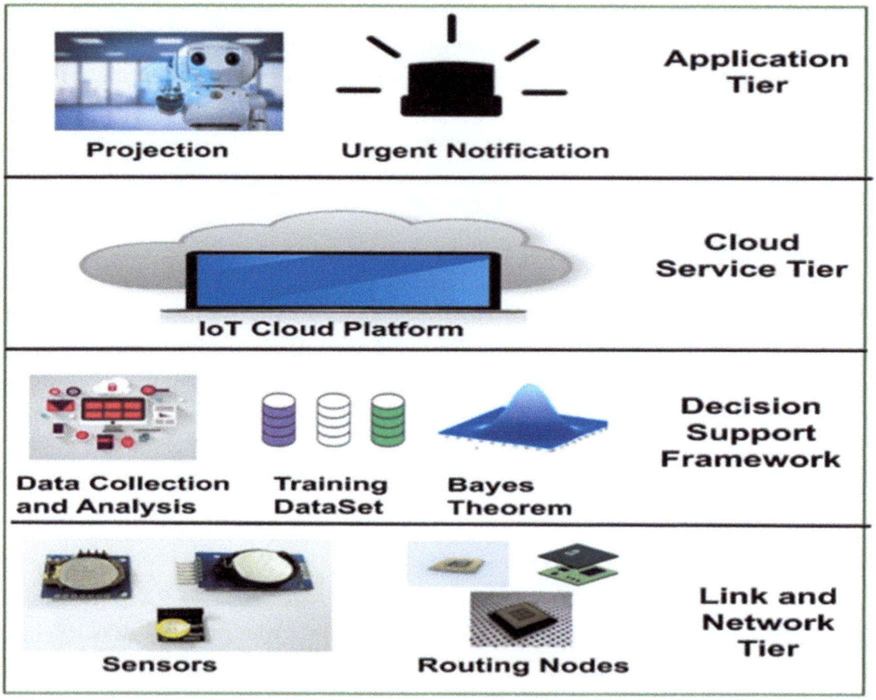

Fig. 7.1 The architecture of the proposed Arduino-based water contamination detection system

Fig. 7.2 pH sensor

Ultrasonic water level Sensor Employing the ultrasonic water level sensor involves emitting sound wave pulses toward the water surface within the tank and subsequently receiving their reflections. This methodology enables the computation of the water

Fig. 7.3 Temperature sensor

level within the tank, thus preventing potential overflow from the water inlet and facilitating the determination of the water volume contained in the tank. The sensor's visual depiction is presented in Fig. 7.4.

Turbidity Sensor The Turbidity sensor quantifies the opacity or haziness within the water, a condition typically attributed to particles imperceptible to the human eye. This sensor capitalizes on light to discern suspended particles within the water, which is achieved by evaluating the light's transmittance and the scattering rate. This behavior correlates with the water's total suspended solids (TSS), reflecting its quality. Acceptable readings for human consumption range from 0 to 5 NTU [28]. Figure 7.5 presents the visual depiction of the Turbidity Sensor.

Water Flow Sensor The water flow sensor is designed to gauge the quantity of water that traverses the system's outlet. With each rotation of the internal pinwheel, the

Fig. 7.4 Ultrasonic sensor

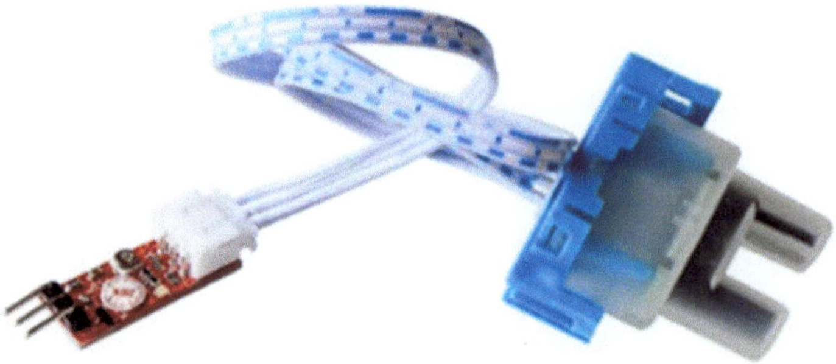

Fig. 7.5 Turbidity sensor

rotor emits an electrical pulse, thereby quantifying the volume of water. The visual representation of this sensor is depicted in Fig. 7.6.

Link and Network Layer These layers assume the responsibility of transmitting the accumulated sensor data to remote servers. Within the proposed system, the data collection is facilitated by sensors integrated with the Arduino platform, while data transmission is facilitated through modules like Wi-Fi, radio, and USB gateway.

Arduino microcontroller Arduino, a cutting-edge IoT platform developed by Eigen Technologies, stands out for its affordability, compactness, and advanced features, making it an ideal choice for research and development endeavors. With versatile applications spanning industries like academia, industry, and research, it offers valuable benefits to students, faculties, and scientists across diverse domains. This platform is bolstered by an intuitive graphical user interface (GUI) and seamless sensor integration, allowing for stimulus monitoring and flexible customization for various applications, as depicted in Fig. 7.7a. It encompasses communication modules, including RADIO, Wi-Fi, and USB GATEWAY, enhancing its connectivity capabilities.

Communication module It may consist of any one of the following modules.

Fig. 7.6 Water flow sensor

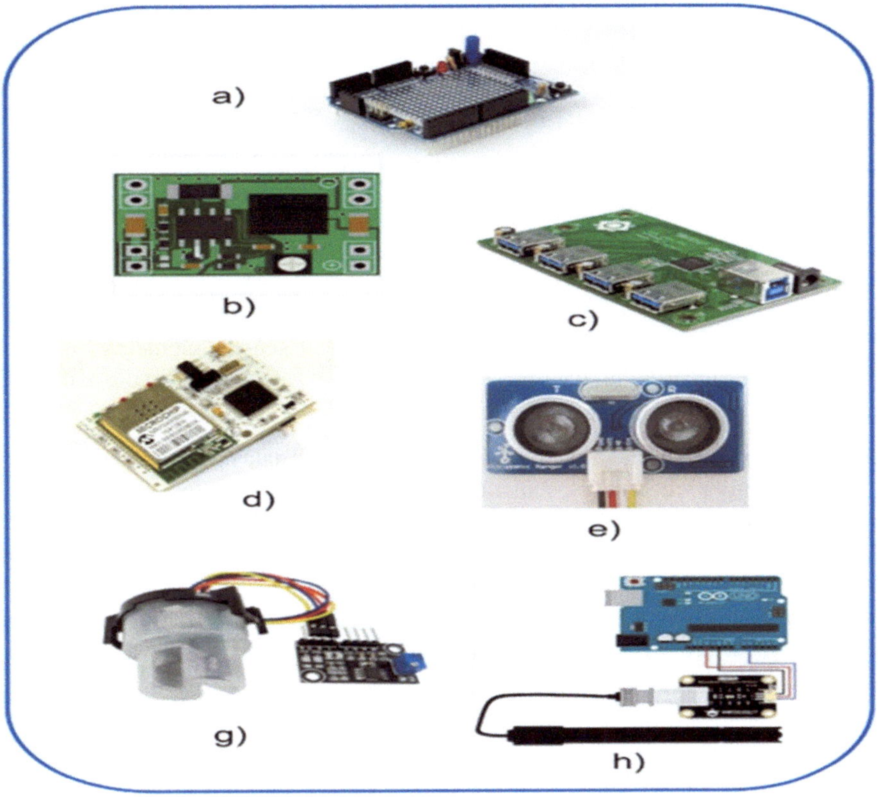

Fig. 7.7 **a** Arduino microcontroller, **b** RADIO module, **c** USB gateway, **d** Wi-Fi module, and **e** sensing nodes

Radio Module It includes a microcontroller and a transceiver to facilitate data transmission, reception, and processing. The setup incorporates a 32-bit RISC JN 5168 Microcontroller with a clock speed ranging from 1 to 32 MHz and 256KB flash memory. Figure 7.7b depicts the USB Gateway module connected to the SENSEnuts platform.

USB Gateway Module This module aims to program the microcontroller and act as an intermediary between the device and the network gateway, facilitating asynchronous serial data transfer. The device manages USB protocols and boasts the following specifications: a Data Transfer rate of 115200 baud, a 128-byte receive buffer, and a 256-byte transmit buffer. As illustrated in Fig. 7.7c, the USB Gateway module is depicted, linked with the Arduino module utilized in the proposed system.

Wi-Fi Gateway Module Arduino incorporates a low-power Wi-Fi module with a single-band 2.4 GHz IEEE 802.11 b/g/n 1 × 1 Wi-Fi transceiver. This module seamlessly integrates SPI-serial flash memory for software powered by the Broadcom

BCM43362 chip. It supports various Wi-Fi security modes, including Open, WPA2-PSK, WEP, and WPA. The Wi-Fi module, exemplified in Fig. 7.7d, boasts 128 kB of SRAM and integrated 1 MB Flash memory, capable of functioning within a temperature range from –30 to +85 °C.

Sensors The sensors (pH, Temperature, Ultrasonic Water Level, Turbidity, Water Flow) are used at the link layer in our proposed system. The details are already described above.

Networking The effectiveness of the Water Contamination Detection System heavily relies on how the various components are positioned and implemented within its operations. In the suggested system, the placement of sensing elements follows a linear topology, incorporating wireless communication gateways like radio and Wi-Fi modules.

Decision Support This tier handles the sensor-generated data by applying mathematical models, probability theory, statistical analysis, and various software applications. Within this system, data falls into two categories: monitored and historical. The central challenge involves effectively utilizing both data sets to trigger emergency alerts. To tackle this challenge, the system employs a Bayesian prediction model. Here's how it works: Initially, it establishes a correlation with a response based on historical data sets. Subsequently, using this correlation, it predicts alerts for newly monitored data.

To ascertain the probability of a threat, let's consider a scenario where N sensors (S) have been deployed, and their readings are observed at various time points, t_1, t_2,……t_n. Let $p_x(t)$ represent the reading of sensor S_x at a given time t and Mn denotes the set comprising all sensor readings at time tn. Once the entire mining system and its array of sensors are set up, Bayes' theorem comes into play to compute the posterior probability, effectively predicting various parameters within the water (W_N)by using Eq. (7.1).

$$P(W_N/M_n) = ((P(M_n/W_N) * P(W_N)))/P(M_n) \tag{7.1}$$

Here, $P(M_n)$ represents the evidence derived from parameters gathered by sensors, while $P(M_n/W_N)$ signifies a conditional likelihood. Additionally, $P(W_N)$ is the prior probability, estimated by training historical data.

The conditional likelihood ($P(M_n/W_N)$) is determined through Eq. (7.2), which involves integrating the likelihood of all parameters across the entire domain. This integration uses the probability distribution function Pdf(N_p, W_N).

$$\text{pdf}\left(\frac{M_n}{W_N}\right) = \int_{D_E} \text{pdf}\left(\frac{n}{n_p}, W_N\right) \cdot \text{pdf}\left(\frac{n_p}{W_N}\right) \cdot D_E \tag{7.2}$$

The likelihood evaluation for the entire monitored set Mn of sensors is performed utilizing Eq. (7.3).

$$\mathrm{pdf}\left(\frac{M_n}{n_p}\right) = \prod_{j=1,i=1}^{j=N,i=n} \mathrm{pdf}\left(\frac{p_j\,(t_i)}{n_p,\, W_N}\right) \tag{7.3}$$

The evaluation of the normal distribution for sensor measurements is conducted according to Eq. (7.4).

$$\mathrm{pdf}(p_j(t_n)|n_p, S_n) = \mathrm{Normal}\{(p_j(t_n); n_{r_j}(n_p t_n t), n\,(\sigma_e)_j\} \tag{7.4}$$

In this context, σ represents the standard deviation computed based on the sensor reading values.

The statistical parameters mean, standard deviation, and normal distribution employed in this method are computed from the readings x utilizing Eqs. (7.5), (7.6), and (7.7).

$$\mathrm{Average}(x) = (1/n)\sum_{i=1}^{n} x_i \tag{7.5}$$

$$\sigma = \sqrt{\left(\frac{1}{n} - 1\right) * \left(\sum_{i=1}^{n} \left((x_i - \overline{x})^2\right)\right)} \tag{7.6}$$

$$\mathrm{NormalDistriution}\, f\left(\frac{x}{\overline{x}}, \sigma^2\right) = \left(\frac{1}{\sqrt{2\pi\sigma^2}}\right) e^{\frac{(-x_i - \overline{x})^2}{2\sigma^2}} \tag{7.7}$$

7.3.2 Cloud service

Within this suggested underground mine safety system, sensor-generated data is handled through the IoT analytics platform ThingSpeak. This platform enables the aggregation, visualization, and analysis of real-time data, streamlining information collection in the cloud. It also offers instant sensor data visualization using built-in tools like Python and MATLAB. ThingSpeak boasts several key functionalities, such as:

- Simple configuration for devices to transmit data to the ThingSpeak platform using IoT protocols.
- Real-time data visualization capabilities.
- ThingSpeak serves as an open API for real-time data collection.
- Automatic execution of IoT analytics based on schedules and events.
- Streamlined creation of IoT systems without needing local server setups or web software development.
- Versatility in creating different applications, including remote logging, location-based services, and network status updates for IoT devices.

7.3.3 Information Sharing and Application Layer

This tier encompasses elements and operations tasked with disseminating information and alerts to other applications and the overseeing authority. The envisioned system identifies contamination in water and can create advanced alerts and share remote information through alarms and emergency lighting, utilizing the functionalities embedded within the application layer. Its foundation lies in the Bayesian prediction model, enabling it to not solely rely on preset threshold values but adapt based on prior occurrences. Alarms transmit warning signals within the visionity of water source and also can be communicated to various IoT-based applications and devices, ranging from smartphones to buzzer alarms and laptops. The proposed system has a specialized focus on evaluating water quality, monitoring pH, humidity, and hardness, and assessing contamination levels within water. Figure 7.1 illustrates the fundamental architecture of this system. Within this setup, sensing units rely on the Arduino module, with sensors connected to the Arduino microcontroller. These sensor nodes capture information regarding various parameters within the water source and relay it to the IoT cloud platform, ThingSpeak. Through the prediction model, different parameter types are identified and their values are predicted based on the training data. As a result, this system facilitates decision-making processes, promptly detecting contamination and generating alerts for concern to take immediate preventive actions.

7.3.4 Working Flowchart

Figure 7.8 delineates the sequential data flow from one process to another within our system. This wireless sensor network application is designed to measure the concentrations of diverse impurities present in the water, utilizing an array of sensors (including impurity and water quality indices).

The collected data is transmitted to the ThingSpeak IoT platform via a Wi-Fi module. Subsequently, this data is accessed from ThingSpeak and subjected to analysis aimed at detecting potential hazards. Furthermore, this system archives all data on a computer for future scrutiny. The primary focus revolves around generating a preliminary alarm for emergencies. Within our system, information stems from monitored data and historical data. Through an analysis of historical data, assumptions are formulated by just exposing and interpreting the monitored information. As a result, the alarm is triggered when sensor values surpass a predetermined threshold level established by monitoring historical data.

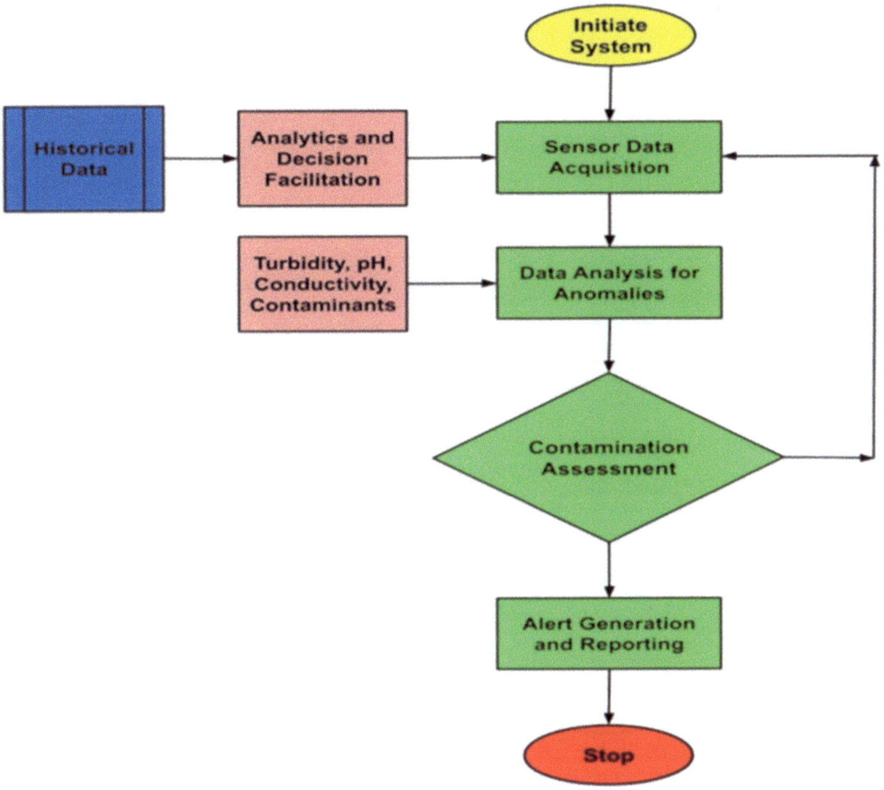

Fig. 7.8 Working flowchart of system

7.4 System Implementation

This part details the operations and interdependencies among various system components, outlining the deployment of a prototype model to assess its functionality and efficiency.

7.4.1 Water Contamination Detection System

Figure 7.9 illustrates the comprehensive setup and proposed system model. It integrates Smart Arduino-based IoT hardware with data analytics employing probability theory, all deployed via the ThingSpeak platform. The system's program executes the probability model, fetching real-time sensor data to generate threat predictions and alerts. Additionally, it concurrently updates historical information stored within the database.

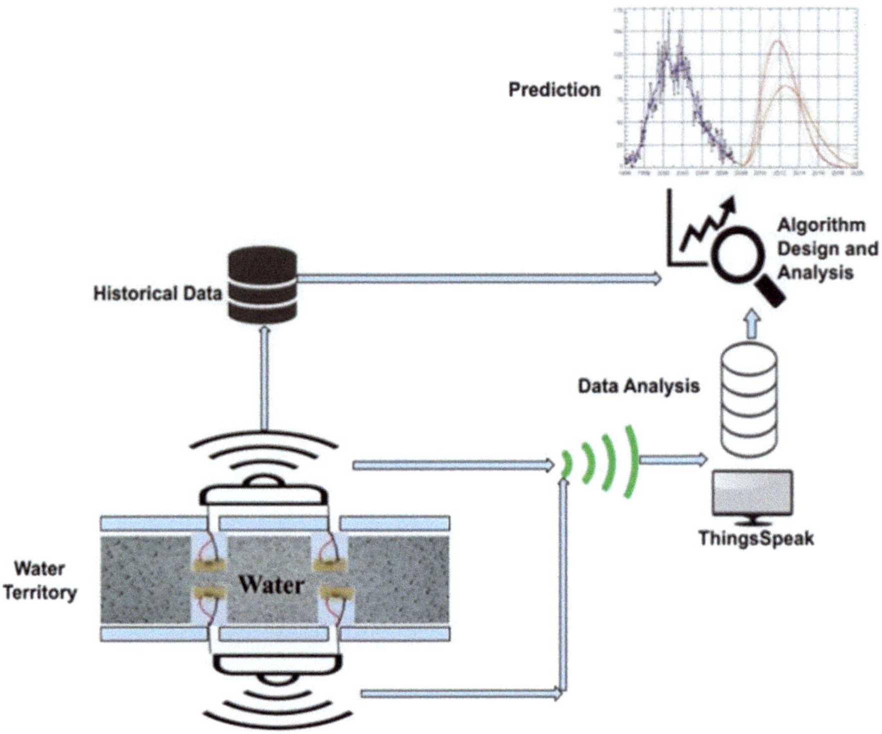

Fig. 7.9 Water source contamination monitoring system

The system is initiated by gathering historical water contamination data through affordable Arduino sensors and ThingSpeak. Subsequently, it commences the analysis of historical data sourced from ThingSpeak. During this phase, the system scrutinizes and refines the data, rectifying missing values, eliminating outliers, and addressing any noise or anomalies. The system then utilizes the processed water data to anticipate forthcoming impurities, employing advanced analytical capabilities within the ThingSpeak platform. A predictive algorithm is crafted using the Bayesian Machine learning model, leveraging diverse input data sets to achieve this. The algorithm undergoes training utilizing the time series tool. Once the performance evaluation is complete, the predictive algorithm is deployed on ThingSpeak. This deployment facilitates the forecasting and presentation of values obtained from various sensors.

7.4.2 *Prototype Deployment*

The prototype system is replicated within a laboratory environment to simulate conditions akin to water containment scenarios. Sensors for monitoring are strategically positioned along the upper sections of containment units, simulating areas where contaminants might concentrate within the water. To mimic this scenario, deliberate introduction of contaminants is carried out, simulating the presence of impurities or pollutants. Wi-Fi-enabled sensors are deployed to detect and capture these simulated contaminations, transmitting the collected data to a central gateway. This data is then forwarded to the cloud for ongoing monitoring and detailed analysis of water quality.

7.5 Results and Analysis

The performance assessment of the water contamination monitoring and prediction system is conducted in alignment with established standards, defined thresholds for contaminants, and specific requirements outlined for drinking water management, as detailed in Table 7.1 .

Initially, instead of manual calibration of different sensors, a linear regression technique is used to train the proposed model, so that the reading of sensors can be matched with the actual values. Figure 7.10 demonstrates the variance between the predicted and measured values of temperature and humidity within the testing environment of the water contamination system. The temperature of water ranges between 5 and 30 °C, while humidity fluctuates within 20–100.

The results obtained exhibit a close resemblance between the values predicted by the proposed model and the actual measured values. This underscores the critical necessity for continuous monitoring to prevent incidents arising from harmful particles and contaminants within water systems.

Measuring the real-time impurity of different parameters in the water is necessary to ensure safety. Therefore, the prototype of the proposed system was tested against the real-time monitoring of pH, turbidity, hardness, TDS, and conductivity in an identical environment. The concentration of these impurities is maintained as per the

Table 7.1 Indian standard parameter range for drinking water

Parameter	Range
pH	6.5–8.5
Turbidity	<10 NTU
Conductivity	200–800 μS/cm
Hardness	300 mg/l Max
Humidity	40–100%
TDS	50–150 PPM
Temperature	10–20 °C

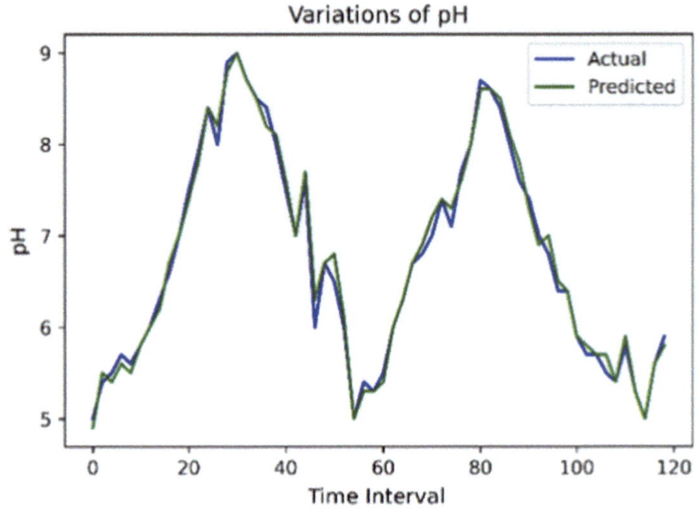

Fig. 7.10 **a** Variation of pH

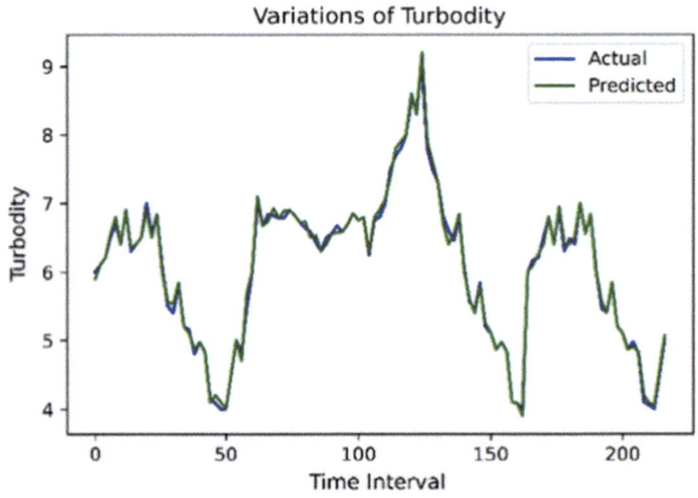

Fig. 7.11 **b** Variation of turbidity

standards of drinking water. Figure 7.11 shows the variations of actual and predicted readings and almost identical results. Figure 7.11a shows the concentration of pH, which varies between 6 to 9. Similarly, Fig. 7.11b–d shows the concentration of turbidity, hardness, TDS, and conductivity, and their values vary from 5 to 11 NTU, 100–350 mg/l, 40–200 PPM and 200–800 μS/cm, respectively. The concentrations of these impurities are measured against time with a set interval of 2 min (Figs. 7.12 and 7.13).

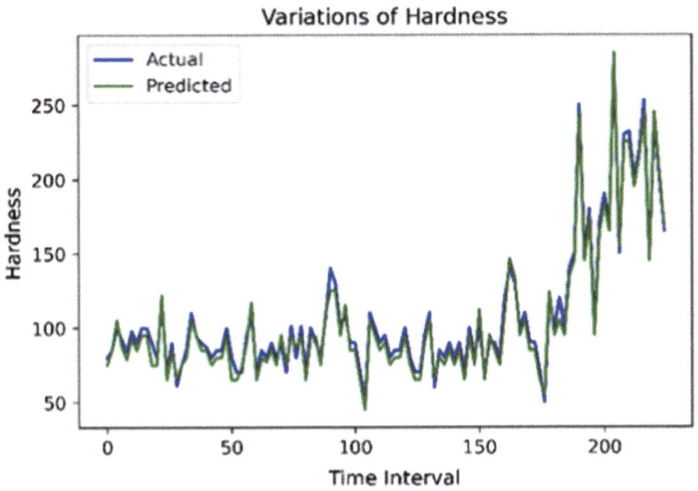

Fig. 7.12 **c** Variation of hardness

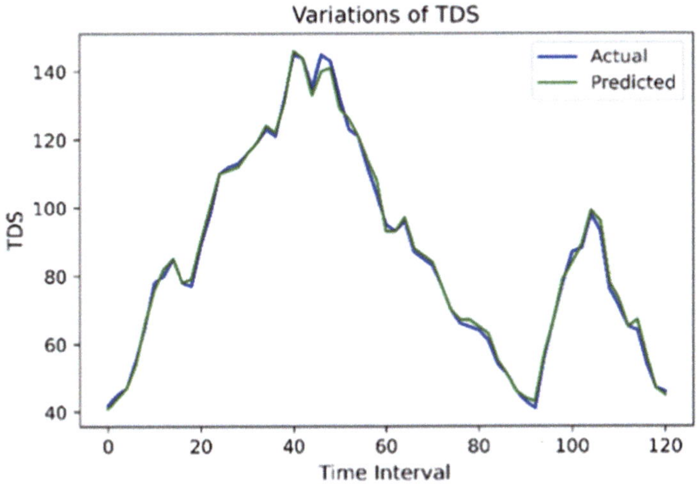

Fig. 7.13 **d** Variation of TDS

Based on the historical data sets, two classes are defined, normal and contaminated. The proposed model was trained and tested using the 80:20 concept. The water source status is classified as normal or contaminated. The predicted readings of sensors are processed using the trained proposed model and if classified as contaminated then an alert is generated.

Our system underwent multiple tests to assess its responsiveness. According to the results presented in Table 7.2, the alert was triggered each time, when the sensor reading was classified as contaminated. A total of 25 observations were performed, out

Table 7.2 Response from the proposed system

Responses	True responses	False responses	Response sensitivity (%)
Positive response	23	2	92
Negative response	22	3	88

of them, 23 were aligned with the true positive response and 22 with the true negative response. This observation underscores the system's sensitivity rate of approximately 92% across all cases.

Based on the analysis of experimental results, several key outcomes of the system have been identified.

- The system sensor reading demonstrates nearly identical prediction accuracy when compared to actual values.
- The proposed system exhibits a high sensitivity in response, hovering around 92%.
- Deployment cost is reduced because it illuminates the requirement of local infra setup.
- The system is cloud-enabled hence sharing with other applications is handy.

7.6 Conclusion

Safety remains a paramount concern within the realm of water containment systems. Water contamination incidents persist despite strides in improving safety compared to past eras. Various safety equipment is available in the market to address these concerns. This paper introduces a water contamination monitoring system built upon the Arduino IoT platform, incorporating ThingSpeak IoT analytics and cloud computing. The system's experimental outcomes demonstrate precise and efficient responses. The amalgamation of ThingSpeak and Cloud infrastructure streamlines data collection, management, analysis, and information dissemination. Furthermore, the system's deployment significantly reduces costs, eliminating the need for setup of web infrastructure and local servers.

References

1. Connor, R., Renata, A., Ortigara, C., Koncagül, E., Uhlenbrook, S., Lamizana-Diallo, B.M., Brdjanovic, D.: The United Nations World Water Development Report 2017: wastewater: the untapped resource. United Nations World Water Development Report (2017)
2. Kumar, G., Tomar, P.: A stateless spatial IPv6 address configuration scheme for internet of things. IETE J. Res. **69**(9), 6039–6052 (2023). https://doi.org/10.1080/03772063.2021.1994037

3. Diène, B., Rodrigues, J.J.P.C., Diallo, O., Ndoye, E.H.M., Korotaev, V.V.: Data management techniques for internet of things. Mech Syst Signal Process **138**, 106564 (2020)
4. McClelland, C.: IoT explained-how does an IoT system actually work? https://www.leverege.com/blogpost/iot-explained-how-does-an-iot-system-actually-work. Accessed 29 Oct. 2016
5. Singh, S.P., Alotaibi, Y., Kumar, G., Rawat, S.S.: Intelligent adaptive optimisation method for enhancement of information security in IoT-enabled environments. Sustainability **14**, 13635 (2022). https://doi.org/10.3390/su142013635
6. Li, C.-Z.-E., Deng, Z.W.: The embedded modules solution of house-hold internet of things system and the future development. Procedia Comput. Sci. **166**, 350–356 (2020)
7. Tomar, P., Kumar, G., Verma, L.P.: Path-rank-based data chunk scheduling for concurrent multipath transmission. Comput. J. **66**(9), 2254–64 (2023)
8. Dachyar, M., Zagloel, T., Saragih, L.: Knowledge growth and development: internet of things (IoT) research, 2006–2018. Heliyon **5**, e02264 (2020). [CrossRef] [PubMed] parameter monitoring. Sensors **14**(7), 13149–13170
9. Pal, A., Kant, K.: Water flow driven sensor networks for leakage and contamination monitoring. In: Proceedings of the 2015, IEEE 16th International Symposium on a World of Wireless, Mobile and Multimedia Networks (WoWMoM), Boston, MA, USA (2015). [CrossRef]
10. Cipolla, S., Maglionico, M., Masina, M., Lamberti, A., Daprà, I.: Real time monitoring of water quality in an agricultural area with salinity problems. Environ. Eng. Manag. J. **18**, 2229–2240 (2019)
11. Kawarkhe, M.B., Agrawal, S.: Smart water monitoring system using IOT at home, vol. 21, no. 1, pp. 14–19 (2019). https://doi.org/10.9790/0661-2101021419
12. Joseph, J., Manju, K.M., Sajith, M.R., Nair, S., Viay, V.P., Krishnan, S.: Water management system using IoT, pp. 4–7 (2018). https://doi.org/10.15662/IJAREEIE.2016.0505080
13. Ashour, M.A., El Attar, S.T., Rafaat, Y.M., Mohamed, M.N.: Water resources management in Egypt. J. Eng. Sci. **37**(2), 269–279 (2009)
14. Doss, P.: Smart water conservation and management system using IOT, vol. 7109, pp. 9–12 (2018)
15. Ahmed Sha, S.K., Sankari, S., Professor, A.: Smart tank water monitoring system using IOT cloud server at home/office. Int. J. Eng. Sci. Comput. **8**(4), pp. 16748–16751 (2018)
16. Aleksic, A., Ljepava, N., Ristic, M.: Smart technologies and innovation for a sustainable future. Smart Technol. Innov. Sustain. Futur. Adv. Sci. Technol. Innov. (January), 333–338 (2019). https://doi.org/10.1007/978-3-030-01659-3
17. Engineering, A., Vidya, B., Poonam, K., Priyanka, G., Gaurav, D., Chandgude, P.A.S.: Water level monitoring system in real time mode using WSN. Int. J. Emerg. Technol. Adv. Eng. **6**(9), 212–214 (2016)
18. Geetha, S., Gouthami, S.: Internet of things enabled real time water quality monitoring system. Smart Water **2**(1), 1–19 (2016). https://doi.org/10.1186/s40713-017-0005-y
19. Perumal, T., Sulaiman, M.N., Leong, C.Y.: Internet of things (IoT) enabled water monitoring system. In: 2015 IEEE 4th Global Conference on Consumer Electronics (GCCE), pp. 86–87 (2015). https://doi.org/10.1109/GCCE.2015.7398710
20. Jain, A., Malhotra, A., Rohilla, A., Kaushik, P.: Water quality monitoring and management system for residents. Int. J. Eng. Adv. Technol. **9**(2), 567–570 (2019). https://doi.org/10.35940/ijeat.b3521.129219
21. Chowdury, M.S.U., et al.: IoT based real-time river water quality monitoring system. Procedia Comput. Sci. **155**, 161–168 (2019). https://doi.org/10.1016/j.procs.2019.08.025
22. Yusri, N.I.A.B., Gödeke, S.H., Mohd Mansor, N.H.B.H.: A water quality database for Brunei-the case of Bukit Barun and Layong. In: Proceedings of the 7th Brunei International Conference on Engineering and Technology 2018 (BICET 2018), Bandar Seri Begawan, Brunei (2018)
23. Kumar, G., Tomar, P.: IPv6 addressing scheme with a secured duplicate address detection. IETE J. Res. **68**(5), 3371–3378 (2022). https://doi.org/10.1080/03772063.2020.1756938
24. Kumar, G., Tomar, P.: A survey of IPv6 addressing schemes for internet of things. Int. J. Hyperconnect. Internet of Things (IJHIoT) **2**(2), 43–57 (2018)

25. Kumar, G., Tomar, P.: SENSEnuts IoT platform and Bayes decision theorem based mine control system. J. MESA **12**(4), 901–914 (2021)
26. Jiao, D., Luo, X.: Water quality monitoring system based on LoRa. DEStech Trans. Comput. Sci. Eng. **10**(IECE), 1107–1116 (2018). https://doi.org/10.12783/dtcse/iece2018/26605
27. Chowdury, M.S.U., et al.: IoT based real-time river water quality monitoring system. Procedia Comput. Sci. **155**, 161–168 (2019). https://doi.org/10.1016/j.procs.2019.08.025
28. Jain, A., Malhotra, A., Rohilla, A., Kaushik, P.: Water quality monitoring and management system for residents. Int. J. Eng. Adv. Technol. **9**(2), 567–570 (2019). https://doi.org/10.35940/ijeat.b3521.129219

Chapter 8
Efficient Utilization of Water Using the Internet of Things and Blockchain Technology

Mahesh Kumar Singh, Kalpana, Suhani, Priyanka Thapa, and Pushpendra Singh

Abstract Water is essential for every living thing in the universe. The article proposes a decentralized system designed to manage water resource information across every stage of the process, "supply-use-consumption-discharge" using blockchain technology. The system enhances traditional methods of storing water data and offers an effective solution to establish trust among stakeholders involved in water resource management. It ensures data security, mitigating risks associated with central institutions' vulnerabilities to disruptions caused by routine operations. Specifically, blockchain technology encrypts monitoring and business data, transmitted via a peer-to-peer network. Shifting from centralized management to distributed management also delegates some responsibilities to each node. This facilitates rapid decision-making and execution upon detecting issues, improving the efficiency of information dissemination and management. Furthermore, two blockchain-driven solutions for water resource management are delineated. This method simplifies the issuance and supervision of water abstraction permits, ensuring the security and authenticity of license data. Additionally, it establishes a reliable system for monitoring water quality, ensuring the precision of data, pinpointing areas with inadequate water quality, assigning responsibility, and protecting the safety of residents' water supply.

Keywords IoT · Blockchain technology · Water conservation · Water treatment · Water utilization

M. K. Singh (✉) · Kalpana · Suhani · P. Thapa
Dronacharya Group of Institutions, Greater Noida, Uttar Pradesh, India
e-mail: maheshkrsg@gmail.com

P. Singh
SRMIST Delhi-NCR Campus, Modinagar, Ghaziabad, Uttar Pradesh, India
e-mail: pushpendra.singh1@gmail.com

S. S. Rawat et al. (eds.), *Unleashing the Power of Blockchain and IoT for Water Informatics*, Water Informatics for Water Resource Management,
https://doi.org/10.1007/978-981-96-3886-4_8

8.1 Introduction

The article explores the potential impact of blockchain and IoT on water management, investigating their applicability in diverse scenarios such as stormwater management, real-time water quality monitoring, direct communication with consumers and stakeholders, and the implementation of smart payment and contract systems. These technologies aim to address the challenges presented by the global water crisis exacerbated by climate change and rapid population growth [1]. Naqash and his team have introduced a framework based on blockchain technology to enhance efficiency in managing water resources and identifying leaks within urban regions [2].

Effective water resource management is crucial for ensuring environmental sustainability, encompassing strategic planning, infrastructure development, equitable distribution, and the optimal utilization of water resources [3]. In recent years, technologies like the Internet of Things (IoT) and blockchain have been increasingly used to enhance water resource management. The Internet of Things (IoT) is a network of interconnected devices that collect and exchange data. In the context of water management, IoT devices like sensors can monitor various parameters such as water quality, temperature, and flow rate in real time [4]. Timely issue detection and effective resource allocation are facilitated by IoT devices, which continuously monitor various parameters in water management. Meanwhile, blockchain technology operates as a decentralized digital ledger, recording transactions across multiple computers. Its primary function lies in ensuring data security and transparency, crucial elements in water resource management. For example, blockchain can establish a reliable trust mechanism among stakeholders, safeguarding data integrity and preventing the collapse of central institutions due to routine system operations. When integrated, IoT and blockchain offer significant potential for improving water management practices. IoT devices gather data and transmit it to a central point, while blockchain technology guarantees the security and transparency of this data, thereby enhancing the overall efficiency and reliability of water management systems [5]. This integration establishes audit trails that facilitate transparent data collection and analysis, ensuring data integrity and immutability through decentralized storage.

The pace of technological advancement is swift, with blockchain emerging as a transformative innovation. In contrast, traditional water management systems face inherent challenges [6]. In urban areas, water supply plants and sources are decentralized, posing challenges to efficient information sharing and delivery. Traditional centralized water information systems lack secure data storage, leaving room for falsification or distortion of data and causing delays in information access due to network congestion.

The intricacy of water usage entails numerous connections, complicating precise monitoring and resulting in elevated expenses for data verification. Moreover, a lack of trust among governmental agencies engaged in water resource management fosters isolated information systems, adversely affecting coordination among businesses and work efficiency.

The distribution and management of water resources pose significant challenges on a global scale. In urban areas, desalination facilities guarantee a dependable water supply. However, in metropolitan areas, monitoring seawater usage and implementing water loss reduction techniques are essential. Issues such as water distribution, pressure regulation, and waste management are prevalent in regions like Madinah Munawara. In cities like Yanbu, flow meters are used to monitor seawater distribution. However, they struggle with accurately measuring water delivery. This complicates distribution planning based on consumption patterns and hampers precise estimation of future demand. The absence of a centralized dashboard system for real-time tracking of seawater usage data further exacerbates these challenges.

Human activities aimed at maximizing benefits from rivers and floodplains can exacerbate costs and damages during periods of droughts, floods, and pollution [7]. These impacts span physical, economic, environmental, and social dimensions, stemming from the disparity between human expectations and nature's provisions. As climate change intensifies, extreme flow conditions beyond the norm are expected to occur more frequently, potentially causing losses for river-dependent human activities unable to adapt to these conditions.

8.2 Components of Water Management

Water management is an extensive field involving diverse tasks associated with the planning, development, distribution, and oversight of water resources [8]. The following are some of the components of water management (see Fig. 8.1).

8.2.1 Resource Management

Effective management of water resources is essential for sustainable development and the overall health of our planet. It involves the optimal utilization of water resources while minimizing waste and ensuring equitable distribution. India has implemented several initiatives to enhance water resource management and conservation. Some of these initiatives include:

National Perspective Plan for Interlinking of Rivers: Established in 1980, this plan aims to transfer water from regions with surplus water resources to those facing deficits.

Command Area Development and Water Management (CADWM) Programme: This program seeks to enhance irrigation potential utilization and improve agricultural production sustainably through Participatory Irrigation Management (PIM).

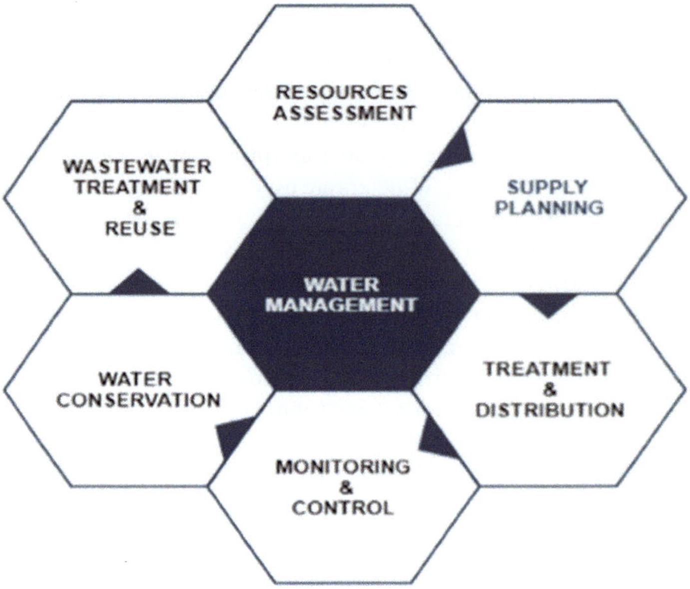

Fig. 8.1 Components of water management system [15]

Jal Jeevan Mission (JJM): This initiative endeavors to deliver safe tap water to every rural residence by 2024, with a specific emphasis on regions experiencing water scarcity and susceptibility to drought.

8.2.2 Waste Water Treatment and Reuse

Wastewater treatment and reuse constitute a vital aspect of water resource management. This entails the purification of wastewater to eliminate impurities, thereby rendering it suitable for reuse. Repurposed wastewater serves multiple purposes such as irrigation, industrial activities, and even potable water supply [9]. The utilization of treated wastewater presents numerous benefits, including the conservation of freshwater resources, the reduction of untreated wastewater discharge into the environment, and the promotion of sustainable development.

In India, the Central Ground Water Board (CGWB) has initiated the National Aquifer Mapping and Management Program (NAQUIM) with the objective of mapping aquifers, understanding their characteristics, and formulating Aquifer Management Plans. This program is geared toward ensuring sustainable management of groundwater resources nationwide. Various methods are employed for wastewater treatment, encompassing physical, chemical, and biological processes. The selection of treatment methods hinges on the quality of the wastewater and the intended use of the treated water. Common treatment processes include sedimentation, filtration, disinfection, and reverse osmosis.

The reuse of treated wastewater can help reduce the demand for freshwater resources and promote sustainable development. However, it is essential to ensure that the treated water is safe for its intended use and does not pose any health risks to humans or the environment.

8.2.3 Water Conservation

Water conservation is a critical component of water resource management, as illustrated in Fig. 8.2. India has implemented numerous initiatives to promote water conservation practices nationwide. Some of these initiatives include:

Jal Jeevan Mission (JJM): This initiative seeks to deliver clean tap water to every rural household by 2024, with a specific emphasis on regions confronting water scarcity and vulnerability to drought.

Pradhan Mantri Krishi Sinchayee Yojana (PMKSY): Introduced to enhance farm water availability and promote efficient irrigation techniques. The scheme prioritizes improving on-farm water utilization efficiency, embracing sustainable conservation strategies, and other related efforts.

Command Area Development and Water Management (CADWM) Programme: Designed to optimize irrigation potential utilization and enhance agricultural productivity sustainably through Participatory Irrigation Management (PIM).

National Perspective Plan for Interlinking of Rivers: Originating in 1980, this plan aims to transfer water from regions with surplus water resources to those facing deficits.

Fig. 8.2 Water conservation [16]

8.2.4 Process Monitoring and Control

Water process monitoring and control are integral aspects of water resource management, ensuring the effective operation of water treatment systems. This involves continuous monitoring to verify that the applied water treatment program for boilers, cooling systems, wastewater treatment, or other industrial water systems is adequately controlled to achieve desired outcomes [10]. Proper monitoring is crucial for mitigating risks associated with chemical underfeeding or overfeeding, maintaining compliance with environmental regulations, optimizing plant operation quality, conserving water, and energy, and enhancing overall plant productivity.

Various methods exist for monitoring water treatment systems, including manual and continuous online monitoring with automatic instrumentation. Manual monitoring typically involves plant operators or technicians conducting chemical tests, such as pH, conductivity, suspended solids, alkalinity, and hardness, and adjusting chemical feed pumps or blowdown valves accordingly based on specified control limits. The frequency of testing varies based on plant resources, ranging from daily to hourly measurements. Manual monitoring is suitable for noncritical water systems or systems with gradual changes in water and plant conditions [11].

In contrast, continuous online monitoring with automatic instrumentation is essential for critical water systems or those experiencing rapid changes in water and plant conditions. This method offers higher precision in monitoring and controlling water treatment programs compared to manual monitoring. Technological advancements in electronics and microprocessor technology have led to a wide range of instrumentation options for monitoring water treatment systems.

8.2.5 Water Treatment and Distribution

Water treatment and distribution are essential aspects of water resource management (see Fig. 8.3) India has enacted various initiatives aimed at fostering water conservation practices nationwide. Some of these efforts comprise:

Jal Jeevan Mission (JJM): Striving to deliver purified tap water to each rural residence by 2024, JJM emphasizes areas confronting water scarcity and drought. **Pradhan Mantri Krishi Sinchayee Yojana (PMKSY)**: PMKSY focuses on improving agricultural water access and promoting efficient irrigation methods. It emphasizes enhancing on-farm water utilization and implementing sustainable conservation practices.

CADWM: CADWM aims to optimize irrigation potential utilization and enhance agricultural productivity through Participatory Irrigation Management (PIM). **National Perspective Plan for Interlinking of Rivers**: Originating in 1980, this plan seeks to redistribute water from surplus to deficit areas to address water scarcity issues.

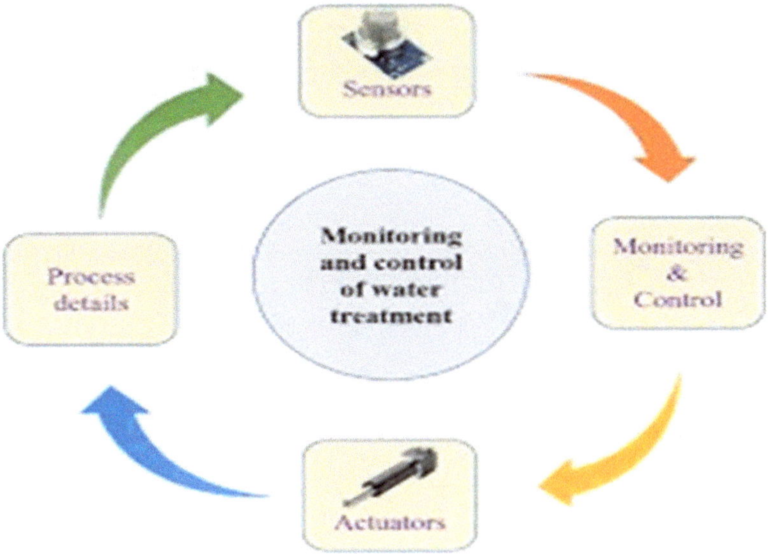

Fig. 8.3 Water treatment and distribution

India anticipates a twofold increase in water demand by 2030, surpassing the current supply. Both public and private sectors are embarking on ambitious projects to develop comprehensive water and wastewater treatment and distribution infrastructure. Acknowledging the urgency, the Indian government has launched various initiatives to promote sustainable water management practices and ensure universal access to safe drinking water.

8.2.6 Water Supply Planning

Water supply planning constitutes a vital procedure, as depicted in Fig. 8.4, encompassing data collection, analysis, and the design of the entire water supply scheme before commencing construction [13]. A well-crafted plan guarantees the development of an efficient and cost-effective system, minimizing expenses. The following stages are integral to water supply planning.

Data Collection Before initiating the water supply project planning process, it is essential to gather the following types of data:

- Hydrological Data
- Geological Data
- Water Demanded by the City
- Currently active Water Supply Projects
- Cleanness status in the Area

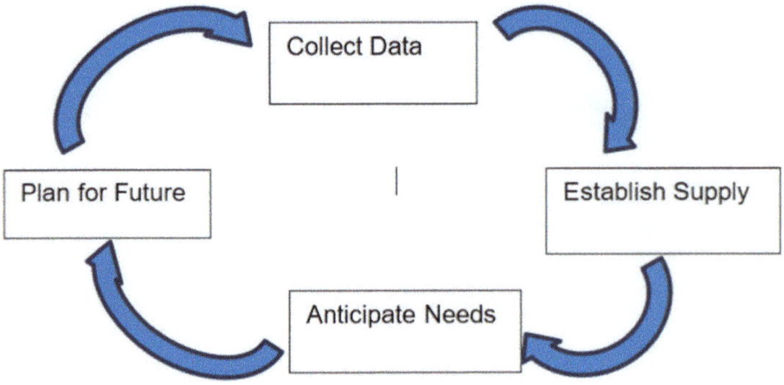

Fig. 8.4 Water supply and planning

- Physical features of the Area
- Legal Information
- Public beliefs.

Project Formulation

- Identifying alternative water sources
- Selecting the optimal water source
- Determining the water supply system's capacity
- Designing the water supply system
- Estimating project costs
- Drafting the project report.

Project Appraisal The project report should be submitted to the concerned authorities for appraisal. The following aspects are considered during the appraisal process:

- Technical feasibility
- Economic viability
- Environmental impact
- Social acceptability.

Project Implementation After the project has been approved, the following activities should be carried out:

- Procurement of materials and equipment
- Construction of the water supply system
- Testing and commissioning of the system
- Operation and maintenance of the system.

Project Evaluation The performance of the water supply system should be evaluated periodically to ensure that it is functioning efficiently and effectively. The following aspects should be considered during the evaluation process:

- Quantity and quality of water supplied
- Cost of operation and maintenance
- Customer satisfaction.

8.3 Blockchain Framework for Water Resource Management System

The proposed framework for optimizing water management and detecting leaks in urban settings utilizes blockchain technology to authenticate and exchange real-time data between sensors and the water distribution dashboard. Additionally, it integrates a modular API intended for leak detection and flow regulation, to reduce water wastage and enhance distribution efficiency. While this strategy shows potential for enhancing water management, its implementation poses complexity [14], necessitating the maintenance of its effectiveness.

To implement this framework, the initial step involves researching the requisite hardware and software requirements for both the sensors and the water distribution dashboard. Subsequently, the creation of the blockchain-driven framework and the adaptable API for detecting water leaks and regulating flow can advance. Ensuring strategic placement of sensors to ensure accurate data provision is crucial. Moreover, prioritizing the security of the blockchain network and encrypting data to prevent unauthorized access is essential. Once the framework is implemented, you can monitor water usage and detect leaks in real time. You can also use the modular API to control the flow of water and reduce wastage. The framework can be customized to suit the specific needs of your water management system. Internet of Things (IoT) and Blockchain technologies are being increasingly used in water resource management. Here is how they work:

IoT in Water Management: IoT functions as a network composed of sensors and devices tasked with collecting and transmitting data to a central data point. Specifically, IoT devices play a pivotal role in monitoring a range of parameters such as water quality, level, flow rate, and available resources.

Blockchain in Water Management: Blockchain technology is a digital ledger system enabling enhanced transparency in accessing and trading online data. Distributing data across multiple computers ensures that records remain immutable without modifications to the original blocks of ordered records. Within water management, blockchain serves to establish a transparent and tamper-proof record of water usage and transactions.

The integration of IoT and Blockchain technologies enables the creation of audit trails. These trails facilitate transparent data collection and analysis, ensuring that the data remains unmodifiable and securely stored in a decentralized manner.

This combination can significantly aid in managing drinking water, especially in areas with water scarcity. However, the implementation of these technologies must be inclusive and should focus on utilization rather than the mechanics behind it. This can help in tracing the water from its source to the end consumer, ensuring its quality and preventing wastage.

Nevertheless, it's crucial to acknowledge that despite decentralized solutions such as blockchain and IoT, centralized governance is necessary to facilitate collaboration among all stakeholders in water management. It's important to recognize that while these technologies offer significant potential, their implementation presents challenges and risks, including the potential to widen knowledge gaps and create interdependent relationships between developing and developed nations. Thus, meticulous planning and regulation are essential for their successful adoption.

The genesis of blockchain technology can be traced to Nakamoto's groundbreaking 2008 manuscript, "Bitcoin: An Electronic Cash System for Peer-to-Peer Transactions." This innovation introduced a decentralized, distributed database architecture. At its core lies an interconnected series of blocks, each representing a discrete unit of information, arranged in chronological order. Significantly, cryptographic methods are utilized to ensure the integrity and security of data transmission. Serving as a communal ledger across a dispersed network, the blockchain offers an immutable mechanism for preserving consistent data. A block comprises two essential components: the block header, containing metadata such as the hash of the preceding block, timestamp, and Merkle root hash, and the block body, housing the actual data.

There exist three distinct categories of blockchains, public chains, consortium chains, and private chains. A public blockchain permits any individual or group to access and record transactions, which undergo validation by the blockchain. Consensus mechanisms are open for participation by any party or individual. Conversely, a consortium blockchain is overseen by multiple consortium institutions. In this setup, predetermined specific nodes serve as bookkeepers, collectively deciding on the creation of each block. While other nodes may interact with the blockchain for transaction handling, they abstain from participating in the consensus mechanism. On the contrary, a private blockchain is employed solely for internal billing operations and remains inaccessible to the public. It imposes stringent restrictions on reading and writing permissions, prioritizing personal data privacy protection. Typically established by corporations, governments, or analogous entities, private blockchains ensure controlled access. Consortium blockchains combine the transparency of public blockchains with the controlled access of private ones. They find utility in scenarios such as water resource information management, and facilitating data sharing among water facilities, users, and associated entities. Furthermore, they assist in centralized water management, safeguarding against malicious tampering with data records.

Blockchain technology offers myriad advantages over traditional distributed databases. Unlike traditional setups where a single central server node holds the data and other nodes serve as backups, blockchain operates on a decentralized model where all nodes actively participate in data maintenance. This stands in contrast to traditional systems where each storage node could potentially manipulate data due to the absence of a verifiable record. In contrast, blockchain employs an immutable ledger system, ensuring the integrity of data. Every node within a blockchain network engages in data maintenance, and even if data on one node is altered or removed, it does not impact the data stored across the entire blockchain. Consequently, data is securely stored, fostering mutual trust among nodes.

8.3.1 Interaction Layer

Interaction denotes the exchange or communication between individuals, groups, or entities through various channels and mediums. This exchange can occur in diverse forms, including verbal discussions, written correspondence, non-verbal cues, and digital communications facilitated by technology. The essence of interaction lies in fostering connections, understanding, and collaboration among people, contributing to the development of relationships, ideas, and solutions. Effective interaction facilitates the sharing of knowledge, experiences, and perspectives, thereby enhancing interpersonal dynamics, teamwork, and societal cohesion.

Service Administration: The process of planning, organizing, and overseeing the provision of services to customers or users, ensuring their satisfaction, and aligning with predefined objectives.

Water Department: The water department, often referred to as the municipal water authority or utility, is a governmental entity tasked with overseeing the management and regulation of water resources within a specific geographical area. Its responsibilities typically include water treatment, distribution infrastructure maintenance, billing, regulatory compliance, and wastewater management. By ensuring the provision of safe drinking water and the proper treatment of wastewater, the water department plays a critical role in safeguarding public health and environmental sustainability within the community it serves.

8.3.2 Application Layer

The stratum where technology or systems are practically employed across diverse settings or sectors.

8.3.3 Block Chain Network Layer

In water resource management, the implementation of blockchain technology could be utilized in various ways at different layers. Let me outline some potential applications of blockchain at the network layer in water resource management:

Data Management and Sharing: Blockchain can assist in securely managing and sharing data related to water quality, usage, distribution, and conservation among different stakeholders in the network.

Smart Contracts for Automatic Transactions: Smart contracts can be deployed on the blockchain network to automate transactions related to water supply, billing, and management, ensuring transparency and reducing manual interventions.

Decentralized Water Trading: Blockchain enables the creation of decentralized water trading platforms where users can buy, sell, or exchange water rights or usage permits directly with each other.

Supply Chain Monitoring: Using blockchain, the supply chain of water resources can be better monitored, allowing for tracking water from its source to its destination, ensuring quality, and reducing wastage.

Monitoring and Auditing: Blockchain can enhance the monitoring and auditing processes in water management by providing a tamper-proof and transparent record of all transactions and activities within the network.

8.3.4 Collection and Transmission Layer

Following are the layers:

Sensor Devices: Devices or instruments utilized for detecting and measuring physical or environmental parameters, converting them into electrical signals for processing, analysis, or transmission.

Internet of Things (IoT) Technology: A network of interconnected devices, sensors, and objects embedded with electronics, software, and sensors that enables them to collect, exchange, and act on data, facilitating automation and efficiency improvements in various applications.

Wireless Data Transmission: The transfer of data, signals, or information between devices or systems without the need for physical wired connections, facilitated through radio waves, electromagnetic fields, or infrared radiation.

8.4 Basic Terms in the Blockchain System for Managing Water Resources

8.4.1 Governance Mechanisms

The procedures and structures involved in overseeing or managing a system, organization, or community, including decision-making processes, regulatory frameworks, and enforcement mechanisms.

8.4.2 Internal Operational Portal

An online platform or system utilized within an organization for managing diverse aspects of its functions, resources, or personnel 4.3. External Service Access and Information Dissemination Portal: An online interface or platform facilitating external users' access to an organization's services or information, typically governed by specific permissions or restrictions.

8.4.3 Maximum Water Resource Allocation Ceiling

The highest permissible quantity of water designated for specific purposes, such as irrigation, industrial usage, or domestic consumption, within a given jurisdiction or timeframe.

8.4.4 Water Resource Management Endeavors

Business initiatives or practices geared toward overseeing water resources, including activities like monitoring, allocation, conservation, and regulatory measures aimed at ensuring sustainable utilization and availability.

8.4.5 Baseline Utilization Metrics

A benchmark or standard against which the effectiveness or efficiency of water resource utilization is gauged and is often utilized for setting targets or benchmarks.

8.4.6 Effectiveness of Upper Limit Sewage Discharge Efficiency

The degree of success or efficacy in implementing measures to control or minimize sewage discharge within the confines of a predetermined maximum permissible threshold.

8.4.7 Maximum Water Supply Network Leakage Threshold

The highest tolerable rate of water loss or leakage from a water distribution network is typically expressed as a percentage of the total volume of water supplied.

8.4.8 System Operational Functions

The fundamental operations or functionalities of a system encompass activities like data collection, processing, storage, and transmission, aimed at achieving specific objectives.

8.4.9 Water Source Origins

The natural or artificial origins or sources from which water is obtained, including reservoirs, groundwater, surface water bodies, or precipitation, are utilized for various purposes.

8.4.10 Water Distribution Mechanisms

The systems and procedures involved in supplying water for consumption, industrial processes, agricultural irrigation, or other uses, to meet the needs of communities or individuals.

8.4.11 Water Utilization Practices

The utilization or consumption of water across different sectors or domains, encompassing residential, industrial, agricultural, or commercial applications.

8.4.12 Water Disposal Strategies

The methods or approaches employed in managing and disposing of wastewater, stormwater, or runoff to prevent flooding, environmental contamination, or waterborne diseases.

8.5 Applications of IoT in Water Resource and Management

The utilization of the Internet of Things (IoT) and blockchain technologies in water management is extensive, with some applications outlined below.

8.5.1 Smart City Water Management

IoT can help city administrators monitor water supply, consumption, and equipment health in real time. For instance, smart sensors can collect real-time data to visualize water distribution across the network1. This can lead to more informed decisions by residents, resulting in a more sustainable city. IoT can further identify issues such as leaks in pipes, enabling operators to promptly receive alerts and initiate necessary repairs.

8.5.2 Water Quality Management

IoT devices play a pivotal role in monitoring the water quality of rivers, lakes, and reservoirs, which is critical due to the potential presence of hazardous contaminants. The degradation of water quality has been exacerbated by factors such as rapid urbanization and population growth.

8.5.3 Stormwater Management

The integration of IoT and blockchain technologies offers opportunities for effective stormwater management. These technologies enable the monitoring and direct reporting of water quality to consumers and other relevant stakeholders.

8.5.4 Smart Water Management for Agriculture

IoT facilitates precise water management in agriculture by assessing individual water requirements based on soil conditions, weather forecasts, and irrigation schedules. In case of anomalies such as leaks, authorities are promptly notified, with the location provided for swift action.

8.5.5 Smart Payment and Contract

Blockchain technology facilitates the creation of smart contracts for water usage, streamlining the issuance and monitoring of water abstraction permits. This enhances the security and verifiability of obtaining license information, ensuring more convenient and transparent water management processes.

8.5.6 Wastewater Management

Blockchain and IoT can address the current challenges in wastewater management. They can ensure that wastewater is disposed of safely and in line with regulations.

These applications illustrate how IoT and blockchain can revolutionize water resource management, making it more efficient, transparent, and sustainable. Nevertheless, it's imperative to acknowledge that the effective deployment of these technologies necessitates government backing, as well as substantial investments from both the public and private sectors, alongside robust local and international cooperation.

8.6 Conclusion

This paper delves into the influence of blockchain and IoT on water management, assessing the viability of their integration across various scenarios. These include stormwater management, direct water quality monitoring and reporting to consumers and stakeholders, as well as the implementation of smart payment and contract systems. Such integration aims to address the challenges posed by the global water crisis, exacerbated by climate change and rapid population growth, in a sustainable manner.

References

1. Dogo, E.M., Salami, A.F., Nwulu, N.I., Aigbavboa, C.O.: Blockchain and internet of things-based technologies for intelligent water management system (2019). https://doi.org/10.1007/978-3-030-04110-6_7
2. Naqash, M.T., Syed, T.A., Alqahtani, S.S., Siddiqui, M.S., Alzahrani, A., Nauman, M.: A blockchain-based framework for efficient water management and leakage detection in urban areas. Urban Sci. **7**, 99 (2023). https://doi.org/10.3390/urbansci7040099
3. Russo, T., Alfredo, K., Fisher, J.: Sustainable water management in urban, agricultural, and natural systems. Water **6**, 3934–3956. https://doi.org/10.3390/w6123934
4. Hassan, M.: Real-time internet of things (IoT) based water quality management system. Procedia CIRP **91** (2020). https://doi.org/10.1016/j.procir.2020.03.107

5. Kharche, A., Badholia, S., Upadhyay, R.K.: Implementation of blockchain technology in integrated IoT networks for constructing scalable ITS systems in India. Blockchain: Res. Appl. 100188 (2024). ISSN:2096-7209. https://doi.org/10.1016/j.bcra.2024.100188
6. Jan, F., Min-Allah, N., Saeed, S., Iqbal, S.Z., Ahmed, R.: IoT-based solutions to monitor water level, leakage, and motor control for smart water tanks. Water **14**(3), 309 (2022). https://doi.org/10.3390/w14030309
7. Ward, P.J., Jongman, B., Aerts, J.C., Bates, P.D., Botzen, W.J., Diaz Loaiza, A., Hallegatte, S., Kind, J.M., Kwadijk, J., Scussolini, P., Winsemius, H.C.: A global framework for future costs and benefits of river-flood protection in urban areas. Nat. Clim. Change **7** (2017). https://doi.org/10.1038/nclimate3350
8. Loucks, P., Beek, E.: Water resources planning and management: an overview (2017). https://doi.org/10.1007/978-3-319-44234-1_1
9. Kesari, K.K., Soni, R., Jamal, Q.M.S., et al.: Wastewater treatment and reuse: a review of its applications and health implications. Water Air Soil Pollut. **232**, 208 (2021). https://doi.org/10.1007/s11270-021-05154-8
10. Silva, J.A.: Wastewater treatment and reuse for sustainable water resources management: a systematic literature review. Sustainability **15**(14), 10940 (2023). https://doi.org/10.3390/su151410940
11. Karre, A.V., Sharma, D., Valsaraj, K.T.: Estimating fouling and hydraulic debottlenecking of a clarifier piping system in the expansion of a chemical manufacturing plant. Chem. Product Process Model. (2020). https://doi.org/10.1515/cppm-2020-0029
12. India Water and Wastewater Treatment Industry (trade.gov)
13. Lyons, K.J., Ikonen, J., Hokajärvi, A.-M., Räsänen, T., Pitkänen, T., Kauppinen, A., Kujala, K., Rossi, P.M., Miettinen, I.T.: Monitoring groundwater quality with real-time data, stable water isotopes, and microbial community analysis: a comparison with conventional methods. Sci. Total Environ. **864**, 161199. ISSN:0048-9697 (2023). https://doi.org/10.1016/j.scitotenv.2022.161199
14. Akkara, S., Thilagaraj, M.: Water leakage detection and management system using IOT (2020)
15. Naqash, M.T., Syed, T.A., Alqahtani, S.S., Siddiqui, M.S., Alzahrani, A., Nauman, M.: A blockchain based framework for efficient water management and leakage detection in urban areas. Urban Sci. **7**(4), 99 (2023)
16. https://www.mygreatlearning.com/blog/ensemble-learning/
17. Xia, W., Chen, X., Song, C.: A framework of blockchain technology in intelligent water management. Front. Environ. Sci. **10**, 909606 (2022)

Chapter 9
IoT-Based Smart Water Resource Management

Neelaksh Seel, Lal Pratap Verma, and Abhinav Gupta

Abstract Water is an invaluable resource essential for sustaining life on Earth. India, with its massive population of 1.4 billion people, holds 4% of the world's freshwater resources, a significant statistic highlighting the need for efficient water management. Effective usage of water across various sectors-household supply, agriculture, industry, electricity production, and research is critical for ensuring the long-term availability of drinking water. Given India's large and growing population, both the government and citizens must prioritize smart water management. Smart water management can be greatly enhanced with the use of technology, particularly the Internet of Things (IoT). IoT technology facilitates efficient distribution and utilization of water, ensures quality management, and improves storage systems. IoT-enabled devices can identify water wastage through leak detection and overflow monitoring, ensuring that precious water resources are not lost unnecessarily. These devices continuously monitor essential quality parameters of water, ensuring it is safe for drinking and other uses. One significant application of IoT in water management is the collection and management of natural water sources, especially rainwater. Rainwater can be harvested from large roofs of buildings, highways, and natural pools. This collected water can then be effectively managed and utilized, reducing dependency on conventional water sources and conserving groundwater reserves. IoT devices also play a critical role in controlling and monitoring water extraction mechanisms. Water pumps, taps, motors, and tube wells can be equipped with IoT sensors that provide real-time data on water usage, helping to optimize the extraction process and reduce wastage. These smart systems can automate water distribution based on actual demand, ensuring that water is delivered where and when it is needed most efficiently. Moreover, IoT technology offers a comprehensive solution for water quality management. By continuously monitoring water quality, IoT systems can detect contaminants and ensure that water supplied to households and

N. Seel · A. Gupta
Moradabad Institute of Technology, Moradabad, UP, India

L. P. Verma (✉)
Manipal University Jaipur, Jaipur, Rajasthan, India
e-mail: er.lpverma1986@gmail.com

S. S. Rawat et al. (eds.), *Unleashing the Power of Blockchain and IoT for Water Informatics*, Water Informatics for Water Resource Management,
https://doi.org/10.1007/978-981-96-3886-4_9

industries meets safety standards. This capability is particularly important in preventing waterborne diseases and maintaining public health. The implementation of IoT-based smart water management systems represents a significant advancement over traditional mechanical systems. Traditional methods often rely on manual monitoring and control, which can be inefficient and prone to errors. In contrast, IoT systems provide automated, real-time data and control, greatly enhancing the efficiency and reliability of water management practices. For developing countries like India, transitioning to smart water management systems is not just beneficial but essential. As the population continues to grow and industrial demands increase, the pressure on freshwater resources intensifies. Smart water management, supported by IoT technology, offers a sustainable solution to these challenges. It ensures that water is conserved, used efficiently, and maintained at high-quality standards.

Keywords Cloud analytics · IOT · National water policy · Smart water · Sensors

9.1 Introduction

The increasing water demand, a finite and essential resource, presents a significant challenge influenced by various factors such as population growth, urbanization, and evolving agricultural practices. Addressing this challenge effectively requires the prudent and sustainable use of water resources to ensure widespread access and support for development.

In response to these challenges, the Indian government has implemented numerous policy-level strategies to tackle water-related issues. A key approach has been the formulation of comprehensive policies aimed at the holistic development of water resources. These policies encompass a range of measures designed to ensure that water is used efficiently and sustainably across different sectors and regions.

One of the critical areas of focus is providing technical support to all states in India. This support includes groundwater exploration, which is vital for identifying new water sources and managing existing ones. With proper exploration, states can better plan for water extraction and conservation, reducing the risk of overexploitation and depletion of groundwater reserves.

Irrigation is another significant area where technical support is provided. Efficient irrigation techniques and projects help optimize water use in agriculture, ensuring that crops receive adequate water without unnecessary wastage. This is crucial for enhancing agricultural productivity and food security in a country with a large agrarian population.

The government also supports adaptable projects that can be tailored to the specific needs and conditions of different regions. These projects address various aspects of water management, including command area development, which focuses on improving the infrastructure and efficiency of irrigation systems within designated areas. Proper development of command areas ensures that water is distributed evenly and used effectively, benefiting farmers, and reducing water scarcity.

Addressing issues of waterlogging and drainage is another priority. Waterlogging can severely impact agricultural productivity and infrastructure, making it essential to develop effective drainage systems. These systems help manage excess water, preventing damage to crops and property. Flood control measures are equally important, given the recurrent and devastating floods in various parts of India. Technical support for flood control includes designing and implementing infrastructure to manage and mitigate the impact of floods and protect lives and property. Similarly, coastal and riverbank erosion issues are addressed through measures to stabilize and protect these areas, preventing the loss of valuable land and resources.

Dam safety is another crucial aspect of water resource management. Ensuring that dams are well-maintained and safe helps prevent catastrophic failures and ensures a reliable water supply for irrigation, drinking, and industrial use. Hydraulic structures for navigation and hydropower are also supported, facilitating transportation, and generating renewable energy, respectively.

India has also made substantial investments in infrastructure, including extensive dams, storage facilities, and canal networks, to meet the country's water and agricultural needs. These efforts focus on promoting technology-based interventions to enhance agricultural productivity. However, despite these initiatives, a significant gap persists between the demand and supply of water across various sectors. The "Water Gap" for India, estimated by the "2030 Water Resource Group," is a concerning 50% [1, 2].

The interconnection and autonomous data transfer among internetwork devices mark a forefront in communication advancements expected to shape the coming decades. Referred to as the Internet of Things (IoT), this technological innovation represents a revolutionary shift, enabling extensive digital connectivity among numerous everyday physical devices. Wireless sensors, seamlessly configured into a network, play a crucial role in collecting information within this technology. Following this data collection, the network transmits sensor readings through a signal communication system to the IoT cloud for subsequent processing and analysis.

The primary components of this process include the following: Fig. 9.1 [3].

- Essential components such as sensors, actuators, and intelligent metering instruments play a pivotal role in gathering data on physical and chemical parameters, encompassing pH, temperature, turbidity, and conductivity.
- Diverse communication technologies such as Bluetooth, LoWPAN, ZigBee, and WiFi are utilized to establish connections among the different elements of the system.
- The IoT cloud serves as a platform for data storage, processing, and analysis, integrating advanced technologies such as "Google Cloud AutoML, Artificial Intelligence (AI), Machine Learning (ML), Edge Computing, and Big Data analytics".
- Additionally, the system relies on power sources like solar power supply with backup and rechargeable batteries, which can be equipped with energy-saving components to ensure sustained and efficient operation.

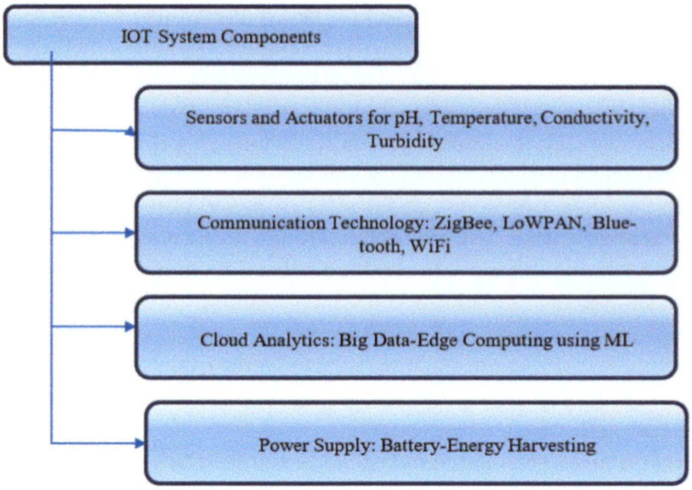

Fig. 9.1 IoT devices

Numerous proposals have been advanced for water management across diverse regions, with a focus on monitoring and addressing various aspects. Some systems aim to reduce wastewater volume, improve the efficiency of water distribution networks [4], and forecast and alert communities about significant environmental water-related issues [5].

These initiatives align with the future development of sustainable IoT solutions. This commitment addresses several factors, including the considerable annual water loss in innercity water supply systems in developing countries, estimated at 32 billion cubic feet [6]. Such water loss contributes to energy wastage and, consequently, contributes to global warming. Recognizing this, there is a shift in urban planning, with 45% of the global urban population intending to embrace new IoT-enabled smart water resource management and monitoring solutions by 2024, according to the IDC (International Data Corporation) [7].

9.2 National Water Policy

The current guiding document is the National Water Policy of 2012; however, recognizing the evolving challenges in the water sector, there is a deliberate intention to revise the National Water Policy with the establishment of a drafting committee for this purpose. Acknowledging water as a matter falling within the jurisdiction of individual states, efforts to enhance, preserve, and effectively manage water resources primarily fall within the purview of respective State Governments. In tandem with these initiatives, the Central Government provides crucial technical and financial support through various schemes and programs.

In collaboration with the States, the Government of India energetically executes the "Jal Jeevan Mission (JJM) - Har Ghar Jal". The purpose of the mission is to provide drinking water in adequate quantity and recommended quality to each poor and rural family through piped water connections till 2024 with a complete projected budget of Rs. 3.60 lakh crore. Water supplies comprise groundwater, lake water (reservoirs, rivers, springs, lakes, and so on), and raindrops gathered in tiny tanks for drinking water delivery projects.

The "Atal Mission for Rejuvenation and Urban Transformation" (AMRUT) was initiated in 2015 as a national urban mission, focusing on achieving general coverage of water sources in 500 Mission cities within 5 years. The mission has been extended until March 2023 for the completion of this project. At the commencement of AMRUT, water resource coverage was at 64%, aiming to encompass 100% of households by the mission's conclusion. The objective is to provide 139 lakh water-piped connections for comprehensive coverage. Under AMRUT, 115 lakh freshwater piped connections have been facilitated in conjunction with other schemes.

AMRUT 2.0, which went live on October 1, 2021, broadens its objective of universal access to water supplies beyond 500 cities to include all democratic tiny villages. AMRUT 2.0 aspires to make cities self-sufficient in delivering fresh drinking water by installing 2.68 crore piped connections. The projected budget for "AMRUT 2.0" is ₹2,77,000 crore, with a central share of ₹76,760 crore over 5 years "(FY 2021–22 to FY 2025–26)". AMRUT 2.0 proposes to establish the sustainable use of water by developing "City Water Balance Plans" for each city, focusing on the recycling or recycling of treated sewage, restoration of water supplies, and water management.

The "Central Ground Water Board (CGWB)" began artificial recharge operations in certain Aspirational Districts in 2018 and plans to complete it by 2020. Check dams, percolation tanks, subsurface barriers, recharging shafts, and recharge wells were built to trap runoff water in streams and store it, thereby increasing groundwater recharge. CGWB's "Aquifer Mapping and Management Program" delineates and characterizes aquifer dispositions across the country. The aquifer mapping program attempts to develop aquifer or area-specific groundwater management methods that involve community engagement. The organizational plans are then shared with specific state governments for relevant execution.

On November 14, 2019, the "National Water Mission" began the "Sahi Fasal" campaign, urging farmers in areas with limited water resources to plant crops that are less water-intensive, economically profitable, and use water efficiently. Training sessions for the "Sahi Fasal" initiative have been held in regions around the country that are experiencing water scarcity.

A different approach effort, "Catch the Rain" with the slogan "Catch the rain, where it falls when it falls" was introduced to motivate participants and states to build "Rainwater Harvesting Structures (RWHS)" suitable to the weather and subsoil divisions, with flexible engagement from the public before the start of the rainy season to verify the storage of water getting through the rain.

The Government of India and the Jal Shakti Ministry launched the "Jal Shakti Abhi-yan-I (JSA-I)", a water-saving and security initiative intended for 256 freshwater-stressed districts around the country. Under the auspices of JSA-I, government officials, water professionals, and researchers from the central government have worked with State and District authorities to encourage water preservation and effective management of resources. The Indian PM started the second "Jal Shakti Abhiyan Catch the Rain" (JSA: CTR) campaign under the water-collecting theme "Catch the Rain where it Falls when it Falls" on March 22, 2021.JSA: CTR is carried out in all regions/districts of the country during the early monsoon and rainy seasons from March 30 to November 30, 2021.

On December 1, 2021, the Indian Government began the third edition of the "Water Heroes-Share Your Stories" program, which will run for one year. The competition targets to boost the perception of the importance of water and support national programs focused on water conservation and sustainable development. Participants submit anecdotes about those who help to conserve water [2].

9.3 Plan for Water Resource Management

A municipality's comprehensive "Water Resource Management Plan" includes a "Water Resource Assessment (WRA)", which evaluates the existing availability of water, current water demand, upcoming water convenience, and future water mandate. It also includes a Demand Management Plan, which outlines rules and activities for efficient water resource management. The WRA calls for a thorough evaluation of the entire water supply service chain, including water allocations for the various sectors covered by metropolitan services. The calculation of current and future water accessibility is based on well-known probable water supply resources for the town, while the evaluation of existing and future water mandates is mainly focused on the water delivery network up to end consumers [11].

In the urban environment, the "Integrated Urban Water Management" (IUWM) approach emerges as a pivotal strategy, consolidating all features of the municipal water cycle (sanitation, water supply, stormwater) under a unified framework. IUWM draws inspiration from Integrated Water Resource Management (IWRM), a concept usually applied at the catchment level within local governance. Subsequent sections will explore the facts of each of these mechanisms.

9.4 Water Resource Assessment

Water resources assessment is a systematic approach that involves the collection, measurement, and analysis of appropriate considerations related to the property and capacity of water resources as shown in Fig. 9.2.

The purpose of this process is to improve the development and management of water assets, as outlined by Keller in 2008. It entails a thorough examination of resources, the status of water services, and trends in demand and accessibility [8, 11].

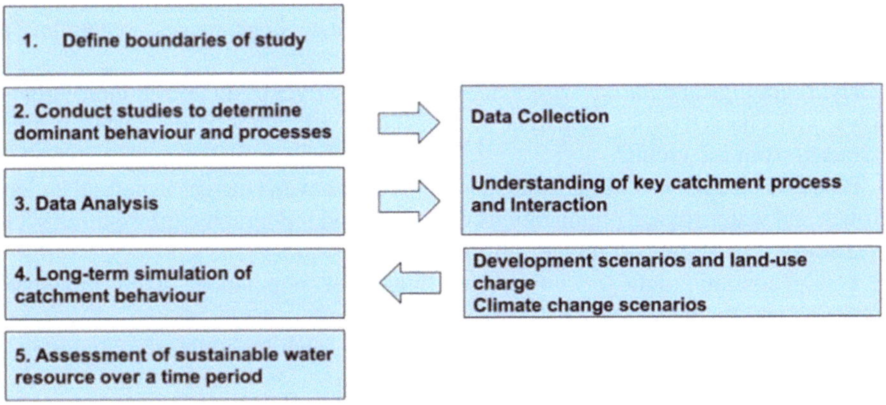

Fig. 9.2 Schematic diagram of water resource assessment development process [11]

An alternative definition presented by the "World Meteorological Organization" in its "Technical Material for Water Resources Assessment [9]" characterizes water resources valuation as the systematic examination of water sources, reliability, extent, quality, and volume of water assets for their utilization and regulation. In this context, water resources refer to the presence of water or its potential availability in sufficient quantity and quality at a designated location over a period suitable for a discernible. demand. The fundamental goals of a "Water Resource Assessment (WRA)" encompass:

- Evaluating the current state of water source availability, taking into account both inter-annual and intra-annual water variability.
- Assessing the environmental and social tradeoffs linked to current patterns of water utilization.
- Identifying factors affecting the availability and reliability of water.

9.4.1 Water Resource Assessment Process

The initiation of the "Water Resource Assessment (WRA)" process involves defining the study's scope, which may extend to catchment, micro-catchment, or city/district levels. The effectiveness of the WRA depends on a thorough understanding of storages, water flows, and their temporal interrelationships, along with their correlation with human demand or impact within the specified boundary. This framework was outlined by the "World Meteorological Organization" in 2012 [9].

Subsequently, a high-level review of the defined boundary is conducted to ascertain dominant behaviors and processes. This phase requires extensive data collection, encompassing current and historical hydrological data, categorized into:

Hydro-meteorological data, encompassing climate appearances, precipitation data, vaporization metrics, and soil moisture levels.

Hydrogeological data, covering catchment details, river basin information, stream flows, soil characteristics, apparent storage, and particulars of the water system extracted from the ground.

Biophysical data, including details on usable land cover, changes in natural undergrowth and water-related organizations over time, and topographic information such as altitudes, curves, and drainage patterns [11].

Socio-economic data, encompassing figures of population, main monetary activities, and the living standard.

Consumed water data used for all purposes, spanning domestic, industrial, commercial, and recreational uses.

Following data collection, the subsequent step comprises thorough analysis to comprehend the main interactions within the feature identification and catchment of long-term and short-term water balances [11]. This analysis, crucially, incorporates factors related to water quality and environmental considerations.

The insights derived from the analysis are then utilized to construct a long-term simulation of catchment behavior, incorporating diverse scenarios related to development, landuse changes, and climate variations. This simulation proves instrumental in identifying and assessing sustainable water sources over an extended period.

9.5 Outline of Water Resource Assessment

As a result of multiple Water Resource Assessments, a framework for the process has been formulated in the given figure. The Water Resource Assessment (WRA) serves as a valuable tool to measure both the present and upcoming demands of water supply, along with an estimation of existing and prospective availability of water within the jurisdiction of municipal committee [11] (Fig. 9.3).

9.5.1 Water Use in the City

This segment should encompass comprehensive details regarding the overall water supply, starting from the water source to the consumer. It should provide insights into the various purposes for which water is demanded shown in Fig. 9.4. The computation includes the entire water inhibited from the different ground surface and groundwater sources for public supply. Parameters like per-unit production demand or per-capita demand are calculated, and inefficiencies within the agencies are pinpointed. Utilizing the computed present demand, the difference between supply and demand can be ascertained. The supply side data is typically sourced from the water supply agencies or water efficacies of the Urban Local Body (ULB). In cases of majority acquisition, it can be obtained from the local State Irrigation Department [11]. On the side of

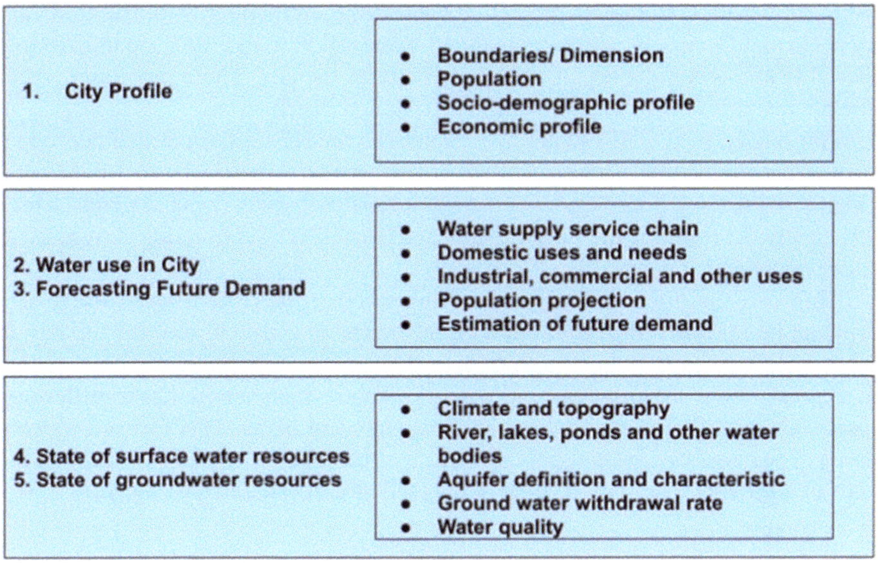

Fig. 9.3 Outline for a water resource assessment

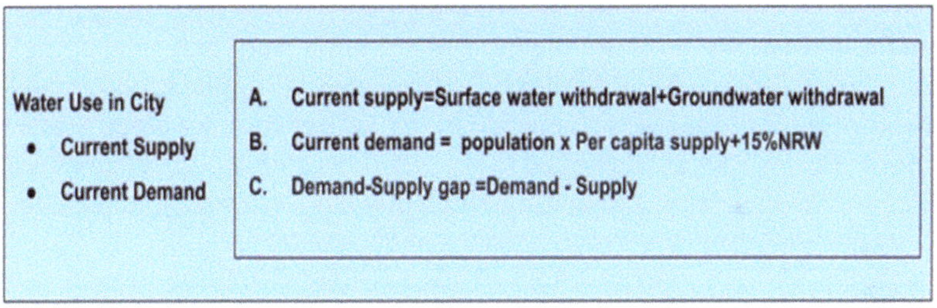

Fig. 9.4 Supply, demand, and demand-supply gap calculation [11]

demand, information is gathered through existing measurable practices or thorough surveys. Existing water usage standards, established by CPHEEO or IS-1172-1993, serve as benchmarks for identifying instances of overuse. To gain a comprehensive understanding, it is recommended that the city undertake a comprehensive water assessment throughout the all-inclusive water supply agency service chain, detailing supply, gaps, demand, and losses.

9.5.2 Projecting Future Demand

Anticipating future water demand necessitates projecting the population over a defined planning horizon for which the water resource management plan is being developed. Various population projection methods recommended by the Central Public Health and Environmental Engineering Organization (CPHEEO) are utilized and tailored to align with the specific characteristics of the city. These projections offer valuable insights into future population growth and distribution.

Additionally, the CPHEEO provides standards for per-unit or per-capita production water requirements. These standards are instrumental in calculating future water demand. Using these benchmarks, planners can evaluate water demand trends, which is crucial for determining the sustainability and feasibility of continuing current water usage practices in the city.

This process not only helps in identifying whether the current water usage scenario can be maintained in the future but also acts as a critical tool for the city to assess its vulnerability to potential stress or shocks due to increasing water demand. By understanding these trends and potential future demands, cities can develop more robust and adaptive water resource management plans. This forward-looking approach ensures that water supply systems are resilient and capable of meeting the needs of a growing population, even in the face of unforeseen challenges.

9.5.3 Smart Water Management System

The comprehensive system architecture for monitoring and managing water resources across industrial, agricultural, and residential applications involves the deployment of multiple sensors connected to the IoT technology cloud via Wireless Sensor Networks (WSN), as illustrated in Fig. 9.5. This architecture enables real-time data collection and analysis, facilitating efficient water resource management.

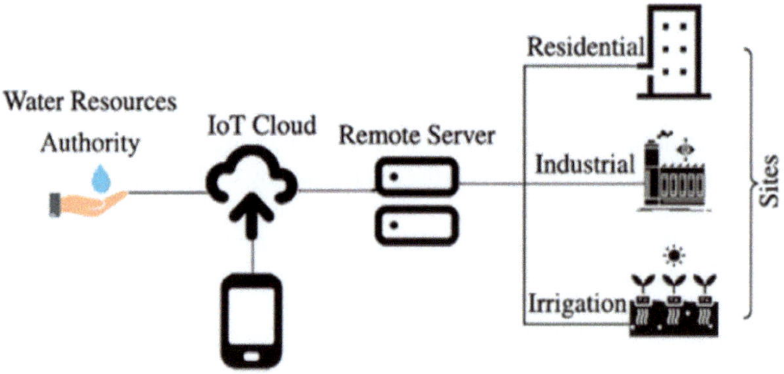

Fig. 9.5 IoT-based smart water management system

Components of the System Architecture

1. **Wireless Sensor Networks (WSN):**

   Sensors: Various types of sensors are used to measure parameters such as water flow, pressure, quality, and usage.

   Nodes: Sensor nodes are strategically placed to cover the targeted areas, ensuring comprehensive monitoring.

   Connectivity: These nodes communicate wirelessly, transmitting data to central gateways that interface with the IoT cloud.

2. **IoT Cloud Platform**:

   Data Aggregation: The IoT cloud aggregates data from multiple sensors, providing a centralized platform for data analysis.

   Real-time Monitoring: Continuous monitoring allows for the immediate detection of anomalies such as leaks, overflows, or quality issues.

   Analytics and Insights: Advanced analytics tools process the data to generate actionable insights, helping in decision-making and resource optimization.

3. **IoT Devices with Sensors**:

   Types of Sensors: These devices are equipped with various sensors, such as temperature, humidity, light, motion, and pressure sensors.

   Functionality: Sensors continuously monitor environmental conditions and collect data.

4. **Communication Protocols**:

   WiFi: Utilized for high data rate and longer range communication, suitable for stable, stationary devices.

   Bluetooth: Ideal for short-range communication, often used in wearable devices and short-distance applications.

   Zigbee: A low-power, low-data-rate protocol that is excellent for battery-operated devices and mesh networking in home automation.

5. **Customization and Utilization**:

   The practical utilization of IoT-based systems allows for efficient customization based on the specific requirements of different applications, focusing on factors such as cost, performance, flexibility, and reliability.

6. **Gateways**:

   Role: Serve as intermediaries that aggregate data from various IoT devices. Gateways bridge the communication between sensors and the central system.

   Functionality: Ensure data integrity, manage communication protocols, and perform initial data filtering or preprocessing.

7. **Cloud Infrastructure:**

   IoT Platform: A centralized system hosted in the cloud for comprehensive data storage, advanced analytics, and management.

   Data Storage: Scalable databases that handle large volumes of incoming data from IoT devices.

   Analytics: Tools and services for analyzing data patterns, generating insights, and predicting trends.

   Management: Interfaces for configuring, monitoring, and controlling IoT devices remotely.

8. **Applications and Dashboards**:

   Monitoring: Real-time dashboards that display current sensor readings, historical data, and alerts.

   Control: Interfaces for users to interact with and control IoT devices, such as adjusting settings or triggering actions.

   Visualization: Graphs, charts, and maps that provide intuitive data representation and actionable insights.

9. **Integrated Security Measures**:

   Encryption: Ensures data privacy and security during transmission and storage by encrypting data end-to-end.

   Authentication: Validates users and devices through secure methods to prevent unauthorized access.

Access Control: Manages permissions to ensure that only authorized entities can access or control the system.

10. **Advantages of IoT-based Water Management Systems**

    Cost Efficiency: IoT systems can be tailored to fit budget constraints without compromising on functionality or performance.

    Scalability: The modular nature of IoT systems allows for easy scaling, accommodating the growing needs of urban and rural areas.

    Reliability: Advanced IoT solutions offer high reliability, ensuring continuous operation and minimal downtime.

    Flexibility: IoT systems can be adapted to various environments and requirements, providing a versatile solution for different water management needs.

An effective "IoT-based Smart Water Management System (SWMS)" necessitates the distribution of numerous sensors throughout water resources or reservoirs at designated sites. These sensors measure essential chemical and physical parameters of water, including flow rate, water level, pH, turbidity, temperature, water salinity, dissolved oxygen, conductivity, and ion concentration [10]. The SWMS then communicates the collected sense data from the sensors installed, storing it on the defined cloud for subsequent processing and then analyzed through a computer program. Smart water measurement devices are also integrated to monitor and maintain the record of consumer usage, automatically uploading water ingestion readings periodically based on inquiries to the IoT technology cloud and the relevant water centralized agency repository responsible for managing overall water-related data. Typically, a web dashboard or mobile application is implemented to interface with end-users, allowing them to access water-related information for their websites, create water consumption accounts for consumers, obtain billing information, and perform other functionalities.

Each reviewed system aims to achieve at least one of the following goals, as identified in the present survey:

- Water source remote monitoring and management.
- Observing equipment and structure conditions to forecast potential failures, leaks, maintenance, or tampering needs.
- Prediction of significant environmental problems connected to water control and features through measurements and analysis of physical and chemical characteristics.
- Monitoring consumed quantities for every resource and confirming rational distribution by examining usage purposes.
- Utilizing collected data for decision-making like billing services and water allocation.

9.6 Conclusions

This chapter provides a comprehensive overview of various investigative efforts related to the design and implementation of Smart water management systems based on the Internet of Things (IoT). It presents a generic architecture for smart water monitoring systems and categorizes these systems into residential, agricultural, and industrial applications. The review delves into the latest research proposals for Smart water management systems, examining their relevance to each application domain. The chapter culminates with the introduction of an innovative optical Smart water management system based on IoT, designed for versatile implementation across all fields. It explores potential solutions and assesses the practical feasibility of each system component. The primary goal of this work is to inspire further research initiatives focusing on the design of IoT-based Smart water management systems, adaptable for various liquid-related applications.

References

1. ADRI India.: Water Resources Management. https://www.adriindia.org/adri/water_resources_management. Accessed 29 Jan. 2024
2. Press Information Bureau, Government of India.: Government of India launches National Hydrogen Mission to promote clean energy. Press Information Bureau (2022). https://pib.gov.in/Pressreleaseshare.aspx?PRID=1782283
3. Sheng, Z., Mahapatra, C., Zhu, C., Leung, V.C.M.: Recent advances in industrial wireless sensor networks toward efficient management in IoT. IEEE Access **3**, 622–637 (2015)
4. Lalle, Y., Fourati, M., Fourati, L.C., Barraca, J.P.: Communication technologies for smart water grid applications: overview, opportunities, and research directions. Comput. Netw. **190**(107940) (2021)
5. Pule, M., Yahya, A., Chuma, J.: Wireless sensor networks: a survey on monitoring water quality. J. Appl. Res. Technol. **15**(6), 562–570 (2018)
6. González-Vidal, A., Cuenca-Jara, J., Skarmeta, A.F.: IoT for water management: towards intelligent anomaly detection. In: Proceedings of the World Forum on Internet of Things, pp. 858–863 (2019)
7. Goldstein, P.: Smart water technology: how iot helps cities save money and conserve water (2021). https://statetechmagazine.com/
8. Keller, S.: Water resource assessment factsheet. SSWM (Sustainable Sanitation and Water Management) (2008). https://sswm.info/sswm-university-course/module-4-sustainable-water-supply/further-resources-water-sources-software/water-resources-assessment
9. World Meteorological Organisation.: Technical material for water resources assessment. World Meteorological Organisation, Geneva (2012)
10. Yaroshenko, I., Kirsanov, D., Marjanovic, M., Lieberzeit, P.A., Korostynska, O., Mason, A., Frau, I., Legin, A.: Real-time water quality monitoring. [Journal/Conference], Volume (Issue), Page Range (n.d.)
11. Climate Centre for Cities, NIUA.: Water Resources Management, Training manual 2013 (2021)

Chapter 10
Agriculture Production Optimization

Rachna Jain, Aziz Nanthaamornphong, and Komal Malsa

Abstract Agriculture is an efficient field exclusively in rapidly rising nations like India. Agriculture and farming are the main sources of income in India. It is also called a country of farmers. In India, the majority of people work in agriculture. Various factors contribute to agricultural activities; soil is one of them which helps to increase the quantity of crops. Utilizing historical datasets in agriculture can change how decisions are made and increase farmer productivity. While farming contributes only 18% of India's GDP, but still it is the primary income source for a significant section of the country's population. The lack of appropriate decision-making on yield forecasts by farmers is one plausible cause. There is no system in place to guide farmers in selecting the right plants. This paper also considers regulatory mechanisms and audits of water resources which have always played a pivotal role in agriculture optimization. Water scarcity and extreme weather occurrences, such as floods and droughts, are major obstacles to the water management widely used in agriculture. This work examines a unique strategy combining blockchain, WSN, and IoT technologies to address these issues. The primary output of the suggested approach is to enhance the drought and flood management techniques' effectiveness, transparency, and resilience. Sensors have been thoughtfully situated in strategic locations to continuously monitor vital metrics like soil moisture, water levels, and weather conditions that make up the IoT and WSN components to improve overall agriculture production.

Keywords Auditing · Crop yield prediction · Logistic regression · K-means algorithm · Supervised learning technique · Water regulatory mechanism

---

R. Jain (✉)
JSS Academy of Technical Education, Noida, India
e-mail: rachnajain@jssaten.ac.in

A. Nanthaamornphong
University of Alabama, Alabama, USA
e-mail: aziz.n@phuket.psu.ac.th

K. Malsa
Lingaya's Vidyapeeth, Faridabad, India

S. S. Rawat et al. (eds.), *Unleashing the Power of Blockchain and IoT for Water Informatics*, Water Informatics for Water Resource Management,
https://doi.org/10.1007/978-981-96-3886-4_10

10.1 Introduction

India has a population of 1.2 billion people, and the majority of people work in agriculture. So, we can say that the main source of income in India is agriculture. Various factors contribute to agricultural activities; the soil is one of them which helps to increase the quantity of crops. Soil testing is essential because it gives information on all nutrients in the earth like Potassium (K), Phosphorous (P), and Nitrogen (N). This will help farmers to decide which crop is best for the soil. The other factor is climate; it also contributes to the high-yield production of crops. If a crop gets a proper temperature and humidity then it will grow fast and give a high yield. Rainfall and pH value are also factors that contribute to the high-yield production. If the crops do not get proper rain, then they will not grow properly and farmers will not get that much yield. If we take rice as an example, it requires heavy rainfall so it should grow in areas where rainfall is heavy. Farmers are unaware and they are using their own experience to plow the crop which has a very less success ratio. Agriculture is a productive sector. Lack of appropriate decision-making on yield forecast by farmers is one possible cause for this.

To help the farmers decide the crop to be plowed for their benefit we are motivated to build this model. This dataset includes the temperature, rainfall, and nutrient availability for a specific crop in the farmer's soil. Based on nutrients our model will predict soil type. According to the soil type, crops that can grow in a particular soil can be suggested. Similarly based on temperature and rainfall model predicts crops that can grow on the earth. The suggested machine learning approach looks at a number of factors, such as rainfall, PH soil, temperature, and crop humidity to yield the most for our country. Figure 10.1 displays the different steps of machine learning used in application areas in agriculture.

Promoting the management of water resource assets and identifying the parties accountable for environmental harm to water, which is made feasible by the senior cadres' water resource assets' departure audit, are further considerations. This essay is based on the Sustainable Development Goals of the United Nations, which deal with green accounting for natural assets and water resource management. The resource, environment, society, and economy serve as the foundation for the assessment index system that is created for the purpose of the outgoing audit and evaluation of the assets associated with water resources.

The main focus is to increase the crop production. It will optimize the yield production. By taking into account numerous elements including soil composition, rainfall, temperature, and other entities, the suggested model seeks to anticipate crop production. Using machine learning techniques, the model creates a predictive model. Here, a variety of machine learning methods are employed such as k-mean algorithms logistic regressions. Utilizing a variety of input data, we will design, build, and deploy the model. So, using machine learning techniques, the model would be in the condition to extract the crop yield from the data and learn the features. This model will predict soil type based on nutrients. The soil type model forecasts a list of crops that can grow in a specific soil. A list of crops that can grow in a specific

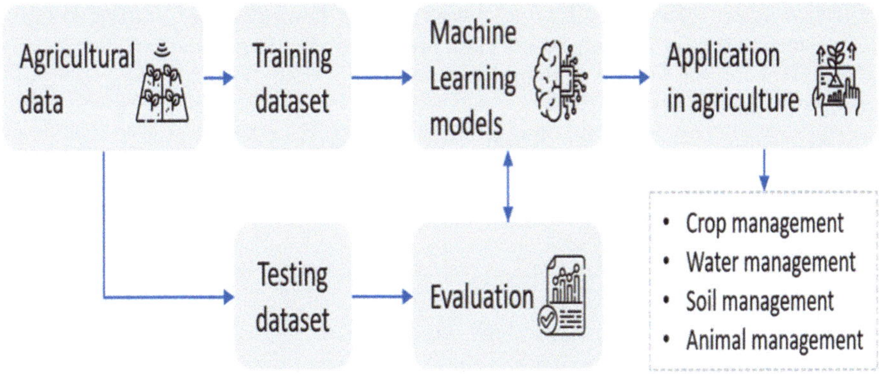

Fig. 10.1 Different steps of machine learning used in application areas in the agriculture

environment is predicted by a model based on temperature and rainfall in a similar way. The suggested machine learning approach tries to forecast the best-yielding crop for our nation by examining a number of variables, including rainfall, soil, pH and temperature, and crop humidity.

Another important point of study is regarding the regulating body, and there is yet another query to be answered. Has the regulating body taken into consideration the findings from past audits in planning for this one? Nothing suggests that this is the case. When a similar nonconformity had previously been noted, at the very least, one should have anticipated finding some remarks in the audit report. Theoretically, in order to prepare future regulatory controls with better information, it is important to regularly search for trends in past regulatory controls.

10.2 Literature Review

A comprehensive literature review for enhanced water management during extreme weather events reveals significant advancements. Blockchain technology is increasingly applied in water management systems, offering benefits such as improved scalability and security. IoT and WSN integration in water systems can provide real-time insights into hydrologic responses to extreme weather, aiding in emergency management efforts. Research emphasizes the importance of long-term commitment, organizational policy updates, and relevant expertise for the successful adoption of distributed ledger technologies in water management. Additionally, IoT systems have been designed for various sectors, including oil exploration, etc. showcasing the versatility and potential of these technologies.

Model entitled "Crop Prediction based on Soil Classification using Machine Learning with Classifier Ensembling" [1]. Based on soil categorization, the authors developed a web solution to forecast the crop. Our main goal is to create an intuitive system based on soil attributes. Data pre-processing has been completed using data transformation. Data is gathered from many sources. Bagged Tree, SVM, etc. algorithms that have been used.

Model entitled "Crop Prediction Using Machine Learning" [2], in it the researchers emphasized on the application of the algorithm in the agricultural field. This work suggests a model so that given inputs of pH and soil nutrient values (NPK values) can forecast the crop.

Model entitled "Crop Yield Prediction based on Climatic Parameters" [3], authors have produced an approachable online application and the specified system's interface will be used by the farmers to interact. The User, Server, and Climate Forecast APIs are the three key components of the system. The user will choose the district, crop, and size of his field before providing these data to the website. On the server side, this data will be examined. The random forest method has been used to train the model.

Model entitled "Demand Based Crop Recommender System for Farmers" [6]. In order to predict agricultural yield and price by analyzing trends from historical data, the author applied the sliding window non-linear regression method. The authors suggested a system that would recommend the greatest kind of crops for farmers to select. Demand levels were classified throughout the system design. The demand for crops is forecasted using the demand level classification.

Model entitled "The System for Maximize the Yielding Rate of Crops using Machine Learning Algorithm" [7] provides an overview of the suggested strategy to aid in identifying crop selection problems, boosting crop net yield rates throughout the course of seasons, and assisting in achieving the highest level of economic growth. The authors talked about the various influencing factors that various forecasting models can use for crops. The proposed method divided crops into four categories: annual, short-term, and long-term plantations.

Model entitled "Crop Yield Prediction based on Climatic Parameters" [8] provides a web-based solution for farmers. The User, Server, and Climate Forecast API are the three key components of the system. The user will choose the district, crop, and size of his field before providing this data to the server. This data will be analyzed on the server.

Model entitled "Yield Prediction using Soil Climatic Data using AI" [9]. The researchers have created a method that would primarily rely on characteristics (such as region, soil type, climate, etc.) necessary for maximum profit in relation to certain crops. These elements will be taken into consideration by the regression model, which will also aid in predicting agricultural production for each crop during the ensuing several years. A few machine learning models, including the XG Boost Regression model, the LGN Boost Regression model, and the Random Forest Regression model, have been tested. The XG Boost linear regression model had the most appropriate outcome. As a result, crop production forecasting is done using this model.

Model entitled "Machine learning approach for forecasting crop yield based on climatic parameters" [5]. Our country's districts were selected according to the area under that particular crop. Based on this criterion, the top five districts with the greatest amount of selected crop areas were chosen. The crops selected for the research were the most common in the district chosen. Among the crops chosen are soy proteins, maize, paddy, and wheat. However, agriculture production is affected by a variety of other input characteristics, including watering, chemical fertilizer, pesticide application, and so on, which were not recognized in the current study.

Model entitled "Design and Implementation of Crop Yield Prediction Model in Agriculture" [10]. In order to assess an issue and decide how to solve it, the author has created a system that aids analysts in predicting or identifying useful information from a set of observations, papers, or business models. Crops that depend on a variety of elements, including soil nutrients like nitrogen, phosphorus, and potassium, as well as environmental conditions like temperature and rainfall, are a novel innovation in the globe today. The suggested approach accurately forecasts the farmer's profitable advanced crop.

Model entitled "Crop Yield Prediction Using Supervised Learning Techniques" [11]. By studying the farming land's past data, the proposed system tries to forecast a model by considering soil properties, the amount of rainfall, the temperature, productivity, and other factors. Here, the authors utilize a variety of machine learning algorithms, including decision trees, polynomial regression, and random forests. Predicted accuracy is used to evaluate performance.

Model entitled "Analysis of Crop Prediction using Data Mining Techniques" [8]. Based on frequent usage, the datasets have been gathered and refined. It is feasible to predict the crop's name and net yield rate from these parameters. The specific crop has been examined and predicted using the KNN algorithm while taking numerous factors like soil type, region, and area into consideration.

Model entitled "Crop Prediction System using Machine Learning" [4]. The suggested approach recommends a mobile app for Android that can accurately forecast the farmer's most lucrative crop. GPS determines the person's specific position. Weather as well as soil information is used to identify the possible crops in each place. To determine the most lucrative crop in the current site, these soils are compared to a database of past year productivity. The user's Android application receives the result after this server-side processing is completed.

Model entitled "Agricultural production optimization and marginal product response climate change" [12]. In this paper, the authors have developed a nonparametric technique. The agricultural field includes equipment and fertilizers. To investigate how climate change will affect these marginal products, The authors utilized a fixed-effects regression model. Labor, Land, Machinery, Fertilizers, and Pesticides are the five inputs that they have used.

Model entitled "A Decision Support Framework for National Crop Production Planning" [13]. The planning crop production metric will be defined by the decision support system that the authors have developed. It includes a decision-supporting tool that guides farmers on crop production planning. 0–1 integer actively learning in linear form serves as the model's basis.

Model entitled "Optimization of agricultural machinery task scheduling algorithm based on multi-objective optimization" [14]. It can carry out accurate real-time inputs, primarily targeted at cooperative farm machinery groups and agricultural machinery cooperatives. In addition, it makes full use of the advantage of mobile communication breakthroughs and the rising penetration of smartphone terminal innovations, thereby overcoming the disadvantages of the previous crop growing monitoring and oversight system's the previous crop growing monitoring and oversight system's lack of mobility and adaptability.

Model entitled "Advanced Computational Methods for Agriculture Machinery Movement Optimization with Applications in Sugarcane Production" [15]. In this paper approaches based on cost criteria such as power, fuel, time consumed, and also algorithms for spatial configuration division, and route planning are discussed. It discusses how algorithmic and economic methodologies can be combined, including how savings and investments are assessed for cost-benefit analysis.

Model entitled "Balancing environmental impacts and economic benefits of agriculture under the climate change through an integrated optimization system" [16]. Under various climate change scenarios, the framework provides a balance of the economic benefits of agriculture (crop production) with the impacts of energy and water consumption on the climate. According to the worst climate change scenario, water usage has to be reduced by around 25%in order to maintain river ecosystems. However, in order to maintain the financial advantages of farming, the optimization model raised energy use by about 16%.

Model entitled "Optimization model of agricultural production system in grain farms under risk, in Sorriso, Brazil" [17]. With the aid of this study, we are able to comprehend double-crop production systems in more depth, which has enabled Brazil to become one of the most prolific and competitive grain-producing countries in the world. It puts into practice this theoretical farm planning framework that uses operations research to determine the different productive scheduling in farms engaged in agricultural output and gives a recommendation framework focused on planning and control in highly diversified farms under risky circumstances.

The use of distributed ledger technology, such as blockchain, in the supply chain, logistics, transportation, and governance is expanding quickly. Blockchain technology is being positioned as the central component of smart cities. This paper examines how blockchain technology might be used in water management systems. We conducted a literature review and categorized prior research into three primary application areas: stormwater management, water quality monitoring, and smart water systems. We also discussed institutional, social, organizational, and technical issues that could prevent Blockchain technology from being widely adopted. Before successfully implementing any distributed ledger technology, water management systems must update their organizational policies, establish a long-term commitment strategy, and gain the necessary knowledge and competence [22].

Blockchain technology has advanced and is now utilized in numerous industries. As a point-to-point network with decentralized, traceable, distrust-free, and flooding is becoming more of an issue as a result of storms being more frequent and severe as a result of climate change. More pervasive sensing capabilities are promised by the Internet of Things (IoT) revolution. IoT has the ability to improve our understanding of how hydrologic systems react to intense rainfall events when it comes to water systems, which will help with disaster management preparations both before and during extreme weather events [23]. In this paper, we present a method for optimizing an IoT sensor network for real-time flood monitoring and converting high rainfall events predicted into flood impacts. Initially, we developed a hydrologic model for the Dell Pond watershed in Charlottesville, Virginia, which served as a research area. We employed ArcGIS to acquire geographic datasets, including elevation, soils, land use, and land cover, in order to generate model parameters. A hydrologic model in HEC-HMS was created by combining the parameters from ArcGIS with rainfall precipitation data from the National Oceanic and Atmospheric Administration (NOAA) and readings from IoT water sensors. Since IoT sensors are battery-powered and lack the ability to collect additional power, we first developed models to calculate the battery life of each sensor in the network in order to optimize the IoT sensor monitoring network and investigate systems integration of the model and sensors. Using the IoT network, we also installed a new water level sensor and a soil moisture sensor for the study watershed. Future research might build on the techniques for estimating the IoT sensor's battery life and the prototype deployment to develop next-generation flood management systems that incorporate IoT monitoring networks and computational models [24].

Blockchain technology has advanced and is now utilized in numerous industries. Blockchain is a point-to-point network that can be used to create Internet of Things networks because it has properties like traceability, decentralization, and de-trust. It offers the chance for Internet of Things networks to flourish. Studying the blockchain consensus mechanism is worthwhile since it is a crucial part of the system. In this research, we thoroughly examine blockchain consensus processes from the standpoint of requirements for Internet of Things networks. To help academics comprehend the relationship between blockchain consensus mechanisms and IoT, we first outline the requirements of consensus mechanisms in IoT networks. Next, we categorize the blockchain consensus mechanism into four groups: security, scalability, energy-saving, and performance-enhancing consensus techniques. Based on our observations, we further investigate such blockchain consensus processes and suggest possible directions for blockchain consensus designs. The purpose of this study is to stimulate further work in this area and offer academic insights into the future development of blockchain consensus mechanisms in the Internet of Things [25].

Computer network technologies have developed steadily and quickly over time. Blockchain (BC) and software-defined networking (SDN) have come to be seen as complementary technologies that support increased network performance and security across a wide range of application domains, including the Internet of Things (IoT) ecosystem, with the ultimate goal of raising everyone's standard of living. The emergence of SDN and BC, along with the growth of IoT devices driven by a wide range of use cases and its ubiquitous availability, gives significant prospects for many upcoming research projects. This paper provides an extensive overview of the research on the integration of BC and SDN into the Internet of Things (IoT) ecosystem, a concept known as BC-enabled Software-Defined IoT (BC-SDIoT). First, we go over the reasons and forces for the integration of BC-enabled SDN and BC-SDIoT, along with the advantages and disadvantages. Second, we classify the pertinent studies based on six major implementation goals and concepts—security, trust management, access control & authentication, privacy, networking, and computing paradigms (edge and fog computing)—that integrate BC, SDN, and IoT technologies to create intelligent, secure, and efficient frameworks. We outline the categories (i.e., problem domains) of the previously mentioned innovative taxonomy and go into great detail about relevant studies (i.e., solutions) in the corresponding sections. In conclusion, we list the main obstacles that would need to be overcome, as well as unresolved problems and opportunities for future study, in order to develop comprehensive and innovative frameworks that will enable the expansion of recently discovered research areas in BC-SDIoT. The reader wishing to learn more about the use of BC in SDN and IoT ecosystems may find this survey report to be a useful starting point [26].

The term "Internet of Things" (IoT) describes how smart devices are connected to each other in order to gather data and make informed decisions. IoT is susceptible to security and privacy risks, nevertheless, because it lacks inherent security protections. Blockchain (BC), with its "security by design," can assist in solving important security requirements in the Internet of Things. An extensive overview of the integration of BC and IoT is presented in this article. This paper's goal is to examine current research trends on the application of BC-related methodologies and technologies in Internet of Things settings. Regarding related work, this paper presents the following novelties: (i) it covers various application domains, classifying existing literature in this manner; (ii) it introduces two usage patterns, namely, data management (open marketplace solution) and device manipulation; and (iii) it reports on the state of development of some of the presented solutions. We also examine the primary obstacles that the research community has had to overcome in order to successfully integrate BC and IoT, and we highlight the primary unresolved problems and potential future research areas. Finally, we also provide a survey about new applications of BC in the machine economy [27].

It is challenging to forecast and control extreme occurrences and disasters brought on by climate change or other ecological variables. By using new unconventional risk assessment and management techniques, the current shortcomings of state-of-the-art approaches to disaster prediction and management could be solved. Future successful disaster management infrastructures will be largely enabled by 5G wireless communication, big data analytics, Wireless Sensor Networks (WSNs), and the next-generation Internet of Things (IoT). We commissioned a survey in this chapter to examine new wireless communication technologies that could improve systems for disaster management, monitoring, and prediction. To give academics in this subject some idea of what they might be working on in the future, challenges, opportunities, and research trends are emphasized [28].

The Internet of Things (IoT) seeks to establish peer-to-peer connections between objects and the Internet to gather and exchange data about our everyday activities. A peer-to-peer network maintains an immutable append-only ledger called a blockchain, to which all participants must agree upon the transactional data to be recorded. The decentralized nature of blockchain and IoT design makes them highly compatible. The Internet of Things has been linked with blockchain technology to address current issues. Our study focuses on examining the academically suggested solutions and the approaches used to combine blockchain technology with the Internet of Things. We obtain information about the current technical approaches being used to integrate blockchain into the Internet of Things by performing a systematic literature review (SLR) on peer-reviewed, published articles on blockchain-based solutions for the Internet of Things. The majority of the research in this field is conceptual or is still in its early stages. Only 35 published studies, on the other hand, really used blockchain technology to apply it to IoT platforms. We identify the issues raised by the Internet of Things and the specific blockchain-based solution design from two angles: data management and item management. Additionally, those works' measurements and evaluation techniques are being tracked down and examined. Apart from the literature review, we offer our perspectives on enhancing the current solutions and research methods, drawing from our proficiency and familiarity with blockchain technology [29].

The blockchain has drawn attention from the scientific community since Satoshi Nakamoto initially unveiled it as an open-source project for safe financial transactions. This has made it possible to address issues in areas other than cryptocurrencies, such as the Internet of Things (IoT). To illustrate this potential, though, one must have a thorough grasp of blockchain technology and whether or not it can meet the fundamental security needs of the Internet of Things. To achieve this, the study aims to present a clear and thorough overview of blockchain integration with IoT, highlighting both the advantages and disadvantages of blockchain technology in IoT applications. The survey outlined the main architectures of blockchain and IoT and provided an overview of each. A review is also conducted of the most recent blockchain initiatives in several IoT domains. Then examines the newly put forth alternatives while outlining the present difficulties in fusing blockchain with IoT. Lastly, several future research avenues for blockchain-IoT integration are explored. It is intended that this survey will act as a resource and source of inspiration for future research directions in this field, given the study's conclusions [30].

The real-time and highly efficient collaboration of the Internet of Things (IoT) has led to its broader acceptance; the Wireless Sensor Network, or WSN, is a key component for enabling IoT operations. Several study studies have taken into consideration the security issue, which is one of the main issues. The objective of this research review is to critically examine the blockchain-based WSN) space. The goal of Blockchain-WSN is to concentrate on the various facets of security issues in wireless sensor networks. Furthermore, this research review is unusual since it critically examines the adoption of blockchain in WSN in contrast to other research reviews. This paper initially addresses WSN and its issues, particularly from a security standpoint by highlighting WSN vulnerabilities. Additionally, a blockchain approach study and its integration with traditional WSNs are introduced in this research review effort. Additionally, a number of current blockchain-WSN mechanisms are examined and evaluated. Finally, the constraints and limitations of blockchain-WSN are emphasized, highlighting the research gap for developing a new blockchain-based WSN security mechanism [31].

The Internet of Things is expanding exponentially these days (IoT). Worldwide, there are more than 8 billion IoT devices, including hardware, cars, and household appliances. IoT is still susceptible to privacy and security risks despite its benefits and effects. This is because most IoT devices have low resources, privacy concerns are not taken into account, and scaling challenges arise. As a result, typical security and privacy strategies are inadequate for IoT. This article's primary objective is to determine whether blockchain technology may be used to address IoT security issues. In order to learn more about the most recent applications of Blockchain technology, a Systematic Literature Review was initially carried out. Out of the 44 use cases of blockchain that we identified in the literature, 18 of them were created expressly to apply blockchain technology to IoT security concerns. The state-of-the-art application cases were divided into four categories: smart homes, smart cities, smart economies, and smart health. We list the accomplishments, discuss the approaches and lessons discovered, and point out restrictions and future research issues [32].

Flooding is becoming more of an issue as a result of storms being more frequent and severe as a result of climate change. More pervasive sensing capabilities are promised by the IoT revolution. IoT can improve our understanding of how hydrologic systems react to intense rainfall events when it comes to water systems, which will help with disaster management preparations both before and during extreme weather events. In this paper, the author presents a method for optimizing an IoT sensor network for real-time flood monitoring and converting high rainfall events predicted into flood impacts. Initially, a hydrologic model is employed in Virginia, which served as a research area. Then, geographic datasets are collected, including elevation, soils, land use, and land cover, to generate model parameters. Since IoT sensors are battery-powered and cannot collect additional power, we first developed models to calculate the battery life of each sensor in the network to optimize the IoT sensor monitoring network and investigate systems integration of the model and sensors. Using the IoT network, we also installed a new water level sensor and a soil moisture sensor for the study watershed. Future research might build on the techniques for estimating the IoT sensor's battery life and the prototype deployment to develop next-generation flood management systems that incorporate IoT monitoring networks and computational models [24].

Events including floods and droughts have become more frequent and severe in recent decades. These human-caused and climate change-related stresses on water resources are the main risks to communities that are associated with water. The risks have also increased due to the population's and infrastructure's increased exposure to these kinds of catastrophes. In order to thoroughly evaluate the risks, it is necessary to assess the impact scope of these events in many subfields using an objective, methodical manner. In order to explore the current multidisciplinary body of knowledge on assessing flood and drought together, this research blends content analysis and scientific mapping. 119 publications were found when specific search phrases were used to search the literature. At first, a variety of contents were taken from these articles, including the research scale, applicable methodologies and indices, and keywords written by the authors. After that, these materials were added to the science mapping method to create communicative networks. Thirteen main study themes emerged from an analysis of these publications, all of which had a consistent focus on hydrological challenges. But more recently, a wider spectrum of themes—such as economics, sociology, insurance, and policymaking was discovered. Insightful findings that can aid in the development of new and existing frameworks to support the management, design, and policymaking sectors in reacting to flood and drought occurrences were discussed through the creation of such computational and visual networks [33].

Floods in the past have ruined infrastructure valued at millions of dollars. All the research, though, has not yet produced a global, all-inclusive system for gathering, storing, analyzing, and forecasting flood data. Researchers from all across the world are working to find a way to gather, store, and process massive amounts of flood data so that flood-based prediction systems can predict their results. This work has developed an IoT-based water and disaster management system using a deep learning mode. A hybrid type of classification technique is used. First, the flood big data collection of information is used to generate the input data. Four types of IoT sensors—to monitor the water flow, water level, rain, and humidity were employed in the system's construction. After that, the repetitive data from the IoT sensed data is reduced using HDFS map-reduce. Once the repetitious data has been eliminated, the data are preprocessed using a normalizing algorithm and missing value imputation. This leads to the creation of a rule using a combination of attributes and attributes approach. Convolutional Deep Neural Network (CDN) and Artificial Neural Network (ANN) classifiers are combined in a hybrid classifier that assigns the rules two classifications: (a) likelihood that flooding will occur and (b) likelihood that it won't at the end. The proposed method's outcomes are compared using metrics including F-score, recall, accuracy, precision, sensitivity, and specificity. In addition, the suggested technique provides a considerably more accurate result than the other ways when compared to other algorithms [34]. Given that sensor nodes are known to be power-hungry devices, implementing the Internet of Things (IOT), Wireless Sensor Networks (WSN) is frequently fraught with difficulties. Particularly as more data is sent to the cloud or when several sensors are connected to a single sensor node, the energy contained in the batteries that power these sensor nodes soon runs out. In the context of flood and environmental monitoring, it is desirable to increase the number of sensor nodes in a Wireless Sensor Network to improve the representation of rising water levels and overall water quality in a given city by improving the spatial resolution of the data. On the other hand, an increased number of sensor nodes in a wireless sensor network presents additional difficulties for the network's overall power supply management. There is a limitation to the number of cycles that a battery can undergo before it is deemed to be completely degraded in sensor nodes, which are typically powered by lithium-ion batteries. Consequently, techniques that can extend the duration of each cycle of charging and discharging will be helpful in extending the battery's lifespan. This paper proposes a method that combines solar energy harvesting with an adaptive sampling algorithm based on fuzzy logic to achieve two goals: a continuous energy source for the sensor nodes and an extended charging and discharging cycle, which leads to longer-lasting batteries. The sensor nodes that were built have been utilized to measure the dissolved oxygen content and river water levels [35].

10.3 Methodology

The methodology is implemented in two parts. Section 10.3.1 gives the steps used in the implementation of smart contracts and architectural design of water management systems whereas Sect. 10.3.3 gives the algorithm for anomaly detection using blockchain.

10.3.1 Steps to Implement

Deployment of sensors, actuators (IoT devices), and set up of Wireless networks for communication between devices.

Data is collected from IoT devices in real time with the help of WSN. Further, this collected data to transmitted to the blockchain network for further processing and storage.

The Ethereum blockchain ledger handles the collected data for the water management system. Smart contracts manage and automate the process of water allocation, distribution, billing, and payments.

Data analysis can be done by applying a suitable machine learning algorithm. It analyses historical trends, optimizes water resource management strategies, and detects anomalies or deviations from normal conditions. It also provides decision support capabilities for stakeholders to make informed decisions based on the analysis results and recommendations generated by the system.

Enable seamless integration with external systems, such as weather forecasting services, water utilities' infrastructure, and consumer-facing applications.

Monitoring tools and dashboards are established to monitor the performance and uptime of the system components in real-time. Establish proactive maintenance procedures to address any issues or failures promptly and ensure the continuous operation of the system, especially during extreme weather events. By integrating these components into a cohesive architecture, the Blockchain-Powered IoT and WSN Integration system can enhance water management practices, improve resilience to extreme weather events, and ensure sustainable use of water resources for the maximization of agriculture production.

10.3.2 Architectural Design for Water Management System

To design an architecture for a Blockchain-Powered IoT and WSN Integration system for enhanced water management in the face of extreme weather events, several key components need to be considered. Below is an architectural overview:

IoT Devices and WSN Nodes A range of sensors and actuators as Internet of Things (IoT) devices to gather information about water quality, amount, temperature, pressure, and other pertinent factors are installed. In order to create a distributed network for data transmission, these devices can communicate with one another using Wireless Sensor Networks (WSNs). The WSN nodes and IoT devices can function dependably in hostile locations and are resistant to severe weather.

Data Acquisition Layer Real-time data is gathered from WSN nodes and IoT devices. Data is then combined and preprocessed using some standard protocols. The gathered data is then sent to the blockchain network for additional processing and storage.

Blockchain Infrastructure Ethereum blockchain platform is used to create a blockchain network architecture with nodes, a consensus method, and smart contracts that are suited for applications related to water management. Smart contracts are created to oversee water allocation, distribution, billing, and payment processes, automate tasks, and enforce business logic.

Data Storage and Management The blockchain ledger is used to store water-related data, such as sensor readings, transaction histories, and metadata, as a decentralized, immutable database. Protocols are established on the blockchain for safe and effective data retrieval, storing, and querying.

Data Analysis and Decision Support A machine learning algorithm is used to process the gathered data and derive useful insights. The algorithm identifies abnormalities or departures from the norm, evaluates past trends, forecasts extreme weather events, and manages water resources more effectively. The well-informed decisions based on the analysis and suggestions made by the system are sent to the stakeholders.

Integration with External Systems This interface can be connected with other external systems, including consumer-facing apps, government databases, water utilities' infrastructure, and weather forecasting services.

Monitoring and Maintenance Dashboards and monitoring tools are used to keep an eye on the uptime, performance, and overall health of the system's constituent parts in real time. Proactive maintenance protocols are created to guarantee the system's continuing operation and quickly handle any problems or malfunctions, particularly during severe weather occurrences.

The Blockchain-Powered IoT and WSN Integration system may guarantee sustainable use of water resources, improve resilience to extreme weather occurrences, and improve water management practices by combining these elements into a coherent design. The smart contract for water management used in agriculture is shown in Fig. 10.2.

This contract introduces a few enhancements: Thresholds for Flood and Drought: The contract now allows setting thresholds for both flood and drought conditions.

```
pragma solidity ^0.8.0;
contract WaterManagementContract {
address public owner;
uint public waterLevel;
uint public constant MAX_WATER_LEVEL = 1000; // Maximum water level allowed
uint public constant MIN_WATER_LEVEL = 0;   // Minimum water level allowed
uint public floodThreshold;        // Threshold at which flood is triggered
uint public droughtThreshold;    // Threshold at which drought is triggered
enum WaterStatus { Normal, Flood, Drought }
WaterStatus public currentStatus;
event WaterLevelChanged(uint newWaterLevel);
event FloodTriggered(uint waterLevel);
event DroughtTriggered(uint waterLevel);
modifier onlyOwner()
 {
   require(msg.sender == owner,"Only contract owner can call this function");
_;}
constructor(uint _floodThreshold, uint _droughtThreshold)
{
   owner = msg.sender;
   waterLevel = MAX_WATER_LEVEL/2; //Start at half the maximum water level
   floodThreshold = _floodThreshold;
   droughtThreshold = _droughtThreshold;
   currentStatus = WaterStatus.Normal;
}//Function to increase water level

function increaseWaterLevel(uint amount) external onlyOwner
{
    require(waterLevel + amount <= MAX_WATER_LEVEL, "Cannot exceed maximum water level");
    waterLevel += amount;
    emit WaterLevelChanged(waterLevel);
    if (waterLevel >= floodThreshold && currentStatus != WaterStatus.Flood)
      {           currentStatus = WaterStatus.Flood;
                  emit FloodTriggered(waterLevel);
      }
    else if (waterLevel <= droughtThreshold && currentStatus != WaterStatus.Drought)
      {
                  currentStatus = WaterStatus.Drought;
                  emit DroughtTriggered(waterLevel);
      }
    else if (waterLevel > droughtThreshold && waterLevel < floodThreshold)
    {
    currentStatus = WaterStatus.Normal;
    }
} // Function to decrease water level
function decreaseWaterLevel(uint amount) external onlyOwner
{
     require(waterLevel - amount >= MIN_WATER_LEVEL, "Cannot go below minimum water level");
     waterLevel -= amount;
     emit WaterLevelChanged(waterLevel);
     if (waterLevel >= floodThreshold && currentStatus != WaterStatus.Flood)
       {
                  currentStatus = WaterStatus.Flood;
                  emit FloodTriggered(waterLevel);
      }
      else if (waterLevel <= droughtThreshold && currentStatus != WaterStatus.Drought)
      {
                 currentStatus = WaterStatus.Drought;
                 emit DroughtTriggered(waterLevel);
      }
      else if (waterLevel > droughtThreshold && waterLevel < floodThreshold)
      {
                  currentStatus = WaterStatus.Normal;
      }
}// Function to check current water level
function getWaterLevel() external view returns (uint)
{
     return waterLevel;
 }// Function to update thresholds
function updateThresholds(uint _floodThreshold, uint _droughtThreshold) external onlyOwner
{
       floodThreshold = _floodThreshold;
       droughtThreshold = _droughtThreshold;
} // Function to get current water status
function getCurrentStatus() external view returns (WaterStatus)
{
       return currentStatus;}}
```

Fig. 10.2 Implementation of smart contract

When the water level reaches these thresholds, events are emitted and the contract's status is updated accordingly.

Water Status Enumeration: Introduced an enumeration of WaterStatus to represent the current state of water conditions—Normal, Flood, or Drought.

Event Emission for Flood and Drought: Events are emitted when flood or drought conditions are triggered, providing a mechanism for external systems to react accordingly.

Update Thresholds Functionality: Added a function to update thresholds, allowing for dynamic adjustment based on changing conditions.

This contract provides a more robust framework for managing water levels in the face of extreme weather events like floods and droughts. However, further enhancements may be needed depending on the specific requirements and environmental factors of the target application.

10.3.3 Algorithm: Anomaly Detection for Blockchain-Powered Water Management

Algorithm 1: Algorithm for Anomaly Detection for Blockchain-Powered Water Management

```
Input: Sensor data
Output: Unnormal pattern detection for Blockchain-Powered Water Management
for Every time step do
  Initialization of sensors, set up of parameters for data collection and establishment of WSN
  nodes and IoT devices.
  Start Data collection.
  3. Repeat for
  a. Read sensor data from WSN nodes
  b. Process the data
  c. check data for anomaly detection
  If 'Yes'  i. notification sent to the monitoring team ( in case of flood/ drought)
  ii. water transfer to another place using smart contract transaction
  iii.verify the transaction
  iv. Broadcast the transaction to all nodes of blockchain
  v. Validation of transaction by the blockchain network
  vi. If âŁ˜validatedâŁ™ action taken for disaster management and go to step 4. go to step 3
  4. Stop the process
end for
```

10.4 Conclusion

Agriculture is largely responsible for increasing a country's economic contribution globally. However, due to the slow uptake of ecosystem control technology, the majority of agricultural fields are still underdeveloped. To avoid these problems, agricultural sectors must use machine learning algorithms to forecast the crop from a given data set. The proposed framework suggests the best harvests that might develop in the ideal natural setting by accounting for temperature, humidity, soil properties, and pH value. It has been determined that the growing human population, along with increased economic activity and climate change, has placed significant pressure on India's government and policymakers to come up with novel and astute solutions to the demand-supply imbalance in the water sector. The tangible result does not sufficiently resonate on the ground level, even though the country has the largest water infrastructure in the world, and worries about the growing water problem have been voiced in national debate at the academic, policy, and governance levels.

References

1. Waikar, V.C., Thorat, S.Y., Ghute, A.A., Rajput, P.P., Shinde, M.S.: Crop prediction based on soil classification using machine learning with classifier ensembling. Int. Res. J. Eng. Technol. **7**(5) (2020)
2. Thomas, Tom, K., Varsha, S., Merin Mary Saji, Lisha Varghese, Er Jinu Thomas. "Crop prediction using machine learning. Int. J. Future Gener. Commun. Netw. **13**(3), 1896–1901 (2020)
3. Veenadhari, S., Misra, B., Singh, C.D.: Machine learning approach for forecasting crop yield based on climatic parameters. In: 2014 International Conference on Computer Communication and Informatics, pp. 1–5. IEEE (2014)
4. Zingade, D.S., Buchade, O., Mehta, N., Ghodekar, S., Mehta, C.: Crop prediction system using machine learning. Int. J. Adv. Eng. Res. Dev. Spec. Issue Recent Trends Data Eng. **4**(5), 1–6 (2017)
5. Raja, S.K.S., Rishi, R., Sundaresan, E., Srijit, V.: Demand based crop recommender system for farmers. In: 2017 IEEE Technological Innovations in ICT for Agriculture and Rural Development (TIAR), pp. 194–199. IEEE (2017)
6. Masare, Y., Mahale, S., Kele, M., Upadhyay, A., Nandwalkar, B.: Maximize the yielding rate of crops using machine learning algorithm. Int. J. Res. Technol. (2020). ISSN:2278-0181
7. Pandhe, A., Nikam, P., Pagare, V., Palle, P., Dalgade, D.: Crop yield prediction based on climatic parameters. Int. J. Res. Eng. Technol. (IJRET) **6**(03) (2019)
8. Gandhi, Mrugank, Kothavade, S., Nehete, S., Arlikar, S., Shinde, K.A.: Agricultural production optimization engine. Int. J. Creat. Res. Thoughts (IJCRT) IJCRT 2205314 (2022)
9. Ge, J., Zhao, L., Yu, Z., Liu, H., Zhang, L., Gong, X., Sun, H.: Prediction of greenhouse tomato crop evapotranspiration using XGBoost machine learning model. Plants **11**(15), 1923 (2022)
10. Sangeeta, S.G.: Design and implementation of crop yield prediction model in agriculture. Int. J. Sci. Technol. Res. **8**(1), 544–549 (2020)
11. Suganya, M.: Crop yield prediction using supervised learning techniques. Int. J. Comput. Eng. Technol. **11**(2) (2020)
12. Liu, D., You, J., Wang, R., Deng, H.: Agricultural production optimization and marginal product response to climate change. Agriculture **12**(9), 1403 (2022)

13. Rasheed, N., Khan, S.A., Hassan, A., Safdar, S.: A decision support framework for national crop production planning. IEEE Access **9**, 133402–133415 (2021)
14. Zheng, L.: [Retracted] Optimization of agricultural machinery task scheduling algorithm based on multiobjective optimization. J. Sens. **2022**(1), 5800332 (2022)
15. Filip, M., Zoubek, T., Bumbalek, R., Cerny, P., Batista, C.E., Olsan, P., Bartos, P., et al.: Advanced computational methods for agriculture machinery movement optimization with applications in sugarcane production. Agriculture **10**(10), 434 (2020)
16. Sedighkia, M., Abdoli, A.: Balancing environmental impacts and economic benefits of agriculture under the climate change through an integrated optimization system. Int. J. Energy Environ. Eng. **13**(3), 1053–1066 (2022)
17. Osaki, M., Batalha., M.O.: Optimization model of agricultural production system in grain farms under risk, in Sorriso, Brazil. Agric. Syst. **127**, 178–188 (2014)
18. Omar, S., Jain, R.: Classification of disease symptoms in tomato leaf with the help of convolutional neural network. In: International Conference on Computational Intelligence and Sustainable Engineering Solutions (CISES) **2022**, 561–565 (2022)
19. Omar, S., Jain, R., Bali, V.: Leaf disease detection using convolutional neural network. In: 2022 International Conference on Machine Learning, Big Data, Cloud and Parallel Computing (COM-IT-CON), pp. 53–56 (2022)
20. Jain, R., Singh, A., Yadav, A.K., Sharma, A., Srivastava, A.S.: Path finder. In: Proceedings of the Advancement in Electronics & Communication Engineering 2022 (2022)
21. Jain, R., Singh, S., Swami, S., Kumar, S.: deep learning-based techniques to identify COVID-19 using medical image segmentation. In: Health Information Sciences, pp. 327–342 (2021)
22. Asgari, M., Nemati, M.: Application of distributed ledger platforms in smart water systems—A literature review. Front. Water **4**, 848686 (2022)
23. Ismail, S., Dawoud, D.W., Ismail, N., Marsh, R., Alshami, A.S.: IoT-based water management systems: survey and future research direction. IEEE Access **10**, 35942–35952 (2022)
24. Khattar, N., Washington, T.M., Mai, A., Malinowski, L., Bowman, A. N., Phumphid, K., et al.: Hydrologic modeling and system optimization for IoT flood management. In: 2023 Systems and Information Engineering Design Symposium (SIEDS), pp. 137–142. IEEE (2023)
25. Wen, Y., Lu, F., Liu, Y., Cong, P., Huang, X.: Blockchain consensus mechanisms and their applications in IoT: a literature survey. In: Algorithms and Architectures for Parallel Processing: 20th International Conference, ICA3PP 2020, New York City, NY, USA, 2020, Proceedings, Part III, vol. 20, pp. 564–579. Springer International Publishing (2020)
26. Turner, S.W., Karakus, M., Guler, E., Uludag, S.: A promising integration of SDN and blockchain for IoT networks: a survey. IEEE Access (2023)
27. Panarello, A., Tapas, N., Merlino, G., Longo, F., Puliafito, A.: Blockchain and IoT integration: a systematic survey. Sensors **18**(8), 2575 (2018)
28. Adeel, A., Gogate, M., Farooq, S., Ieracitano, C., Dashtipour, K., Larijani, H., Hussain, A.: A survey on the role of wireless sensor networks and IoT in disaster management. In: Geological Disaster Monitoring Based on Sensor Networks, pp. 57-66 (2019)
29. Lo, S.K., Liu, Y., Chia, S.Y., Xu, X., Lu, Q., Zhu, L., Ning, H.: Analysis of blockchain solutions for IoT: a systematic literature review. IEEE Access **7**, 58822–58835 (2019)
30. Abubakar, M., Jarocheh, Z., Al-Dubai, A., Liu, X.: A survey on the integration of blockchain and IoT: challenges and opportunities. In: Big Data Privacy Security in Smart Cities, pp. 197–221 (2022)
31. Darla, S., Naveena, C.: Survey on securing internet of things through block chain technology. In: 2022 International Conference on Electronics and Renewable Systems (ICEARS), pp. 836–844. IEEE (2022)
32. Ekramifard, A., Amintoosi, H., Seno, A.H.: A systematic literature review on blockchain-based solutions for IoT security. In: From Research to Application, Data Science, pp. 311–321 (2020)
33. Fasihi, S., Lim, W.Z., Wu, W., Proverbs, D.: Systematic review of flood and drought literature based on science mapping and content analysis. Water **13**(19), 2788 (2021)

34. Badholia, A., Sharma, A., Chhabra, G.S., Verma, V.: Implementation of an IoT-based water and disaster management system using hybrid classification approach. In: Deep Learning Technologies for the Sustainable Development Goals: issues and Solutions in the Post-COVID Era, pp. 157–173. Singapore, Springer Nature Singapore (2023)
35. Yazid, M.A.M., Jazlan, A., Rodzi, M.Z.M., Husman, M.A., Afif, A.R.: A method for preserving battery life in wireless sensor nodes for LoRa based IOT flood monitoring. J. Commun. **17**(4), 230–238 (2022)
36. Araújo, S.O., Peres, R.S., Ramalho, J.C., Lidon, F., Barata, J.: Machine learning applications in agriculture: current trends, challenges, and future perspectives. Agronomy **13**(12), 2976 (2023)

Chapter 11
Conservation of Water Using Smart IoT-Based Sensors: A Methodical Study

Arman Raj

Abstract Water Scarcity is one of the biggest challenges across the world. As per the US Geological Survey, the water layer is getting depleted at a very fast pace. The factors like groundwater extraction, climatic changes, rapid growth in population, industrialization, deforestation, and existing water infrastructure are some of the major loci which contribute significantly to the depletion of water. In this comprehensive study, the authors present how the integration of smart Internet of Things (IoT) sensors can be helpful in providing an effective solution for safeguarding water resources. This study presents an extended examination of the existing methodologies used to manage water resources and how the integration of Smart IoT (Internet of Things) Sensors can be beneficial in the conservation of water. This chapter also presents a detailed comparative analysis of various IoT sensors on the basis of parameters like real-time monitoring, leak detection and prevention, optimization of water usage, predictive analytics, data-driven decision-making, etc. This chapter also presents an in-depth performance analysis which has been conducted based on the past study and how the outcomes with Smart IoT-equipped sensors have improved the traditional paradigm has been discussed.

Keywords Internet of things (IoT) · Sensors · Ground water extraction · Predictive analytics · Real-time monitoring

11.1 Introduction

Water is an indispensable resource for everyone and all living beings cannot even imagine a life without water. Conserving Water resources is essential for sustaining individuals' life, strengthening ecology, and employing socio-economic development [1]. "Water for Everyone" is one important Sustainable goal that will help in enhancing public health, food security, and mitigating poverty. Water is very crucial in implementing sustainable farming. Some of the best sustainable techniques

A. Raj (✉)
Galgotias University, Greater Noida, India
e-mail: armanraj095@gmail.com

S. S. Rawat et al. (eds.), *Unleashing the Power of Blockchain and IoT for Water Informatics*, Water Informatics for Water Resource Management,
https://doi.org/10.1007/978-981-96-3886-4_11

which help in establishing sustainable farming are: sustainable irrigation techniques, soil moisture monitoring, and crop distinction which can together be helpful in the optimization of water allocation, supplementing agricultural productivity, and also slackens the impacts of water scarcity on food production [1, 2].

The depletion of the water layer is posing a global challenge. It is one of the serious challenges that globally affect to achievement of sustainable water practices. The multitude of challenges like the extrication of groundwater resources, natural climatic shifts, increase in population, rapid growth in industrialization, and deforestation are some of the major factors that contribute significantly to the depletion of the water layer [3]. Apart from these factors, there is a need to improve the existing infrastructure of water resources [4].

Dams and reservoirs need to be reconstructed and existing irrigation system needs to be improved in order to maximize crop productivity. In the face of these challenges, unique solutions are needed that can be helpful in mitigating water depletion and ensuring the sustainable management of our indispensable water resources.

The Internet of Things (IoT) with its numerous sensors capability offers a wide range of cutting-edge solutions for safeguarding water and enhancing existing water management methodologies. Research has proven that IoT-enabled systems can significantly strengthen water regulation, mitigate undesired wastage, and optimize resource allocation [5]. Here we have discussed some of the advantages that how IoT sensors can be helpful in conserving water and achieving sustainable practices. Some of the potential advantages are:

11.1.1 Real-Time Regulation

IoT sensors with their ability to collect and transmit data can be helpful in continuous monitoring, covering aspects like water usage, flow rates, pressure intensity, and other important parameters like determination of pH and turbidity. Real-time observation further provides valuable insights into water distribution topology, identifying leaks, disorganization, and anomalies promptly [6].

11.1.2 Leak Sensing

IoT devices with their numerous features can be helpful in detecting leakage. The unexpected increase in water flow rates, continuous water usage, etc. can lead to water leakage. In this situation, IoT sensors with their ability to alert signals help in notifying stakeholders of water leakage. IoT sensors help in detecting the location where leakage has incurred and the damage that can be caused by such leaks. These sensors help in enabling prompt repairs, minimizing water loss, and diminishing the damage that has occurred due to such leakage [7].

11.1.3 Ultramodern Irrigation System

In modern agricultural practice, there is wide usage of soil moisture IoT-based sensors which help in improving the existing irrigation system [8]. By leveraging these features IoT-enabled irrigation system can improve crop productivity and optimize water resource usage and crop yield.

11.1.4 Demand-based Water Distribution

IoT sensors can be helpful in identifying patterns of data based on different locations and times. By dynamically changing water distribution based on demand fluctuations, utilities can improve resource assignment and mitigate energy costs, which altogether helps in corroborating balanced access to water [9].

11.1.5 Examining Water Quality

IoT sensors help in examining water quality attributes like temperature, dissolved oxygen, and contaminants. With the ability to provide real-time data on water quality, these IoT-based sensors help in the early detection of pollution events, ensuring timely interventions in preserving public health and environmental unification.

11.1.6 Smart Quantification

IoT-enabled sensors equipped with smart meters have the ability to provide consumers with real-time feedback on their water consumption and related costs [10]. These IoT-based smart meters encourage water conservation behaviors among consumers which leads to reduced usage and minimized water bills.

11.1.7 Predictive Analytics

IoT devices have the ability to analyze massive volumes of data which further helps in identifying patterns, predicting future water usage, and helpful in evaluating system performance [11]. By using this ability of predictive analytics, water utilities can enhance decision-making procedures.

11.1.8 Remote Monitoring and Control

IoT-based sensors can be helpful in remote monitoring and control of water systems which further allows operators to govern assets, identify issues, and optimize operations from anywhere with a secure Internet connectivity [12]. Remote monitoring increases overall efficiency, decreases downtime, and strengthens system resilience.

The Internet of Things with its wide advantages can bring significant changes in water management and conservation. IoT with its wide sensors can enhance efficiency and make water management systems more scalable. All these advantages together can be helpful in ensuring sustainable practices of this precious resource.

The organization of this chapter is classified in the following ways: Section 11.1 consists of an introduction in which the author has shown the essence of conserving water resources for Sustainability and also highlighted some of the potential advantages of IoT-based sensors in managing water resources. Section 11.2 consists of related work in which the author has shown some of the latest surveys that have been conducted in order to improve existing water conserving paradigms with IoT-equipped sensors. Section 11.3 deals with Comparative Analysis which provides a holistic view between traditional water allocation and water management using IoT-based sensors. Section 11.4 consist of performance evaluation which has been performed based on past studies carried out by researchers. Followed by Conclusion and Future Work. Kindly ensure that the Contact Volume Editor is given the name and email address of the contact author for your paper. The Contact Volume Editor uses these details to compile a list for our production department at SPS in India. Once the files have been worked upon, SPS sends a copy of the final pdf of each paper to its contact author. The contact author is asked to check through the final pdf to make sure that no errors have crept in during the transfer or preparation of the files. This should not be seen as an opportunity to update or copyedit the papers, which is not possible due to time constraints. Only errors introduced during the preparation of the files will be corrected.

11.2 Related Works

There are numerous studies that have been conducted in view of how IoT sensors can significantly enhance existing water management systems. The wide features of IoT sensors along with their advantages like real-time monitoring, predictive analytics, improved irrigation systems, etc. considered to be one of the best ways to improve existing water management systems. The authors in [13] explained the use of IoT sensors in community-based water conservation processes further entitles tenants to manage their water usage and collectively help in reducing water consumption.

The research in [11] examined the development of IoT-based water management system accumulates sensors, actuators, and data analysis which altogether helpful in mitigating water consumption across numerous sectors like agriculture, municipal, power conservation and provides a holistic view of water management practices. The authors in [14] discussed the usage of IoT sensors which can examine groundwater levels which will be helpful in avoiding the exploitation of water.

Jan et al. [15] discusses the recent state-of-the-art IoT-enabled water management systems and also discussed the various IoT-based sensors and how those sensors can improve the existing practice. Arshad et al. [16] explores the use of IoT-based sensors which can be helpful in detecting flood management and also discussed the different types of data analytics process.

Bouramdane [17] discussed the improved decision system for sustainable groundwater resource management.

The research in [18] discussed the numerous data fusion techniques like sensor fusion, spatial data fusion, model-based fusion and distributed fusion which would be helpful in water resourcing and can significantly increment the reliability and robustness of smart water management practices. The authors in [19] discuss about the different IoT-based sensors like soil moisture sensors, climate sensors, crop sensors, etc., and how these types of sensors can be helpful in the water management process and enhancing crop production.

Singh et al. [20] discussed about the different IoT-based sensors like rainfall sensors, and temperature sensors, and how these sensors help in flood prevention has been discussed.

The authors in [21] developed an IoT-based smart water quality monitoring (SWQM) which can be helpful in measuring the quality of water on the basis of parameters like pH, temperature, Haziness, and electric conductivity.

The researchers in [22] developed a solar-powered water quality system with the use of WSN technology. This model would be helpful in places where access to electricity may be restricted, solar-powered systems allow for the remote monitoring of water quality indicators. This makes continuous water quality monitoring possible in isolated or rural locations where conventional monitoring techniques would not be feasible.

11.3 Comparative Analysis Between Traditional Water Management System and Enhanced IoT-Based Water Management System

In the view of water management, the integration of IoT-based sensors has significantly strengthened the traditional water management system. IoT sensors with their wide features and high performance have improved water management systems. This analysis is a blend of traditional water management systems and IoT-based water managing systems on the basis of several key parameters which highlight the transformative capabilities of IoT sensors in water allocation management. By leveraging real-time monitoring, Leak Detection, Integrated IoT-ML algorithms for optimization of water conservation, predictive analytics, and data-driven decision-making. These factors of IoT-based ultramodern water management systems offer

Table 11.1 Comparative Table

Parameters	Traditional water Management system	IoT-based water management system
Real-time monitoring [6, 24]	Not able to monitor in real time	Continuous real-time analysis
Leak detection [7, 25]	Often follows manual ways to check leakage	Real-time detection using IoT-enabled sensors
Optimization of water resources [26]	Not able to optimize the water resource as this methodology was based upon manual adjustments	Complete optimization of water resources can be realized with the help of data-driven insights provided by IoT sensors
Predictive analytics [11]	Prediction is usually carried out by past data or by using manual steps	IoT sensors help in providing real-time analysis which altogether helps in resource optimization
Data driven decision system [27]	In this methodology, decision system was usually carried out based upon manual process which does not lead in making informed decision	IoT-enabled sensors help in gathering actionable insights which helps in improved decision-making process

unprecedented efficiency, robustness, and sustainability. As research continues to evolve in this wide study of water conservation for a better sustainable future, it is evident that the integration of IoT sensors will play a major role in addressing the existing challenges like water scarcity, infrastructure resilience, and environmental protection, which will definitely helpful in paving the way toward a more resilient, efficient, and sustainable water future (Table 11.1).

11.4 Performance Analysis of IoT-Based Sensors for Improved Water Management System

In order to perform this performance analysis we have taken a few papers that have been recently published in IoT with a view to improve existing water management. We have taken parameters like name of IoT-based sensors, efficiency, robustness, accuracy, sustainability, and cost-effectiveness. After going through the study we have taken a standard scale of 10 (Minimum–Maximum) and shown which factors have contributed the most and likewise, we have given them points. In this performance comparison, we have also highlighted the specific sensors which has been used by the researchers in that particular study. This performance analysis provides a comprehensive view of different types of sensors which are in use to improve the existing water management system. With the help of this analysis, we can draw few important conclusions. Some of them are:

11.4.1 Identification of Effective IoT-Based Sensors

With the help of this study, water managers can easily get to know which sensors are available to improve the different aspects of water management.

11.4.2 Performance Evaluation

This analysis would be helpful in evaluating the performance of different IoT sensors based on the different criteria as shown in Table 11.2. It would further help stake-

Table 11.2 Performance evaluation

Study reference robustness cost-effectiveness sustainability	IoT sensors used	Efficiency	Robustness	Cost-effectiveness	Sustainability
Barriga et al. [26]	Water quality sensors, pressure sensors	8	7	9	9
Sarminingsih et al. [27]	pH sensors, turbidity sensors	8	8	10	10
Singh et al. [28]	Crop sensors, weather sensors	10	8	8	9
Chhaglani et al. [29]	Flow sensors, acoustic sensors	10	7	10	8
Aliar et al. [30]	Rainfall sensors, temperature sensors	9	9	7	8
Naqash et al. [31]	Smart water meters, leak detection sensors	10	8	10	10

holders in making informed decisions while selecting sensors for their specific water management needs.

11.4.3 Optimized Water Resource Management

The performance evaluation of these IoT sensors would be directly helpful in resource utilization.

11.4.4 Sustainability

These IoT-based sensors would be helpful in the sustainable management of water resources by improving efficiency, optimizing cost, mitigates environmental impact which would be altogether helpful in leading to more resilient and sustainable water systems.

11.5 Conclusion and Future Work

This chapter has provided an extensive overview of water management using IoT-based sensors and how the existing paradigm of water management systems can be significantly improved with the transformative capabilities of IoT-based sensors has been addressed. We have highlighted some of the major factors which are responsible for water depletion. We have listed some of the challenges which caused due to Water depletion like exploitation of water resources, climatic changes, etc. These challenges can be overcome with the help of IoT-based sensors as it has potential advantages like predictive analytics, real-time monitoring, ultramodern irrigation systems, etc., and with the help of these, existing loopholes present in the water management can be improved. This chapter also presents a comprehensive comparative analysis of traditional water management systems and IoT-based water management systems and with the help of these detailed analyses readers can get to know how decision systems along with optimized water resource management can be exponentially improved with the help of IoT-enabled sensors. This chapter also presents a performance analysis of IoT-based sensors in water management systems further draw insights from past studies examined by researchers in the field of water management with the goal of achieving sustainability. This analysis also underlines the specific IoT sensors that are in use in strengthening various aspects of water management. The potential advantages of IoT sensors hold paramount importance in the sustainable management of water resources. Future research should focus on the seamless integration of IoT sensors with the existing infrastructure. Secondly, there is a need to have more operative sensors which can strengthen existing water management practices. The research can also be carried forward in the development of an innovative predictive analytics model which can leverage IoT data that will help in forecasting water demand, anticipate water quality trends, and optimize resource allocation in real time.

References

1. Chen, S.-L., et al.: An intelligent water monitoring IoT system for ecological environment and smart cities. Sensors **23**(20), 8540 (2023)
2. Bouramdane, A..-A..: Optimal water management strategies: paving the way for sustainability in smart cities. Smart Cities **6**(5), 2849–2882 (2023)
3. Davis, G..B., Rayner, J..L., Donn, M..J.: Advancing "Autonomous" sensing and prediction of the subsurface environment: a review and exploration of the challenges for soil and groundwater contamination. Environ. Sci. Pollut. Res. **30**(8), 19520–19535 (2023)
4. Chen, T., et al.: Application of internet of things (IoT) technologies in green stormwater infrastructure (GSI): a bibliometric review. Sustainability **15**(18), 13317 (2023)
5. Rajak, P., et al.: Internet of things and smart sensors in agriculture: scopes and challenges. J. Agric. Food Res. **14**, 100776 (2023)
6. Syrmos, E., et al.: An intelligent modular water monitoring IoT system for real-time quantitative and qualitative measurements. Sustainability **15**(3), 2127 (2023)
7. Bakhtawar, B., Zayed, T.: State-of-the-art review of leak diagnostic experiments: toward a smart water network. Wiley Interdiscip. Rev. Water **10**(5), e1667 (2023)
8. Zhao, L.: Design of intelligent water-saving irrigation system based on internet of things. Wirel. Eng. Technol. **13**(3), 33–40 (2022)
9. Di Nardo, A., et al.: Smart urban water networks: solutions, trends and challenges. Water **13**(4), 501 (2021)
10. Bhardwaj, A., et al.: Smart IoT and machine learning-based framework for water quality assessment and device component monitoring. Environ. Sci. Pollut. Res. **29**(30), 46018–46036 (2022)
11. Kamyab, H., et al.: The latest innovative avenues for the utilization of artificial Intelligence and big data analytics in water resource management. Results Eng. 101566 (2023)
12. Mezni, H., et al.: Smartwater: a service-oriented and sensor cloud-based framework for smart monitoring of water environments. Remote Sens. **14**(4), 922 (2022)
13. Barbhuiya, M.R., Bharadwaj, M., Shukla, S.: IoT as an assistive technology for community-based water management practices during COVID-19 pandemic and beyond. In: Impact of COVID-19 on Emerging Contaminants: one Health Framework for Risk Assessment and Remediation. Springer Nature Singapore, Singapore, pp. 153–175
14. Patel, A., et al.: Review of artificial intelligence and internet of things technologies in land and water management research during 1991–2021: a bibliometric analysis. Eng. Appl. Artif. Intell. **123**, 106335 (2023)
15. Jan, F., et al.: IoT-based solutions to monitor water level, leakage, and motor control for smart water tanks. Water **14**(3), 309 (2022)
16. Arshad, B., et al.: Computer vision and IoT-based sensors in flood monitoring and mapping: a systematic review. Sensors **19**(22), 5012 (2019)
17. Bouramdane, A..-A..: Optimal water management strategies: paving the way for sustainability in smart cities. Smart Cities **6**(5), 2849–2882 (2023)
18. Nagy, M., Lăzăroiu, G.: Computer vision algorithms, remote sensing data fusion techniques, and mapping and navigation tools in the industry 4.0-based Slovak automotive sector. Mathematics **10**(19), 3543 (2022)
19. Raj, A., et al.: Modern farming using IoT-enabled sensors for the improvement of crop selection. In: 2023 4th International Conference on Intelligent Engineering and Management (ICIEM). IEEE (2023)

20. Singh, V.K., et al.: IoT based rainfall surveillance system with sensor integrated infrastructure. In: 2022 7th International Conference on Communication and Electronics Systems (ICCES). IEEE (2022)
21. Mukta, M., et al.: IoT based smart water quality monitoring system. In: 2019 IEEE 4th International Conference on Computer and Communication Systems (ICCCS). IEEE (2019)
22. Amruta, M.K., Satish, M.T.: Solar powered water quality monitoring system using wireless sensor network. In: 2013 International Mutli-Conference on Automation, Computing, Communication, Control and Compressed Sensing (iMac4s). IEEE (2013)
23. da Costa, T.P., et al.: A systematic review of real-time monitoring technologies and its potential application to reduce food loss and waste: key elements of food supply chains and IoT technologies. Sustainability **15**(1), 614 (2022)
24. Islam, M.R., et al.: A review on current technologies and future direction of water leakage detection in water distribution network. IEEE Access (2022)
25. Du, Z., Dong, Z.: Dynamic data-driven modelling of water allocation for the internet of things. Wirel. Commun. Mob. Comput. **2022** (2022)
26. Barriga, A., et al.: IoT-based expert system for fault detection in Japanese Plum leaf-turgor pressure WSN. Internet Things **23**, 100829 (2023)
27. Sarminingsih, A., et al.: Water quality monitoring system for temperature, pH, Turbidity, DO, BOD, and COD parameters based on internet of things in the Garang Watershed. Ecol. Eng. Environ. Technol. (EEET) **25**(2) (2024)
28. Singh, D.K., et al.: LoRa based intelligent soil and weather condition monitoring with internet of things for precision agriculture in smart cities. IET Commun. **16**(5), 604–618 (2022)
29. Chhaglani, B., et al.: Flowsense: monitoring airflow in building ventilation systems using audio sensing. Proc. ACM Interact. Mob. Wearable Ubiquitous Technol. **6**(1), 1–26 (2022)
30. Aliar, A.A.S., et al.: A comprehensive analysis on IoT based smart farming solutions using machine learning algorithms. Bull. Electr. Eng. Inform. **11**(3), 1550–1557 (2022)
31. Naqash, M.T., et al.: A blockchain based framework for efficient water management and leakage detection in urban areas. Urban Sci. **7**(4), 99 (2023)

Chapter 12
Intelligent Water Management: Implementing IoT and AI for Enhanced Efficiency and Sustainability

Bishnu Kant Shukla, Ruchi Saraswat, Nikunj Agarwal, Nitya Singh, Hans Kumar Singh, and Shivam Verma

Abstract Water scarcity and management are concerns that extend worldwide and the combination of Internet of Things (IoT) and Artificial Intelligence (AI) technologies holds promise, in addressing these issues. This article explores the role of IoT and AI in enhancing water resource management by discussing their advantages, challenges, and future prospects. The utilization of hardware like sensor networks and software solutions is vital for implementing water management at different levels. Notable platforms such as ThingSpeak, IBM Watson IoT, and Adafruit excel in handling real-time data by employing machine learning techniques and providing analysis tools. These platforms are supported by infrastructures like OpenStack and CloudStack. However, it is important to address challenges such as system complexity, data security and ethical considerations. The integration of devices with AI algorithms significantly improves water systems by enabling real-time monitoring detecting anomalies promptly and conducting predictive analyses. This leads to the utilization, distribution, and management of water resources while automating tasks such as monitoring water levels or predicting resource allocation. Furthermore, AI enhances water distribution optimization efforts while improving quality monitoring

B. K. Shukla (✉) · R. Saraswat · H. K. Singh
Department of Civil Engineering, JSS Academy of Technical Education, Noida, India
e-mail: bishnukantshukla@gmail.com

R. Saraswat
e-mail: rsaraswat@jssaten.ac.in

N. Agarwal
Department of Mathematics, JSS Academy of Technical Education, Noida, India
e-mail: nikunjagarwal@jssaten.ac.in

N. Singh
Department of Civil and Environmental Engineering, University of Liverpool, Brownlow Hill, Liverpool L69 7ZX, UK
e-mail: nityasingh615alg@gmail.com

S. Verma
New Jersey Institute of Technology, Newark (New Jersey), USA
e-mail: ssv8@njit.edu

S. S. Rawat et al. (eds.), *Unleashing the Power of Blockchain and IoT for Water Informatics*, Water Informatics for Water Resource Management,
https://doi.org/10.1007/978-981-96-3886-4_12

procedures to prevent contamination. The combination of IoT and AI plays a role in advancing water resource management by offering optimized solutions that are real-time oriented while promoting sustainability. However, it is imperative to ensure robust security measures are implemented along, with considerations to guarantee the use of technology while safeguarding data privacy. *abstract* environment.

Keywords Internet of things (IoT) · Smart water harvest system · Artificial intelligence (AI) · Consumption monitoring · Devices used for integration

12.1 Introduction

Conserving resources of water, water harvesting, preparing the resources of water that are available, and distributing it wisely to customers are all duties that fall under the umbrella of water management. It also entails building up procedures and regulations to carry out the duties with dispersed controls. To keep the supply of water sustainable over the long period of time, water management strategies must be fully considered. A whopping 97% of water found across the globe is too salty to drink. Water supply is also impacted by pollution [1, 2]. Water pollution is primarily caused by a number of industries, including industrial output, rigorous agriculture, mining, wastewater, and unprocessed inner-city runoff [3–5]. Effective use of water from multiple sources is required, which traditional water management techniques fall short of. The current water usage practices are not very effective as far as costs are involved [6] and there exists a reluctance to use the most recent information and communication technology (ICT) among the population.

Recent findings highlight the precarious condition of worldwide water resources. According to the World Resources Institute, it is projected that by 2025, over two-thirds of the world's population may experience water shortages. These shortages will be intensified by climate change, leading to catastrophic droughts in several places, including California and Sub-Saharan Africa [7]. Case studies, such as the smart water management system built in Cape Town, South Africa, exemplify the efficacy of Internet of Things (IoT) and Artificial Intelligence (AI) technology in emergency situations. In the midst of the 2018 water crisis, the utilization of IoT sensors and AI-driven analytics played a crucial role in diminishing water usage by 60 thereby averting the depletion of the city's water supplies [8]. In India, IoT-based systems have been implemented to effectively manage and distribute water in dry areas, resulting in a substantial decrease in water wastage and enhanced availability of clean water for rural communities [9]. These instances emphasize the pressing necessity for the extensive implementation of intelligent technologies in water management to alleviate the effects of imminent worldwide water scarcity.

In the fields of agriculture, public supply, industry, mining, producing hydropower, aquaculture, and livestock housing, water management is necessary [10, 11]. The main issues in agriculture relate to effective water usage, sustainable strategies for water harvesting, conservation, and methods for gaining access to water [12]. The water for the industries comes from either surface or groundwater. The choosing of selection is based on a number of variables, including the availability of surface water, groundwater, demand, and cost for fresh potable water from local civic corporations [13]. Systems of water level monitoring and quality monitoring systems of water are the two primary categories into which the water management system can be roughly grouped. Systems that use sensors to attempt to detect the water level of a reservoir in real time are referred to as level monitoring systems. The system of water quality monitoring uses a variety of sensors to measure the pH, conductivity, TDS, and other water quality factors present in the water. The smart algorithms' models of the water distribution infrastructure promote effective public water supply distribution that is both safe and sustainable. The model created using intelligent techniques would suggest water-saving smart equipment, put limits on how much water is used at home, and levy fees for water use. Three groups of characteristics-physical, biological, and chemical-are used to evaluate water quality. Dissolved oxygen, Chlorophyll, pH, heavy metal concentrations, pH, lead, and chloride are a few of the contaminants of water (quality indicators) [2, 14, 15].

A few researchers have developed various techniques employing machine learning to predict pollution using the location and elevation of water bodies [16]. Deep learning [17], IoT, and machine learning algorithms are examples of intelligent systems that can be used for processes like contamination, leak management, overuse, flow monitoring, and developing plans for appropriate water use. The research was conducted on a system for monitoring the water level on campuses in 2015. The system made use of a reasonably priced, 10-meter-capable ultrasonic sensor. A system of real-time monitoring of water level based on IoT in a smart house was presented by Perumal et al. in 2016. Sensor actuators, power sources, and wireless communication make up the system [18]. The present work presents the advancements and key contributions of various researchers in employing AI and IoT technologies for monitoring water qualities, present challenges in applications of smart technologies, and future aspects for further research.

12.2 Smart Water Harvesting Systems

A system that uses cutting-edge technology, such as IoT sensors and AI algorithms, to optimize the collection, storage, and distribution of water resources is known as a smart water harvesting system.

The natural water cycle has been significantly altered by rising urbanization, climate change, and phenomena including runoff, floods, and water scarcity. The use of water harvesting systems is a promising solution in this situation to conserve water and improve its management. The rainwater harvesting (RWH) system accumulates rainwater from rooftops, impermeable surfaces rooftop terraces and for on-site reuse for various tasks, such as flushing toilets and watering gardens and green roofs (Fig. 12.1). Although conventional RWH systems are widely used, the development

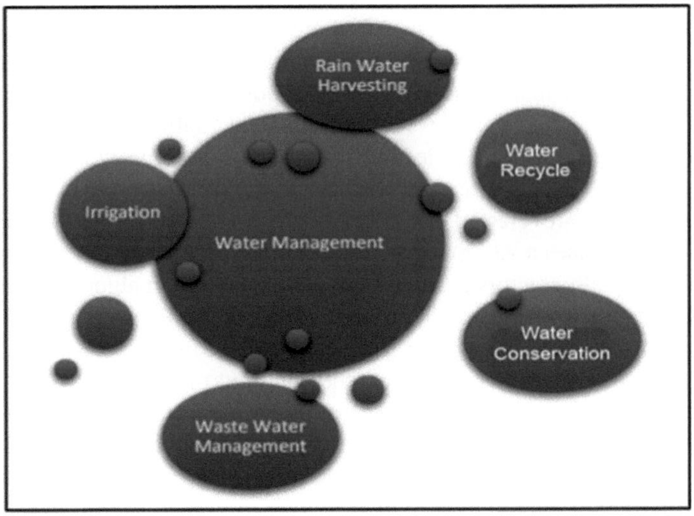

Fig. 12.1 Parameters of water management

of IoT technologies has had an impact on their use, creating new problems for optimization. Smart water harvesting technologies are thus becoming more and more common in the literature [19]. Several famous examples demonstrate the efficacy of smart water collection technologies. In Singapore, the introduction of an integrated IoT and AI-driven rainwater harvesting system has greatly improved water conservation efforts. The method has allowed for the collection and reuse of rainwater, lowering the demand for potable water by up to 15 and demonstrating significant cost savings for municipal water supplies [20]. Similarly, in Australia, smart water management technologies have been used to optimize stormwater utilization. These technologies significantly reduced urban runoff while increasing water availability for non-potable users by 20 demonstrating a novel method to sustainable urban water management [21]. This assigned task examines several similar water management strategies that offer help with resource harvesting, recycling, and conservation. The present review examines a number of studies that have been conducted by researchers on the contribution of artificial intelligence using software that is powered by machine learning and deep learning methods. Additionally, it discusses current trends and numerous obstacles to the implementation of efficient water management systems and various water management strategies and case studies.

12.3 Recent Technological Advancements

The management and conservation of water resources could be completely changed by technological developments in "Smart Management of Water" using the Internet

Table 12.1 Literature survey of recent technological advancements in water management system

Advancements in water resource management system	References
Various AI methods in relation to the treatment of wastewater	[22]
Discussions on how to use genetic algorithms (GA) to measure the key variables in wastewater, including chemical oxygen demand (COD), nitrogen, biological oxygen demand (BOD), pH levels and turbidity	[23]
Reviews of various AI methods that might be useful in detecting heavy metals in sources of water	[24]
Discussed how a floating solar power-driven system in an effluent pond loses water as a result of surface evaporation	[25]
Numerous improvements to the supply of water and effective delivery of service are possible as a result of the employment of AI in smart systems in water management. Designed an IoT as well as a data analytics	[26]
Solution or intelligent management of water that employs time series forecasting	[27]
The researcher looks at current problems that had an impact on the system for managing the water supply in rural India	[28]
The water delivery mechanism ensures that houses have received water from the distributed network	[29]
IoT-related discussion on the smart water management platform (SWAMP)	[30]
A technology called Smart AgroTech was suggested, which uses the IoT platform and measures soil moisture, humidity and temperature for urban farming	[31]
Discussed employing inexpensive sensors to decentralize water infrastructure in ingenious ways	[32]
The IoT framework's potential for managing water supply in a smart city	[33]
Outlined a strategy for using IoT and big data analytics to manage water in smart cities	[34]
Proposes the use of a REFlex water architecture to manage the water independently	[35]
With the help of IoT and sensing systems, SMART irrigation solves the Sustainable Development Goals (SDGs)	[36]
Reduces water waste through dam water management system (DWM) employing IoT-based technology	[37]
IoT was used to develop intrusion detection systems and efficient water management	[38]

of Things. Real-time monitoring and data collecting are made possible by the usage of IoT sensors and devices, which may then be analyzed by AI algorithms to find trends, spot abnormalities and make predictions (Table 12.1). These forecasts can subsequently be utilized to reduce water waste, optimize water use and distribution, and enhance the management of water resources in general.

Although recent technical breakthroughs have greatly improved water management, there are still numerous constraints that hinder their general adoption and efficiency. The main difficulties were the expensive nature of implementation, the intricacies of maintenance, and the requirement for specialized training in operating the system [29]. Furthermore, the use of these systems often involves handling sensitive information, which raises issues about data privacy and security. It is necessary to implement strong cybersecurity measures to address these concerns, although this is not always done effectively [40]. The absence of dependable Internet access in rural regions can impede the efficacy of solutions based on the Internet of Things (IoT) [41]. The issues are tackled by proposed solutions through the integration of affordable sensor technology, streamlining user interfaces to minimize the requirement for lengthy training, and enhancing data encryption methods to enhance security. Moreover, our architecture is specifically engineered to function well even in situations where there is sporadic or unreliable internet connection. This allows to expand the advantages of smart water management to areas that lack adequate access to such technologies.

12.4 Water Consumption

Utilizing the technology of the Internet of Things (IoT), it is possible to monitor and track water consumption in real time. Utilizing this technology will enable the detection of leaks and other inefficiencies, as well as the optimization of water use. The automated system of real-time monitoring has been created recently for smart management of the consumption of water and accurate quantification of it. Smart meters of water that employ cloud computing and the Internet of Things (IoT) to discriminate between regular and excessive water use are used to manage consumption. This encourages sustainable water management and increases consumers' knowledge of water use. Additionally, IoT for water use can be coupled with other intelligent systems, including intelligent irrigation systems, allowing for the use of water in the most efficient way. Water Consumption can also be used to monitor water quality, by connecting water quality sensors to the network and analyzing the data to detect any anomalies or contaminants. Table 12.2 presents some of the existing works describing the utilization of smart devices in the measurement of water consumption.

Traditional methods for monitoring the consumption of water mostly depend on manual meter readings, which are labor-intensive and susceptible to human mistakes, frequently leading to inaccuracies and delayed data analysis. On the other hand, approaches based on the Internet of Things (IoT) provide notable progress by allowing the collection and analysis of data in real time. Traditional approaches often offer monthly consumption statistics, which lack the level of detail needed

Table 12.2 Summary of the existing works on water consumption measurement utilizing artificial intelligence

Method	Outcomes	References
ANN-artificial neural networks; Bi-LSTM-Bidirectional long short-term memory RNN-recurrent neural networks; GRU-gated recurrent unit LSTM-long short-term memory	Mean absolute error (MAE): 13.4% correlation coefficient (CC): 0.85% Nash-Sutcliffe efficiency coefficient (NS): 0.65 root mean square error (RMSE): 21.16%	[42]
Hybrid model; Convolutional Long short-term memory (LSTM); Neural network (CNN)	MSE:0.055 NS: 0.75 TOC: 0.832 TP: 0.899 TN: 0.987	[43]
U-net; CNN tensor flow libraries	Accuracy: 99% recall: 88% precision: 99%	[44]
SVM (Support Vector Machine)	Accuracy: 81.6%	[45]
Belief rule-based model (BRDM); Deep learning neural network models	Ph value: 4.28 temperature: 46.19 °C	[46]
Deep neural networks (DNNs)	MSE:0.52	[47]
Feed-forward deep neural networks (FF-DNNs); RMSprop optimization algorithm	NSE:0.89	[48]
Long short-term memory (LSTM), SVM	Accuracy: 94%	[49]

to identify specific periods of high usage or rapidly uncover leakage. IoT systems have the capability to continually and in real-time detect irregularities and optimize water usage. This level of precision not only boosts efforts to conserve water but also enables fast corrective actions, enhancing overall system efficiency and minimizing loss. Comparative studies have demonstrated that the utilization of IoT approaches can lead to a significant reduction in water usage, up to 30 in both residential and industrial environments. This is achieved by facilitating the provision of timely data and alarms [50].

12.5 Research Background

This section provides background details of the work.

12.5.1 Internet of Things (IoT)

The terms "Internet" and "Things" refer to a global network of interconnected devices that uses technology for sensing, communicating, networking, and processing information. These gadgets can be remotely operated with a smartphone, computer, or other device and collect and transmit data using embedded sensors and CPUs.

The capability of real-time collection of data and analysis is one of the major advantages of IoT. This enables effective system and device monitoring and control, which can raise the efficacy and efficiency of many sectors. IoT has the ability to automate a variety of processes and functions. The effectiveness of these methods for water conservation and runoff extenuation has been the subject of several research [51, 52]. In a different study, Behzadian et al. [53] looked into an IoT-based system that automatically regulates the tank's water level to ensure there is enough space to store stormwater runoff. Information and communication technology (ICT) may have undergone a change as a result [54, 55].

Water management infrastructures can be improved by increasing their efficiency, lowering energy costs, and minimizing the need for human intervention, among other advantages of the integration of the paradigm of IoT into activities of water management.

12.5.2 Overview of Smart Water Management Technologies

Utilizing technology and data to improve the usage, distribution, and treatment of water resources is known as smart water management. This can involve employing sensors to track water levels and flow rates, predicting water demand using weather forecasts, and adjusting water distribution and treatment systems in real time in response to changing environmental circumstances. Water may be more efficiently used, wasted less, and provided to areas where it is most needed with the help of smart water management. Smart water management systems can also assist with leak detection and prevention, water contamination detection and response, and general water quality improvement.

A great way to increase the effectiveness of water distribution systems is through smart water management, which employs sensors and telemetry for communication and measurement [55–58] to the monitoring system for the immediate surroundings [60]. The sensors empower involuntary monitoring, hydraulic data real-time monitoring, and reports via the cloud platform for situations like water leaks or overuse. The key benefit of smart water systems is remotely controlled pumps and valves, which can monitor pressure, usage, and flow [59]. Figure 12.2 (prepared based on the comprehensive discussion detailed in [60]) explains a few of the most prominent sensors and demonstrates how they're employed in smart cities.

Although smart water management systems have demonstrated success in small-scale pilot projects, there are numerous hurdles to implementing these technologies

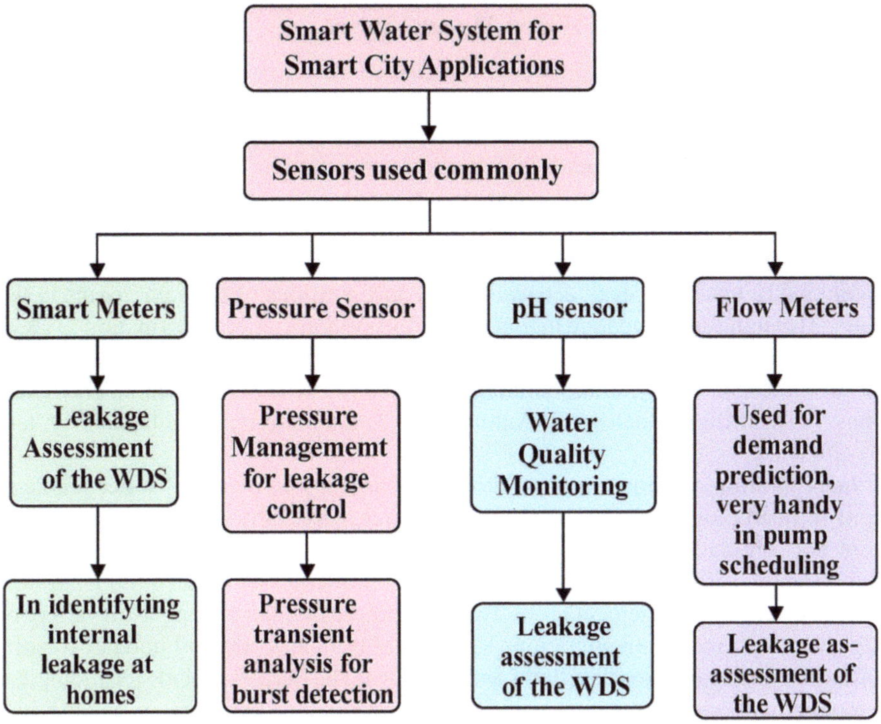

Fig. 12.2 Application of sensors used in intelligent water management system

in larger urban settings. Financial constraints are the main obstacles, as the initial expenditure required for mass technology adoption can be substantial. Another crucial problem is the seamless integration of technology with the current infrastructure, without causing any disturbances [61]. In addition, the regulatory and policy frameworks may not consistently facilitate the swift incorporation of cutting-edge technologies. To achieve successful scaling, it is imperative to overcome these obstacles by employing strategic planning, involving stakeholders, and implementing the process in stages. Pilot projects frequently act as valuable demonstrations for stakeholders, showcasing the possible return on investment (ROI) and operational advantages, thus facilitating the implementation of large-scale applications. Collaboration among government, business, and academia is crucial in creating favorable conditions for the expansion of smart water technology. This strategy not only guarantees the adjustment of technology to various urban sizes but also improves the sustainability and resilience of water management systems in response to increasing urban needs and climate fluctuations [62, 63].

12.5.3 Monitoring of Water Management

Monitoring water management entails measuring and keeping track of the quantity, quality, and distribution of water resources using a variety of instruments and methods. Sensors make it possible to control consumption, keep an eye on system performance, and start the proper repairs when something breaks or an alarm goes off. This can involve things like employing sensors to monitor water levels in reservoirs and aquifers, flow meters to measure water flow in rivers and streams, and water quality testing tools to determine the concentrations of different toxins in the water. Through this preventive maintenance, the system gathers information to identify the root causes of any errors and automatically corrects them [64]. Lastly, as per recent research [65], smart buildings have the following five essential characteristics: (1) Multifunctionality; (2) Automation (3) Interactivity; (4) adaptability; and (5) efficiency.

Incorporating contemporary monitoring technology into current water management infrastructures presents notable difficulties, especially in older systems that were not originally planned to accommodate these improvements. Implementing such systems sometimes necessitates significant alterations to accommodate new sensors and data management tools. These modifications can encompass a variety of improvements, including alterations to physical infrastructure and updates to software systems that oversee data flows and analytics. The hurdles include technological compatibility issues, the requirement for significant capital expenditure, and the possibility of disruptions during the changeover phase [66]. Furthermore, the existing workforce frequently experiences a deficiency in skills, which might impede the efficient adoption and continuous upkeep of these sophisticated systems. Although faced with these obstacles, the incorporation of intelligent monitoring technologies can greatly improve the effectiveness and adaptability of water management systems, resulting in improved resource management and decreased operational expenses [67]. Effective integration plans frequently incorporate gradual implementations and comprehensive training initiatives to minimize disturbances and optimize the advantages of new technologies.

12.5.4 Interdisciplinary Contributions to Smart Water Management

The integration of environmental science, engineering, and information technology is essential in the creation of smart water management systems. From an environmental science standpoint, it is crucial to comprehend the ecological consequences and sustainability factors. This field of study offers crucial knowledge about the hydrological processes, methods for preserving water, and the environmental consequences of exploiting water resources. It helps in making ethical and sustainable decisions on the use of technology in natural ecosystems. Engineering proficiency is essential for designing the tangible elements and systems that enable efficient water management. Engineers utilize ideas from civil, mechanical, and electrical fields to build robust systems that can survive environmental challenges and satisfy the requirements of diverse geographies and climates.

Information technology is the essential infrastructure that enables the integration and operation of Internet of Things (IoT) devices within these systems. IT workers are responsible for creating the software and algorithms that are essential for collecting, analyzing, and transmitting data. They guarantee that the systems possess the ability to monitor and respond in real-time, while also being secure and effective in managing the vast quantities of data produced [68]. This integration facilitates the utilization of predictive analytics and adaptive reactions, which are distinctive features of sophisticated smart water management systems.

By integrating these several areas of specialized knowledge, intelligent water management systems may be comprehensively designed to effectively tackle both human requirements and environmental conservation. Interdisciplinary collaborations improve the functionality, sustainability, and flexibility of systems in response to changing environmental conditions [69].

12.6 Building Application and Operation

The integration and usage of smart water management systems in buildings are referred to as "building applications" and "building operations." An element of the receiver that picks up the reflected wave and an emitter that produces the ultrasonic signal make up most water measurement equipment [70]. An IoT-based system of water monitoring that uses IEEE802.11 communiqué standards and incorporates a gateway (wireless) into the network of consumer was proposed by Syrmos et al. [71] and measures the level of water in real-time. In a different study [72], the authors suggested a water-saving device that uses a fuzzy logic algorithm enabled and an ultrasonic sensor (HC-SRF04) employed Arduino Uno to decide whether to turn on or off the water tap.

A wireless water utilization monitoring system that relies on flow rate and sensors measuring temperature to gather data, which is then transmitted to a remotely located server over the Internet and home Wi-Fi. This can help building managers to monitor water usage, identify areas for improvement, and make adjustments to water systems in response to changing conditions. Figure 12.3 constructed based on the detailed discussions presented in [73]).

A system to track water use, prevent overflow, and discover water-saving techniques was created in a recently proposed urban water resources management strategy [74]. A sensor device (YF-S201) detects the rate of flow of water and total consumed volume, while an ultrasonic sensor (HC-SR04) gauges reservoir level. Figure 12.4 (constructed based on the detailed discussion extracted from [19, 75–82]) explains step-by-step process of harnessing intelligent water resource management

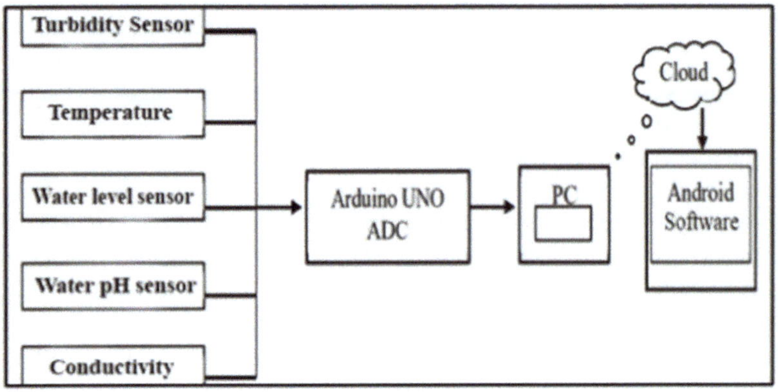

Fig. 12.3 Block diagram of IoT environment implementation for smart water quality monitoring system

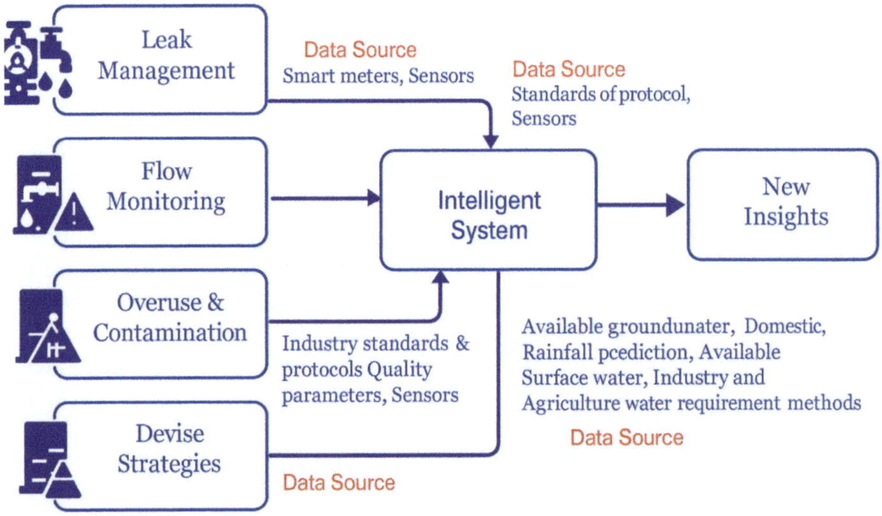

Fig. 12.4 Harnessing intelligent systems for water management

system and Table 12.3 proposes literature survey of various hardware and software components used in such management system.

12.7 Discussion, Current Challenges and Future Directions

IoT-based systems for monitoring and controlling smart water, with a primary focus on systems that are practical at the building size before moving on to the urban

Table 12.3 Application of IoT and sensors in water quality monitoring

Hardware components	Software components	References
Microcontroller ultrasonic sensor	GSM modem; Arduino IDE	[75]
Ultrasonic sensor; Arduino; ESP8266 Wi-Fi module	Application of Android; firebase	[76]
Raspberry Pi; ultrasonic sensor	Bluetooth and wireless LAN	[77]
ESP8266 used as microcontroller; ultrasonic sensor	Application of Android; firebase cloud	[78]
HC-SR04 Ultrasonic sensor; ESP8266 Wi-Fi module; motor	Arduino IDE using C; Adaftruit web-application	[79]
Water overflow sensor; ultrasonic sensor HC-SR04; ATMega 328 microcontroller; tank flush sensor	Future idea: implement wireless connectivity between the device and user application by including a Wi-Fi module	[80]
Arduino Uno; ultrasonic sensor HC-SRF04	Database; using fuzzy logic to make decisions	[81]
Sensor of flow (Hall-effect-based); motor; ultrasonic sensor AG222VXCM0800US1 pump; ESP8266 Wi-Fi module; relay; Arduino Mega 2560 microcontroller	Mobile application; Wi-Fi	[82]

scale. This overview makes it clear that there are two main categories into which the essential parts of an IoT-based system of water management may be divided: hardware and software units. Furthermore, as stated in [83], it is impossible to ignore the use of networks of wireless sensors, which were taken into account in several studies for this overview. An open IoT data platform called ThingSpeak Cloud Platform enables users to simply configure devices to communicate data using industry-standard protocols of IoT and to view sensor data in real-time [84] using Arduino and the ThingSpeak IoT Platform.

With free channel hosting, app integration, and event planning, IoT Cloud enables data collecting in private channels [85]. Smart homes can leverage the IBM Watson IoT Platform, which offers services employing machine learning to incorporate into applications of IoT and data analytics [86], whereas Adafruit offers a variety of statistical tools with just a few clicks [87]. Finally, in order to monitor, administer, and provide an infrastructure to install Cloud platforms, many Cloud infrastructures have been developed (including OpenStack, OpenNebula, and CloudStack). The perceived ramification of smart systems of water in relation to installation, maintenance, and operation tasks is also a significant barrier [88]. As a result of all of this discussion, a thorough examination of the articles under consideration aids readers in recognizing the principal difficulties, pertinent suggestions, and future directions for applications of IoT for the smart management of water.

With the growing integration of IoT and AI technologies in the water management industry, it is crucial to carefully examine and solve ethical concerns and the broader societal effects. Primary ethical considerations encompass data protection, necessitating cautious management of data gathering and analysis via IoT devices to safeguard individual private rights. The General Data Protection Regulation (GDPR) and similar regulations establish guidelines for safeguarding data, but their implementation in the context of IoT in water management requires further examination [89]. Moreover, there is a potential for worsening socioeconomic disparities due to the unequal availability of these technologies. If modern water management systems are not provided equally, underprivileged populations may experience greater differences in water quality and availability, while rich regions may reap the benefits [90]. Future strategies should prioritize the implementation of inclusive policies that guarantee universal access to technology benefits across all societal groups. This approach will not only foster technical progress but also promote equitable allocation of water resources. In order to effectively address ethical concerns and societal challenges, it is imperative that technologists, legislators, and the public maintain an open discourse as we progress [91].

12.8 Conclusion

The incorporation of Internet of Things (IoT) sensors and artificial intelligence (AI) algorithms in the management of water resources enables the continuous monitoring and collecting of data in real time. This enables the recognition of patterns, detection of anomalies, and formulation of anticipatory judgments that improve the overall effectiveness of water utilization and greatly minimize wastage.

Internet of Things (IoT) sensors are installed in different water systems to constantly monitor and assess water levels and quality. Simultaneously, artificial intelligence systems analyze this data to forecast future alterations in water conditions, empowering managers to take preventive measures, therefore averting potential problems and optimizing resource utilization.

Artificial intelligence algorithms play a vital role in analyzing data gathered by Internet of Things (IoT) sensors to identify patterns and anomalies in the quality of water. This skill is crucial for guaranteeing the safety and healthiness of water supplies for consumption. It aids in the prevention of water-borne diseases by promptly identifying contaminants.

The implementation of Internet of Things (IoT) and Artificial Intelligence (AI) technologies in water management entails the management of confidential data, which gives rise to substantial apprehensions surrounding the security and privacy of the data. Implementing strong cybersecurity measures is crucial in order to safeguard this data and guarantee the responsible and secure usage of these technologies.

Subsequent investigations should focus on the formulation of policies and strategies that provide equal access to smart water management technologies for all communities. Preventing the worsening of current discrepancies in water quality and availability across various locations is of utmost importance.

Additional research is required to enhance the development of advanced AI models capable of accurately predicting long-term water resource requirements. These models must possess the ability to handle intricate datasets and deliver dependable predictions to facilitate decision-making in water management.

Investigating the utilization of sustainable energy sources for powering IoT devices in water management systems is a crucial field for future research. Implementing this strategy will improve the long-term viability of these systems, decrease operational expenses, and support the overall objectives of environmental preservation.

References

1. Smith, T.F., Waterman, M.S.: Identification of common molecular subsequences. J. Mol. Biol. **147**, 195–197 (1981)
2. Shukla, B.K., Bhowmik, A.R., Raj, R.B., Sharma, P.K.: Physico-chemical parameters and status of ground water pollution in Jalandhar-Phagwara region. Green Eng. **9**(2), 212–23 (2019)
3. Shukla, B.K., Gupta, A., Sharma, P.K., Bhowmik, A.R.: Pollution status and water quality assessment in pre-monsoon season: a case study of rural villages in Allahabad district, Uttar Pradesh, India. Mater. Today: Proc. **32**, 824–830 (2020)
4. Berthet, A., Vincent, A., Fleury, P.: Water quality issues and agriculture: an international review of innovative policy schemes. Land Use Policy **109**, 105654 (2021)
5. Shukla, B.K., Bashir, M., Sharma, P.K., Abhimanyu.: An analytical investigation of surface water quality and pollution status in Srinagar, Jammu and Kashmir, India. J. Green Eng. **11**, 952–962 (2021)
6. Shenoy, A., Shukla, B.K., Bansal, V.: Sustainable design of textile industry effluent treatment plant with constructed wetland. Mater. Today: Proc. **61**, 537–542 (2022)
7. Depetris-Chauvin, N., Fernandez Olmos, M., Hu, W., Malorgio, G.: Costs and benefits of sustainability-oriented innovation in the agri-food industry: a review. New Medit **22**(3), 23–45 (2023)
8. Huang, Z., Yuan, X., Liu, X.: The key drivers for the changes in global water scarcity: water withdrawal versus water availability. J. Hydrol. **601**, 126658 (2021)
9. Dogo, E.M., Salami, A.F., Nwulu, N.I., Aigbavboa, C.O.: Blockchain and internet of things-based technologies for intelligent water management system. In: Artificial intelligence in IoT, pp. 129–150 (2019)
10. Vani, V.G.: Integrating IoT and machine learning for sustainable water management in agriculture. J. Surv. Fish. Sci. 1083–1092 (2022)
11. Saad, A., Gamatié, A.: Water management in agriculture: a survey on current challenges and technological solutions. IEEE Access **8**, 38082–38097 (2020)
12. Ismail, S., Dawoud, D.W., Ismail, N., Marsh, R., Alshami, A.S.: IoT-based water management systems: survey and future research direction. IEEE Access **10**, 35942–35952 (2022)
13. Sharma, P.K., Ayub, S., Shukla, B.K.: Cost and feasibility analysis of chromium removal from water using agro and horticultural wastes as adsorbents. In: 3rd International Conference on Innovative Technologies for Clean and Sustainable Development: ITCSD 2020, vol. 3, pp. 449–463. Springer International Publishing (2021)
14. Shenoy, A., Bansal, V., Shukla, B.K.: Treatability of effluent from small scale dye shop using water hyacinth. Mater. Today: Proc. **61**, 579–586 (2022)
15. Shukla, B.K., Khan, A., Saikiran, G., Sriram, M.: A comparative study on effect of variation in opening shape on oxygenation performance of surface jet aerators used in water and wastewater treatment. J. Green Eng. **9**(3), 427–440 (2019)

16. Oberascher, M., Rauch, W., Sitzenfrei, R.: Towards a smart water city: a comprehensive review of applications, data requirements, and communication technologies for integrated management. Sustain. Cities Soc. **76**, 103442 (2022)
17. Banerjee, K., Bali, V., Nawaz, N., Bali, S., Mathur, S., Mishra, R.K., Rani, S.: A machine-learning approach for prediction of water contamination using latitude, longitude, and elevation. Water **14**(5), 728 (2022)
18. Uppal, M., Gupta, D., Juneja, S., Sulaiman, A., Rajab, K., Rajab, A., Elmagzoub, M.A., Shaikh, A.: Cloud-based fault prediction for real-time monitoring of sensor data in hospital environment using machine learning. Sustainability **14**(18), 11667 (2022)
19. Adedeji, K.B., Hamam, Y., Abe, B.T., Abu-Mahfouz, A.M.: Towards achieving a reliable leakage detection and localization algorithm for application in water piping networks: An overview. IEEE Access **5**, 20272–20285 (2017)
20. Kamaruidzaman, N.S., Rahmat, S.N.: Water monitoring system embedded with internet of things (IoT) device: a review. IOP Conf. Ser.: Earth Environ. Sci. **498**(1), 012068 (IoP Publishing) (2020)
21. Samant, S., Desta, P., Nakanishi, T.: A review of three case studies in Singapore. Climate, Society and Health. The Routledge Handbook on Greening High-Density Cities (2024)
22. Dieperink, C., Koop, S.H., Witjes, M., Van Leeuwen, K., Driessen, P.P.: City-to-city learning to enhance urban water management: the contribution of the City Blueprint approach. Cities **135**, 104216 (2023)
23. Zhao, L., Dai, T., Qiao, Z., Sun, P., Hao, J., Yang, Y.: Application of artificial intelligence to wastewater treatment: a bibliometric analysis and systematic review of technology, economy, management, and wastewater reuse. Process Saf. Environ. Protect. **133**, 169–182 (2020)
24. Malviya, A., Jaspal, D.: Artificial intelligence as an upcoming technology in wastewater treatment: a comprehensive review. Environ. Technol. Rev. **10**(1), 177–187 (2021)
25. Bhagat, S.K., Tung, T.M., Yaseen, Z.M.: Development of artificial intelligence for modeling wastewater heavy metal removal: state of the art, application assessment and possible future research. J. Clean. Prod. **250**, 119473 (2020)
26. Soltani, S.R.K., Mostafaeipour, A., Almutairi, K., Dehshiri, S.J.H., Dehshiri, S.S.H., Techato, K.: Predicting effect of floating photovoltaic power plant on water loss through surface evaporation for wastewater pond using artificial intelligence: a case study. Sustain. Energy Technol. Assess. **50**, 101849 (2022)
27. Jenny, H., Alonso, E.G., Wang, Y., Minguez, R.: Using artificial intelligence for smart water management systems (2020)
28. Liu, H.: Agricultural water management based on the internet of things and data analysis. Acta Agric. Scand. Sect. B-Soil Plant Sci. **72**(1), 300–311 (2022)
29. Maroli, A.A., Narwane, V.S., Raut, R.D., Narkhede, B.E.: Framework for the implementation of an internet of things (IoT)-based water distribution and management system. Clean Technol. Environ. Policy **23**, 271–283 (2021)
30. Huo, D., Malik, A.W., Ravana, S.D., Rahman, A.U., Ahmedy, I.: Mapping smart farming: addressing agricultural challenges in data-driven era. Renew. Sustain. Energy Rev. **189**, 113858 (2024)
31. Kamienski, C., Soininen, J.P., Taumberger, M., Dantas, R., Toscano, A., Salmon Cinotti, T., Filev Maia, R., Torre Neto, A.: Smart water management platform: IoT-based precision irrigation for agriculture. Sensors **19**(2), 276 (2019)
32. Podder, A.K., Al Bukhari, A., Islam, S., Mia, S., Mohammed, M.A., Kumar, N.M., Cengiz, K., Abdulkareem, K.H.: IoT based smart agrotech system for verification of Urban farming parameters. Microprocess. Microsyst. **82**, 104025 (2021)
33. Rawat, S., Shukla, B.K., Sihag, P., Srivastav, Y., Singh, H.K.: Environmental effects and sustainable hydropower development: a review of deployment research, environmental valuation and IoT sensors integration. AIP Conf. Proc. **3050**(1) (AIP Publishing) (2024)
34. Gautam, G., Sharma, G., Magar, B.T., Shrestha, B., Cho, S., Seo, C.: Usage of IoT framework in water supply management for smart city in Nepal. Appl. Sci. **11**(12), 5662 (2021)

35. Nie, X., Fan, T., Wang, B., Li, Z., Shankar, A., Manickam, A.: Big data analytics and IoT in operation safety management in under water management. Comput. Commun. **154**, 188–196 (2020)
36. Gonçalves, R., Soares, J.M. J., MF Lima, R.: An IoT-based framework for smart water supply systems management. Future Internet **12**(7), 114 (2020)
37. Obaideen, K., Yousef, B.A., AlMallahi, M.N., Tan, Y.C., Mahmoud, M., Jaber, H., Ramadan, M.: An overview of smart irrigation systems using IoT. Energy Nexus 100124 (2022)
38. Chellaswamy, C., Nisha, J., Sivakumar, K., Kaviya, R.: An IoT based dam water management system for agriculture. In: 2018 International Conference on Recent Trends in Electrical, Control and Communication (RTECC), pp. 51–56. IEEE (2018)
39. Nandhini, R., Poovizhi, S., Jose, P., Ranjitha, R., Anila, S.: Arduino based smart irrigation system using IoT. In: 3rd National Conference on Intelligent Information and Computing Technologies (IICT '17), pp. 1–5 (2017)
40. Rousso, B. Z., Lambert, M., Gong, J.: Smart water networks: a systematic review of applications using high-frequency pressure and acoustic sensors in real water distribution systems. J. Clean. Prod. 137193 (2023)
41. Lone, A.N., Mustajab, S., Alam, M.: A comprehensive study on cybersecurity challenges and opportunities in the IoT world. Secur. Privacy **6**(6), e318 (2023)
42. García-Martín, J.P., Torralba, A., Hidalgo-Fort, E., Daza, D., González-Carvajal, R.: IoT solution for smart water distribution networks based on a low-power wireless network, combined at the device-level: a case study. Internet Things **22**, 100746 (2023)
43. Apaydin, H., Feizi, H., Sattari, M.T., Colak, M.S., Shamshirband, S., Chau, K.W.: Comparative analysis of recurrent neural network architectures for reservoir inflow forecasting. Water **12**(5), 1500 (2020)
44. Baek, S.S., Pyo, J., Chun, J.A.: Prediction of water level and water quality using a CNN-LSTM combined deep learning approach. Water **12**(12), 3399 (2020)
45. Wu, Y., Kim, K., Henry, M.F., Youcef-Toumi, K.: Design of a leak sensor for operating water pipe systems. In: 2017 IEEE/RSJ International Conference on Intelligent Robots and Systems (IROS), pp. 6075–6082. IEEE (2017)
46. Saraiva, M., Protas, É., Salgado, M., Souza, C., Jr.: Automatic mapping of center pivot irrigation systems from satellite images using deep learning. Remote Sens. **12**(3), 558 (2020)
47. Vij, A., Vijendra, S., Jain, A., Bajaj, S., Bassi, A., Sharma, A.: IoT and machine learning approaches for automation of farm irrigation system. Procedia Comput. Sci. **167**, 1250–1257 (2020)
48. Chowdury, M.S.U., Emran, T.B., Ghosh, S., Pathak, A., Alam, M.M., Absar, N., Andersson, K., Hossain, M.S.: IoT based real-time river water quality monitoring system. Procedia Comput. Sci. **155**, 161–168 (2019)
49. Karamoutsou, L., Psilovikos, A.: Deep learning in water resources management: the case study of Kastoria Lake in Greece. Water **13**(23), 3364 (2021)
50. Thai-Nghe, N., Thanh-Hai, N., Chi Ngon, N.: Deep learning approach for forecasting water quality in IoT systems. Int. J. Adv. Comput. Sci. Appl. **11**(8), 686–693 (2020)
51. Zia, H., Rehman, A., Harris, N.R., Fatima, S., Khurram, M.: An experimental comparison of IoT-based and traditional irrigation scheduling on a flood-irrigated subtropical lemon farm. Sensors **21**(12), 4175 (2021)
52. Palermo, S.A., Talarico, V.C., Pirouz, B.: Optimizing rainwater harvesting systems for non-potable water uses and surface runoff mitigation. In: International Conference on Numerical Computations: theory and Algorithms, pp. 570–582. Springer International Publishing, Cham (2019)
53. Campisano, A., Butler, D., Ward, S., Burns, M.J., Friedler, E., DeBusk, K., Fisher-Jeffes, L.N., Ghisi, E., Rahman, A., Furumai, H., Han, M.: Urban rainwater harvesting systems: research, implementation and future perspectives. Water Res. **115**, 195–209 (2017)
54. Behzadian, K., Kapelan, Z., Mousavi, S.J., Alani, A.: Can smart rainwater harvesting schemes result in the improved performance of integrated urban water systems. Environ. Sci. Pollut. Res. **25**, 19271–19282 (2018)

55. Kranenburg, V.: Moscow futurodesign lab co-create urban intelligence: designing smart interfaces between people and city (2013)
56. Dallaev, R., Pisarenko, T., Ţălu, Ş., Sobola, D., Majzner, J., Papež, N.: Current applications and challenges of the Internet of Things. New Trends Comput. Sci. **1**(1), 51–61 (2023)
57. Zeng, H., Dhiman, G., Sharma, A., Sharma, A., Tselykh, A.: An IoT and blockchain-based approach for the smart water management system in agriculture. Expert Syst. **40**(4), e12892 (2023)
58. Shukla, B.K., Maurya, N., Sharma, M.: Advancements in sensor-based technologies for precision agriculture: an exploration of interoperability. Analytics and deployment strategies. Eng. Proc. **58**(1), 22 (2023)
59. Murdan, A.P., Hardin, A.: Exploring the economic viability of LoRaWAN based smart water meters for sustainable water management. In: IRC Conference on Science, Engineering and Technology, pp. 216–225. Springer Nature Singapore, Singapore (2023)
60. Hemdan, E.E.D., Essa, Y.M., Shouman, M., El-Sayed, A., Moustafa, A.N.: An efficient IoT based smart water quality monitoring system. In: Multimedia Tools and Applications, pp. 1–25 (2023)
61. Ghobadi, F., Kang, D.: Application of machine learning in water resources management: a systematic literature review. Water **15**(4), 620 (2023)
62. Adelani, F.A., Okafor, E.S., Jacks, B.S., Ajala, O.A.: Exploring theoretical constructs of urban resilience through smart water grids: case studies in African and US cities. Eng. Sci. Technol. J. **5**(3), 984–994 (2024)
63. Bouramdane, A.A.: Optimal water management strategies: paving the way for sustainability in smart cities. Smart Cities **6**(5), 2849–2882 (2023)
64. Di Nardo, A., Boccelli, D.L., Herrera, M., Creaco, E., Cominola, A., Sitzenfrei, R., Taormina, R.: Smart urban water networks: solutions, trends and challenges. Water **13**(4), 501 (2021)
65. Yu, T., Chen, X., Yan, W., Xu, Z., Ye, M.: Leak detection in water distribution systems by classifying vibration signals. Mech. Syst. Signal Process. **185**, 109810 (2023)
66. Smart Building Report.: (2021). https://www.energystrategy.it/osservatorio-di-ricerca/intelligent-building/. Accessed 1 Jan. 2024
67. Bawankar, N., Kriti, A., Chouhan, S.S., Chaudhari, S.: IoT-enabled water monitoring in smart cities with retrofit and solar-based energy harvesting. IEEE Access (2024)
68. Olatunde, T.M., Adelani, F.A., Sikhakhane, Z.Q.: A review of smart water management systems from Africa and the United States. Eng. Sci. Technol. J. **5**(4), 1231–1242 (2024)
69. Dinar, A.: Challenges to water resource management: the role of economic and modeling approaches. Water **16**(4), 610 (2024)
70. Shen, Y., Zhang, X.: Intelligent manufacturing, green technological innovation and environmental pollution. J. Innov. Knowl. **8**(3), 100384 (2023)
71. Lê, Q., Nguyen, H.B., Barnett, T.: Smart homes for older people: positive aging in a digital world. Future internet **4**(2), 607–617 (2012)
72. Syrmos, E., Sidiropoulos, V., Bechtsis, D., Stergiopoulos, F., Aivazidou, E., Vrakas, D., Vezinias, P., Vlahavas, I.: An intelligent modular water monitoring IoT system for real-time quantitative and qualitative measurements. Sustainability **15**(3), 2127 (2023)
73. Jamroen, C., Yonsiri, N., Odthon, T., Wisitthiwong, N., Janreung, S.: A standalone photovoltaic/battery energy-powered water quality monitoring system based on narrowband internet of things for aquaculture: Design and implementation. Smart Agric. Technol. **3**, 100072 (2023)
74. Mantoro, T., Istiono, W.: Saving water with water level detection in a smart home bathtub using ultrasonic sensor and Fuzzy logic. In: 2017 Second International Conference on Informatics and Computing (ICIC), pp. 1–5. IEEE (2017)
75. Xiang, X., Li, Q., Khan, S., Khalaf, O.I.: Urban water resource management for sustainable environment planning using artificial intelligence techniques. Environ. Impact Assess. Rev. **86**, 106515 (2021)
76. Gaikwad, K.: IoT based water management system using MQTT protocol. In: 2021 5th International Conference on Trends in Electronics and Informatics (ICOEI), pp. 408–414. IEEE (2021)

77. Zeng, H., Dhiman, G., Sharma, A., Sharma, A., Tselykh, A.: An IoT and blockchain-based approach for the smart water management system in agriculture. Expert Syst. **40**(4), e12892 (2023)
78. Naqash, M.T., Syed, T.A., Alqahtani, S.S., Siddiqui, M.S., Alzahrani, A., Nauman, M.: A blockchain based framework for efficient water management and leakage detection in urban areas. Urban Sci. **7**(4), 99 (2023)
79. Bogdan, R., Paliuc, C., Crisan-Vida, M., Nimara, S., Barmayoun, D.: Low-cost internet-of-things water-quality monitoring system for rural areas. Sensors **23**(8), 3919 (2023)
80. Parenreng, J.M., Lamada, M.S., Baktiar, N.I.H., Adibah, F., Risal, A.A.N.: A smart water tank for control and monitoring based on IoT technology. Internet Things Artif. Intell. J. **3**(82), 204–219 (2023)
81. Praveen, A., Radhika, R., Sidharth, D., Ambat, S., Anjali, T.: Smart water level monitoring and management system using IoT. In: 2021 6th International Conference on Communication and Electronics Systems (ICCES), pp. 482–487. IEEE (2021)
82. Veselinović, A., Popić, S., Lukać, Ž.: Smart home system solution with the goal of minimizing water consumption. In: 2020 International Symposium on Industrial Electronics and Applications (INDEL), pp. 1–5. IEEE (2020)
83. Mantoro, T., Istiono, W.: Saving water with water level detection in a smart home bathtub using ultrasonic sensor and Fuzzy logic. In: 2017 Second International Conference on Informatics and Computing (ICIC), pp. 1–5. IEEE (2017)
84. Khan, N., Kumar, P., Sadistap, S.: IoT enabled embedded ultrasonic sensor-based water tank level system with pump switching control. AIP Conf. Proc. **2335**(1) (AIP Publishing) (2021)
85. Adedeji, K.B., Hamam, Y., Abe, B.T., Abu-Mahfouz, A.M.: Towards achieving a reliable leakage detection and localization algorithm for application in water piping networks: an overview. IEEE Access **5**, 20272–20285 (2017)
86. Ray, A., Goswami, S.: IoT and cloud computing based smart water metering system. In: 2020 International Conference on Power Electronics & IoT Applications in Renewable Energy and its Control (PARC), pp. 308–313. IEEE (2020)
87. El Sayed, H. Y., Al-Kady, M., Siddik, Y.: Management of smart water treatment plant using IoT cloud services. In: 2019 International Conference on Smart Applications, Communications and Networking (SmartNets), pp. 1–5. IEEE (2019)
88. Díaz, M., Martín, C., Rubio, B.: State-of-the-art, challenges, and open issues in the integration of Internet of things and cloud computing. J. Netw. Comput. Appl. **67**, 99–117 (2016)
89. Djalilov, A., Sobirov, E., Nazarov, O., Urolov, S., Gayipov, I.: Study on automatic water level detection process using ultrasonic sensor. IOP Conf. Ser.: Earth Environ. Sci. **1142**(1), 012020 (IOP Publishing) (2023)
90. Saad, A., Gamatié, A.: Water management in agriculture: a survey on current challenges and technological solutions. IEEE Access **8**, 38082–38097 (2020)
91. Colding, J., Nilsson, C., Sjöberg, S.: Smart cities for all bridging digital divides for socially sustainable and inclusive cities. Smart Cities **7**(3), 1044–1059 (2024)
92. Ashok, M., Madan, R., Joha, A., Sivarajah, U.: Ethical framework for Artificial Intelligence and Digital technologies. Int. J. Inf. Manag. **62**, 102433 (2022)

Chapter 13
Synergising Water Management with Blockchain and Artificial Intelligence: Empowering Sustainable Solutions for the Future

Namrata Prakash, Reeta Rautela, Shravan Kumar, Harleen Kaur, and Parul Dixit

Abstract Population growth, urbanization, and climate change make water management more important. Traditional water management methods can't keep up with these complexities, but Blockchain and AI might transform water resource management and conservation. This chapter examines how Blockchain and AI might improve water management for efficiency, transparency, and sustainability. Blockchain's decentralized and immutable ledger may improve data security and trust among water management players including governments, utility providers, industry, and individuals. To optimize water consumption and reduce water hazards, AI-powered data analytics and predictive modeling may provide real-time monitoring, early warning systems, and intelligent decision-making. The chapter analyzes Blockchain and AI water management applications from diverse countries and highlights successful case studies. Data privacy, interoperability, and legal frameworks are also discussed as implementation issues. The study also discusses how Blockchain's decentralization might secure AI systems and prevent data tampering. In contrast, AI can improve Blockchain protocols for speed and scalability. Blockchain and AI will combine to improve water management transparency, efficiency, and sustainability, according to this report. To accept and adapt to this shift, governments, technology developers, water specialists, and communities must collaborate. These innovative technologies may help mankind secure water for future generations.

N. Prakash
Graphic Era Hill University, Dehradun, India

R. Rautela · S. Kumar (✉)
School of Liberal Arts Uttaranchal University, Dehradun, India
e-mail: kumar4shravan@gmail.com

R. Rautela
e-mail: reetarautela@uumail.in

H. Kaur
Jaypee Institute of Information Technology, Noida, India

P. Dixit
Department of Law DAV PG College, Dehradun, India

S. S. Rawat et al. (eds.), *Unleashing the Power of Blockchain and IoT for Water Informatics*, Water Informatics for Water Resource Management,
https://doi.org/10.1007/978-981-96-3886-4_13

Keywords Artificial intelligence · Blockchain · Data integrity · Sustainable solution · Water management

13.1 Introduction

Water is one of our most precious resources since it is essential to the correct functioning of our ecosystems, businesses, and cities. A combination of factors, including more urbanization, rising populations, more industry, and warmer temperatures, is putting a heavy strain on the world's water resources [1]. Minimizing water consumption sustainably without sacrificing conservation efforts requires the development of innovative technological solutions. The reason for this is the inefficiency of conventional approaches to water management. Managing water resources might be drastically altered by the recent advent of AI and blockchain technology. Blockchain refers to the technology that enables Bitcoin to function. Blockchain is an immutable distributed ledger that transparently records transactions [2]. Implementing a fresh method of data administration aims to guarantee safety, immutability, and confidence among water management stakeholders.

Artificial intelligence (AI) can accomplish everything from intelligent decision-making to real-time monitoring to predictive modeling thanks to data processing and sophisticated algorithms. By analyzing massive amounts of data collected from sensors, satellites, and other sources, artificial intelligence may enhance water distribution, detect leaks, predict future water needs, and mitigate water-related dangers. Artificial intelligence has many more potential uses.

13.1.1 Areas Where Blockchain Technology and AI Can Be Used in Water Management

Figure 13.1 shows different arenas where Blockchain and AI can be implemented like customer information, leakage information, flow information, and pressure management. It can also be used for smart physical distribution of water. Water quality monitoring is also possible and this aids in bringing more efficiency in the whole process. Flood prediction is also possible with accuracy thus reducing losses caused due to floods. Water quality monitoring is also possible.

Water Rights and Allocation: In many regions, water rights and allocation have been historically complex and prone to disputes. Blockchain technology can facilitate transparent and immutable water rights registration, ownership, and transfers. For instance, in a pilot project in California, a Blockchain-based platform was used to manage water rights, allowing farmers and other stakeholders to trade water securely and efficiently. This streamlined process fosters water marketplaces where water can be allocated to its most valuable uses dynamically.

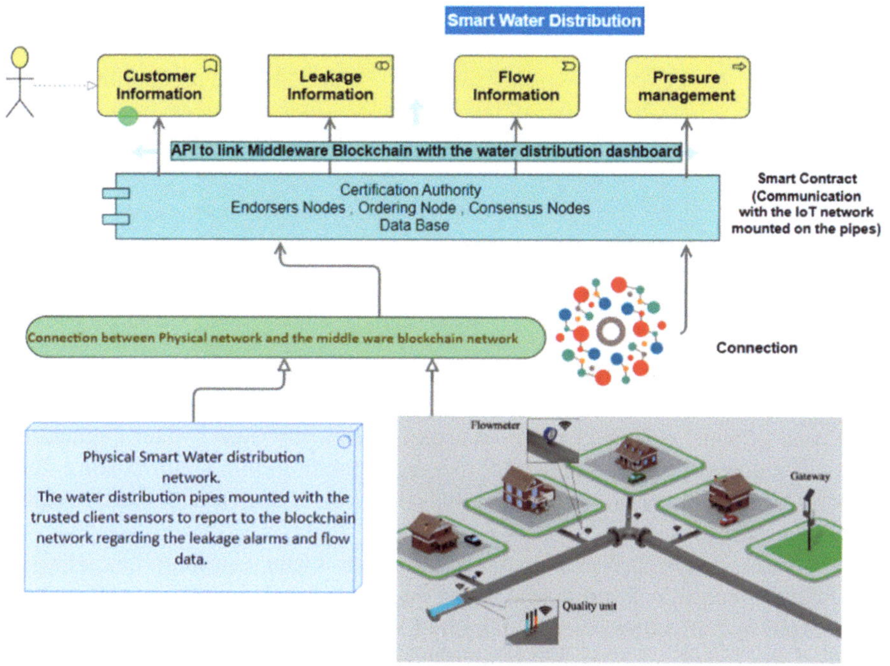

Fig. 13.1 Blockchain and AI in water management

Smart Water Infrastructure: AI integrated with smart sensors can revolutionize water infrastructure management. For instance, in a city facing water distribution challenges, AI-powered sensors installed in pipelines can detect leaks or bursts in real time. The AI algorithms can analyze the data and immediately alert authorities, enabling prompt response and reduced water loss [3].

Water Quality Monitoring: Blockchain and AI can work in tandem to ensure the integrity of water quality data. By storing water quality measurements and analysis results on a Blockchain ledger, the data becomes tamper-proof and verifiable. AI can also analyze this data to identify patterns and trends in water quality, which is crucial for identifying pollution sources and taking timely remedial actions.

Flood Prediction and Management: In areas prone to flooding, AI can analyze weather data, river levels, and historical flood patterns to create predictive models. By combining these predictive models with Blockchain technology, emergency response agencies can issue real-time flood alerts to residents and use smart contracts to trigger automated responses such as opening floodgates or redirecting water flow. These areas illustrate the potential of synergizing Blockchain and AI with water management practices. By harnessing the power of these technologies, we can transform the way we manage and conserve water, leading to a more resilient and sustainable water future for humanity. However, challenges remain, and in the subsequent sections, we will explore existing applications, benefits, and obstacles in implementing these technologies in water management. Figure 13.1 shows how both Blockchain and AI are being used to manage various levels of water management business from water sourcing to operations. Blockchain and AI can make a significant difference in water management by revolutionizing the way water resources are monitored, allocated, and conserved.

13.1.2 The Water Management Challenge: Growing Pressures and Complexities

Some of the challenges are as follows:

Population Growth and Urbanization: The Global Demographic Shift and rapid population growth, especially in urban areas, leads to increased water demand for domestic, industrial, and agricultural purposes. Expanding cities strain existing water infrastructure, resulting in water scarcity, pollution, and challenges in providing equitable access to water.

Industrialization and Water Demand: Industrial Water Consumption: The rise of industries necessitates substantial water usage, leading to potential conflicts with other sectors and affecting water availability for communities and ecosystems. Water Pollution and Industrial Effluents: Industrial activities contribute to water pollution, necessitating proper management and treatment to protect water quality. Climate Change Impacts on Water Resources: Altered Precipitation Patterns and changes in rainfall and snowfall patterns affect water availability and exacerbate droughts or floods in various regions. Rising Sea Levels and Saline Intrusion: Coastal areas face threats of saltwater intrusion into freshwater sources, impacting water supplies for coastal populations.

13.1.3 Blockchain's Impact on Water Management

Blockchain impact on water management is as follows:

Transparency and Trust: Blockchain's decentralized and transparent nature ensures that water-related data, including usage, quality, and ownership, is securely recorded, and shared among stakeholders. This promotes trust and accountability in water management practices, reducing the likelihood of disputes and manipulation of data.

Efficient Water Allocation: Blockchain can facilitate efficient water allocation by enabling water rights to be tokenized and traded as digital assets. Farmers, industries, or municipalities can participate in transparent water markets, allowing water to flow to its most valuable use dynamically.

Secure Water Quality Monitoring: Data from water quality sensors can be stored on the blockchain, creating an immutable record of water quality levels. This prevents tampering and ensures the integrity of data, critical for decision-making and identifying pollution sources.

Decentralized Management: Blockchain's decentralized structure reduces the reliance on centralized authorities, enabling more democratic and inclusive water governance. Local communities and water users can have a greater say in managing their water resources.

Cross-Border Water Management: In transboundary water basins, where multiple countries share water resources, blockchain can facilitate secure data sharing and collaboration, fostering cross-border water cooperation and conflict resolution.

Depleting Groundwater Resources through unsustainable groundwater pumping: Excessive groundwater extraction for agriculture and urban use leads to aquifer depletion and land subsidence in some areas.

Groundwater Contamination: Pollution from industrial activities and inadequate waste disposal practices pose risks to groundwater quality.

Water-Energy Nexus: Energy Production and Water Consumption: The water-intensive nature of energy generation, such as in thermoelectric power plants, puts additional stress on water resources. Reciprocating Impact: Water scarcity can also hinder energy production, affecting hydropower generation and cooling processes for thermal power plants.

Conflicts Over Transboundary Water Resources: Cross-Border Water Management: Shared rivers and basins between countries necessitate collaborative agreements and management mechanisms to prevent disputes. Water scarcity and inequitable access can exacerbate tensions and conflicts between neighboring nations.

Aging Infrastructure: Many countries grapple with outdated water infrastructure, leading to leakages, inefficiencies, and challenges in meeting growing demands.

Investment and Maintenance Gaps: Limited financial resources hinder the construction and maintenance of modern water infrastructure.

Global Water Access Disparities: Millions of people lack access to clean drinking water and proper sanitation facilities, leading to health issues and socio-economic disparities.

13.1.4 AI's Impact on Water Management

AI impact on water management is as follows:

Real-Time Monitoring and Early Warning Systems: AI-powered sensors can continuously monitor water levels, quality, and infrastructure performance in real time. This enables early detection of leaks, floods, or water quality issues, allowing swift responses and minimizing damages.

Data-Driven Decision-Making: AI can analyze vast datasets from various sources to provide valuable insights into water usage patterns, demand trends, and climate impacts. This supports evidence-based decision-making for efficient water resource management.

Water Demand Optimization: AI-driven predictive models can forecast water demand, helping utilities and authorities optimize water supply to meet fluctuating needs. This avoids wastage and ensures adequate supply during peak periods.

Sustainable Agriculture and Irrigation: AI can optimize irrigation systems based on weather forecasts, soil conditions, and crop water requirements, reducing water usage in agriculture and promoting sustainable farming practices.

Flood Prediction and Mitigation: AI algorithms can analyze historical flood data and real-time weather patterns to create flood prediction models. This allows authorities to implement proactive measures to mitigate flood risks and protect communities.

By leveraging the strengths of Blockchain and AI technologies, water management practices can become more efficient, transparent, and sustainable. The synergy of these technologies offers a powerful framework for addressing water challenges in a data-driven, collaborative, and forward-looking manner, ultimately leading to a more secure and resilient water future for our planet.

13.1.5 The Promise of Emerging Technologies: Blockchain and AI-Transforming Water Governance

Decentralized Decision-making and Transparent Accountability: Blockchain's decentralized nature enables distributed governance, allowing stakeholders to actively participate in water management decisions, leading to more inclusive and democratic processes [4]. The transparency provided by blockchain ensures that water-related transactions and data are traceable, holding stakeholders accountable for their actions and fostering responsible water usage.

Securing water rights and allocation and trustworthy water rights management: Blockchain's tamper-proof ledger ensures the secure registration and transfer of water rights, minimizing disputes and enhancing the credibility of water allocations.

Efficient water trading and enhancing water quality monitoring: Blockchain-based smart contracts facilitate seamless and automated water trading, enabling efficient allocation and utilization of water resources.

Immutable Data Integrity: Storing water quality data on the blockchain guarantees its integrity, preventing unauthorized alterations and ensuring reliable information for decision-making and regulatory compliance. Rapid Response to Pollution Incidents: AI-powered sensors can continuously monitor water quality, and in combination with blockchain, enable real-time detection of contaminants, leading to prompt responses and mitigating environmental risks.

Data-Driven Decision Support: AI's data analysis capabilities provide valuable insights into water usage patterns, demand forecasts, and ecosystem health, facilitating informed decisions to optimize water allocation and usage.

Adaptive Water Management: Combining blockchain and AI enables adaptive water management, allowing authorities to respond quickly to changing water conditions, climate shifts, and population dynamics.

Leak Detection and Reduction: AI-driven monitoring systems can detect leaks and inefficiencies in water infrastructure, reducing water losses and conserving valuable resources.

Water Demand Forecasting: AI models can forecast water demand, helping communities and industries plan more efficiently and reduce unnecessary water usage.

Trust-Building Mechanism: Blockchain's transparency and immutability foster trust among neighboring countries sharing transboundary water resources, encouraging collaborative efforts and conflict resolution. Data Sharing and Information Exchange: Blockchain facilitates secure and standardized data sharing, enabling countries to exchange hydrological data and coordinate water management efforts effectively.

Data Collaboration and Insights: The integration of AI and blockchain encourages data sharing among researchers and institutions, accelerating water-related research and innovation.

Resilient Water Systems: Blockchain and AI offer the foundation for building resilient water systems capable of adapting to changing environmental conditions and population dynamics.

The promise of blockchain and AI in water management lies in their ability to bring transparency, efficiency, and intelligence to a sector facing increasing pressures and complexities. Embracing these technologies offers opportunities to tackle water-related challenges effectively and empower stakeholders to work collectively toward a sustainable water future.

13.1.6 Addressing Challenges and Barriers in Integrating Blockchain and AI Technologies

While the integration of Blockchain and AI technologies holds great promise for water management, several challenges and barriers need to be addressed to fully realize their potential [5]. Overcoming these obstacles will require collaborative efforts from governments, technology developers, water experts, and communities. Some of the key challenges include:

Data Privacy and Security Concerns: As water-related data becomes more accessible through blockchain and AI applications, ensuring data privacy and security becomes paramount. Robust encryption and authentication mechanisms are necessary to protect sensitive information from unauthorized access or data breaches.

Interoperability and Integration Challenges: Existing water management systems often use diverse data formats and standards. Achieving seamless integration between different technologies and platforms is essential to enable effective data sharing and collaboration.

Regulatory and Legal Frameworks: The adoption of blockchain and AI in water management may require updates to existing regulations and the creation of new frameworks. Legal challenges related to data ownership, liability, and compliance must be addressed to foster confidence in these technologies. Limited Technology Literacy: Implementing blockchain and AI solutions demands a level of technological literacy from water management stakeholders. Ensuring adequate training and support to enable their effective use is crucial, especially in rural and less technologically advanced regions.

Initial Investment and Costs: Implementing and maintaining blockchain and AI systems can require significant initial investment. Convincing stakeholders of the long-term benefits and cost savings will be essential to secure funding for these projects. Limited Data Availability: In some regions, access to comprehensive and reliable water-related data may be limited. This can hinder the development and effectiveness of AI models and blockchain applications. Efforts to improve data collection and sharing mechanisms are essential.

Resistance to Change: Embracing new technologies can face resistance from established systems and stakeholders. Overcoming inertia and fostering a culture of innovation are necessary to drive adoption and acceptance.

Scalability: As water management involves vast and complex systems, ensuring the scalability of blockchain and AI solutions is crucial. These technologies must handle increasing amounts of data and users without compromising performance.

Environmental Impact: Blockchain, particularly in the case of some cryptocurrencies, can consume significant energy. Efforts to implement more energy-efficient consensus mechanisms and promote sustainable practices in the blockchain space are essential.

Ethical and Social Considerations: Decisions made using AI algorithms should be transparent, fair, and accountable. Avoiding biases and ensuring inclusivity is essential to prevent unintended social and environmental consequences.

To address these challenges, collaboration between the public and private sectors, research institutions, and civil society is essential. Pilot projects and partnerships can help demonstrate the effectiveness of blockchain and AI in water management while providing valuable insights into potential improvements and adaptations. Public awareness campaigns can also play a role in fostering support for these technologies and highlighting their importance in addressing the growing water challenges faced by societies worldwide.

13.1.7 Worldwide Successful Implementations of Blockchain and AI in Water Management

Some of the applications built on blockchain and AI are as follows: Blockchain-based Water Trading in Australia: Australia is known for its arid climate and water scarcity challenges and has implemented a successful blockchain-based water trading platform to manage water rights and allocations. The platform, developed by an Australian tech firm, utilizes blockchain's transparency and immutability to create a secure and efficient marketplace for water trading. Farmers, industries, and other water users can buy and sell water rights in real time, based on market demand and supply [6]. The decentralized nature of the platform has increased transparency, reduced transaction costs, and minimized the risk of fraud, ensuring a fair and reliable water trading system.

Impact: The blockchain-based water trading platform has enabled water users to optimize their water usage, particularly during dry periods, and promote efficient water allocation. Farmers have been able to access water when needed, enhancing agricultural productivity and resilience during droughts. The success of this project has garnered interest from other regions facing water scarcity, showcasing the potential of blockchain in water management.

AI-powered Water Quality Monitoring in Singapore-Singapore: a densely populated island nation, faces challenges in ensuring water quality across its water supply network. The Singapore Public Utilities Board (PUB) has integrated AI-powered sensors and analytics into its water quality monitoring system. These sensors continuously collect data on water quality parameters such as pH, turbidity, and contaminants. AI algorithms analyze the data in real time, detecting anomalies and identifying potential pollution incidents. Automated alerts are sent to PUB authorities, allowing rapid response and appropriate remedial actions.

Impact: The AI-powered water quality monitoring system has significantly improved the detection of water quality issues, allowing PUB to respond promptly to contamination incidents. This has led to better protection of Singapore's water resources, ensuring the delivery of safe and clean drinking water to its residents. Additionally, the system's early warning capabilities have minimized the impact of pollution on aquatic ecosystems, reinforcing Singapore's commitment to sustainable water management.

Blockchain-based water management in the State of Karnataka, India has been facing water management challenges due to its rapidly growing population and varying water availability. In the state of Karnataka, a pilot project was launched to implement a blockchain-based water management system. The project aimed to address water allocation issues by providing a transparent and tamper-proof platform for recording water usage and enforcing regulations. Water authorities, farmers, and industries participated in the platform, which allowed for the efficient allocation of water resources based on real-time data.

Impact: The blockchain-based water management system in Karnataka has improved water allocation, reducing conflicts over water rights and usage [7]. The transparent and auditable nature of the platform has instilled trust among stakeholders, leading to better compliance with water regulations. The pilot project's success has encouraged further exploration of blockchain applications in water management across other states in India.

These studies demonstrate the successful implementation of blockchain and AI in water management, showcasing their potential in addressing water challenges globally. By leveraging the strengths of these technologies, countries like Australia, Singapore, and India have made significant strides toward more efficient, transparent, and sustainable water management practices. As technology continues to evolve, these innovations hold promise for further advancements in water resource management worldwide.

13.1.8 Future of Water Management in the Era of Blockchain and Artificial Intelligence Scalability and Expansion of Applications

As technology continues to evolve, scalability will become a crucial factor for widespread adoption. Innovations in blockchain consensus mechanisms and AI algorithms will enable these technologies to handle larger datasets and cater to the needs of growing water management systems.

Collaborative Governance Models: The integration of blockchain and AI can foster collaborative governance models, where multiple stakeholders actively participate in decision-making [8]. Decentralized platforms will facilitate more inclusive water management, incorporating the insights and preferences of local communities and water users.

Potential for Global Water Crisis Mitigation: The combination of blockchain and AI holds the potential to address the global water crisis by providing innovative solutions to water scarcity, pollution, and mismanagement. Widely adopted blockchain-based water markets and AI-driven water allocation models can optimize water use on a large scale.

Role of Academia, Industry, and Governments: Collaboration between academia, industry, and governments will be critical in advancing research, development, and policy frameworks for blockchain and AI in water management [9]. Partnerships and knowledge exchange will accelerate innovations and ensure responsible implementation.

Enhanced Disaster Resilience: AI-powered early warning systems, integrated with blockchain data sharing, will enhance disaster resilience. Governments and communities will receive real-time alerts about potential floods, droughts, or water quality issues, enabling proactive responses to mitigate risks.

Smart Water Infrastructure and Cities: The integration of blockchain and AI will pave the way for smart water infrastructure and cities. AI-driven sensors, connected through blockchain, will monitor water networks, optimizing usage and minimizing water losses in urban areas.

Improved Water Resource Prediction: AI models will become more accurate and sophisticated, improving water resource prediction and forecasting [10]. This will enable long-term planning and proactive measures to manage water availability and demand effectively. Decentralized Water Management in Developing Regions: Blockchain's decentralized nature can be particularly advantageous in developing regions with limited centralized infrastructure. By using blockchain and AI, these areas can leapfrog traditional water management approaches, improving access and efficiency.

Incentivizing Water Conservation: Blockchain-based water trading platforms can incentivize water conservation by providing rewards for sustainable practices. Water users who efficiently manage water resources can earn tokens that can be traded or used for other benefits.

Global Data Sharing and Collaboration: Blockchain's ability to facilitate secure and standardized data sharing will foster international collaboration on water-related research and management. Governments and organizations can share hydrological data and best practices, collectively addressing global water challenges.

13.2 Conclusion

Population growth, urbanization, and climate change make sustainable water management crucial. Using Blockchain and AI to secure water is new. Combining these advanced methods might change water resource allocation, management, and conservation. Blockchain's openness, trust, and efficiency may allow decentralized decision-making, secure water rights management, and efficient water trading. AI data analysis and forecasting enhance decision-making, water distribution, water quality detection, and water event response.

Case studies in Australia, Singapore, and India demonstrate blockchain and AI water management success. AI-driven water quality monitoring and water trading platforms have solved water issues and improved resource management. Water management using blockchain and AI sounds promising. Scalable applications, collaborative governance, and global water crisis mitigation are coming. Smart water infrastructure and cities, early warning systems, and decentralized water management are possible in developing countries. Governments, industries, colleges, and communities must protect water using these revolutionary technologies. Data protection, interoperability, and early investment are essential. Raising awareness, sharing knowledge, and creating deployment rules need collaboration. Blockchain and AI can enhance water management transparency, efficiency, and sustainability, ensuring equal access to clean water, ecosystem conservation, and future water resource protection. Creative ideas and technology can help everyone and the community live in peace with nature's most valuable resource: water. Blockchain and AI will improve water management, making it more resilient, equitable, and sustainable. These technologies will transform water governance and resource optimization, assuring future water security. To benefit from these achievements, challenges must be solved and execution assured.

References

1. Anderson, M.K., Jackson, S.R.: Blockchain Applications in Water Management. Springer (2021)
2. Bordel, B., Martin, D., Alcarria, R., and Robles, T.: Blockchain-based water control system for the automatic management of irrigation communities. In: 2019 IEEE International Conference on Consumer Electronics (ICCE) (IEEE), pp. 1–2 (2019). https://doi.org/10.1109/ICCE.2019.8661940
3. Dogo, E.M., Salami, A.F., Nwulu, N.I., Aigbavboa, C.O.: Blockchain and internet of things-based technologies for intelligent water management system. In: Al-Turjman, F. (ed.) Artificial Intelligence in IoT, pp. 129–150. Springer Publishing (2019). https://doi.org/10.1007/978-3-030-04110-6_7
4. Grigoras, G., Bizon, N., Enescu, F.M., Lopez Guede, J.M., Salado, G.F., Brennan, R., et al.: ICT based smart management solution to realize water and energy savings through energy efficiency measures in water distribution systems. In: 2018 10th International Conference on Electronics, Computers and Artificial Intelligence (ECAI) (IEEE), pp. 1–4 (2018). https://doi.org/10.1109/ECAI.2018.8679012
5. Lee, C., Williams, R.: AI-driven water demand prediction for smart water allocation. In: Proceedings of the International Conference on Water Resources Management, pp. 45–58. Springer (2023)
6. Mahmoud, H.H.M., Wu, W., Wang, Y.: Secure data aggregation mechanism for water distribution system using blockchain. In: 2019 25th International Conference on Automation and Computing (ICAC) (IEEE), pp. 1–6. https://doi.org/10.23919/IConAC.2019.8895146
7. Pahontu, B., Arsene, D., Predescu, A., Mocanu, M.: Application and challenges of blockchain technology for real-time operation in a water distribution system. In: 24th International Conference on System Theory, Control and Computing (ICSTCC) (IEEE), pp. 739–744 (2020). https://doi.org/10.1109/ICSTCC50638.2020.9259732
8. Smith, J.D., Johnson, A.B.: Leveraging blockchain and AI for sustainable water management. Water Resour. Res. **48**(5), 123–137 (2022)
9. United Nations World Water Assessment Programme (WWAP).: The use of AI and blockchain in water management. UNESCO (2019)
10. World Bank.: Blockchain and AI in water management: a global perspective. World Bank (2020)

Chapter 14
Sustainability Through Water Informatics Using Blockchain and Future Prospects

Kashika Jain and Hiti Bansal

Abstract To address issues of leakage, inefficient distribution, and water scarcity, sustainable urban water management is crucial. An introduction, a summary of water management techniques, the features and operation of water distribution systems, smart systems for optimization, monitoring, and control systems for effective distribution, strategies for water conservation and waste management, analysis of per capita water demand and overviews of desalination plants are all included in this paper on water management in urban areas. A blockchain-based water management architecture incorporating Internet of Things sensors is suggested in the article for precise reporting. To verify and transfer data in real time between sensors and the dashboard for water distribution, the framework makes use of blockchain technology. In order to reduce water waste and improve distribution, it also features a modular API for flow control and leak detection. The recommended strategy might improve water management; its execution is intricate, nevertheless. This paper provides information on water management and proposes a technology for dependable data reporting and effective water distribution that leverages blockchain technology and Internet of Things sensors.

Keywords Blockchain technology · IoT · Hydro informatics · Sensors · Sustainability · Water leakage · Water management

14.1 Introduction

Being an interdisciplinary field that crosses the lines between computer science, data science, and water science, hydro informatics is always changing and reinventing itself. The process of critically evaluating oneself and the discipline's past, present,

K. Jain (✉)
Amity University, Noida, India
e-mail: kashikajainsinghal@gmail.com

H. Bansal
Shiva Shiksha Sadan, Sonepat, Haryana, India

S. S. Rawat et al. (eds.), *Unleashing the Power of Blockchain and IoT for Water Informatics*, Water Informatics for Water Resource Management,
https://doi.org/10.1007/978-981-96-3886-4_14

and future progress is fundamental to its evolution because it fosters a constructive feedback loop between goals, reality, and legacy. The success of hydro informatics thus far, which has arguably been able to mobilize broad research and development and bring the water sector more in line with the digital revolution of the previous 30 years, attests to the potency of this process.

Though water covers two-thirds of the world, just one percent of it is suitable for human use. Freshwater makes up 2.5%, but most of it is confined to the poles or the deep earth. With 7 billion individuals, this leaves us with around 0.4% to divide among ourselves. Water scarcity means that almost 4.5 billion of the population does not have access to clean water. Approximately one in three individuals worldwide faces the scarcity of drinking water. Figure 14.1 displays how severe water scarcity is predicted to get by 2040 below. Humans are the only ones to blame for the rapidly increasing global warming under the guise of civilization and the industrial revolution, which has led to a serious water shortage worldwide [11–14]. A few years ago, Cape Town, South Africa, experienced the worst-case scenario of water scarcity. Lack of water can have serious repercussions for agriculture, energy, and other related industries, affecting not only the socioeconomic environment but also the ability of humans to survive on a fundamental level. Increasing urbanization-related deforestation, population expansion that is happening far faster than expected, growing industrialization, and commercialization are the main causes of the dangerously high levels of climate change and the plague of water scarcity.

Using data and information technology to effectively manage water resources and guarantee their availability and quality for both the present and future generations is known as sustainability through water informatics [15–18]. An outline of the ways in which water informatics supports sustainability can be found by finding essential elements of Water Informatics using data gathering and tracking. Sensors

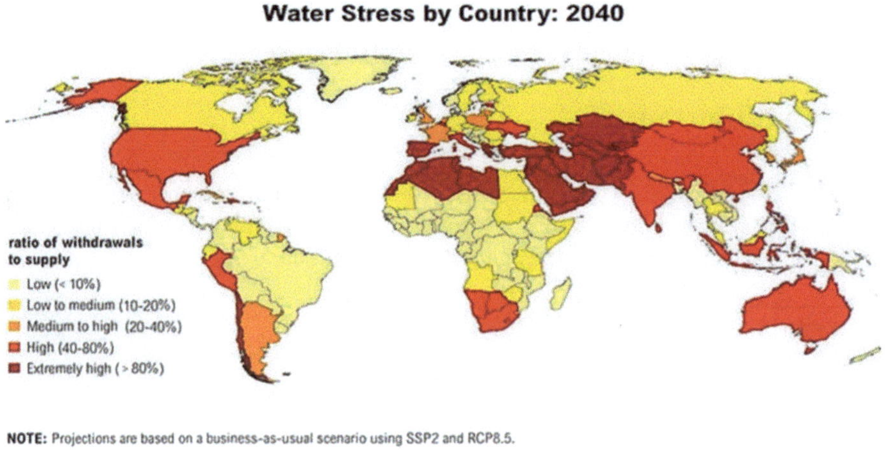

Fig. 14.1 Projected water stress in different countries by 2040 [19]

and Internet of Things devices are positioned in pipes, reservoirs, and water bodies to continuously check the water's quality, level, and flow rate.

Data on water bodies, land usage, and weather patterns are gathered using remote sensing, which uses satellites and drones. Smart meters are installed in homes and businesses to monitor water usage in real time. Modeling and Data Analysis have to be performed by processing massive amounts of data to find trends, patterns, and anomalies which is known as big data analytics. Using AI and machine learning, it can be forecasted using future water demand, locating possible sources of contamination, and distributing water as efficiently as possible.

Hydrological modeling is the technique of simulating the water cycle in order to comprehend and forecast how different water systems will behave. Graphical representation of spatial data pertaining to water resources. Combining information from multiple sources to present an all-encompassing picture of the infrastructure, utilization, and resources. Water managers and policymakers can use Decision Support Systems (DSS) to help them make decisions on the basis of modeling results and data analysis. Public awareness campaigns can help in teaching local populations about sustainable practices and water conservation. Encouraging collaboration across communities, businesses, and governments in order to efficiently manage water resources is known as stakeholder collaboration. Giving accurate and easily obtainable information on the state of water resources and management initiatives results in transparency. By weighing the advantages of water informatics systems against the price of installation and upkeep is a tedious task.

14.1.1 Water Management Techniques

An essential component of agriculture, urban development, and environmental sustainability is water management. Techniques for managing water resources effectively guarantee their efficient use, conservation, and protection from pollution. The following are a few popular and useful methods for managing water:

Rainwater Harvesting This method involves gathering and preserving rainwater for use in drinking, irrigation, and other applications. Its benefits include lowering the pressure on groundwater, offering a substitute water source, and lessening the effects of flooding.

Effective Watering Systems Drip irrigation uses a network of emitters, valves, and tubes to supply water to the plants. Water is dispersed through the atmosphere in a fashion akin to rainfall. Its benefits include less evaporation loss, increased crop output, and decreased water waste.

Wastewater Treatment and Reuse Removing impurities from wastewater in order to safely repurpose it for industrial, agricultural, or even drinking purposes. Its benefits include lowering pollution, protecting freshwater resources, and supplying water in a sustainable manner.

Groundwater Recharge Methods to augment the quantity of water that seeps into the earth to restore aquifers. Techniques: Permeable pavements, recharge wells, and infiltration basins. It helps to prevent land subsidence, maintains groundwater levels, and guarantees long-term water supplies.

Desalination The process of creating fresh water by filtering out salt and other contaminants from brackish or saltwater by distillation and reverse osmosis. It supports expanding populations in coastal areas and offers a dependable supply of water in desert places.

Water-Sparing Fixtures and Appliances It helps in utilizing water-efficient appliances like low-flow showerheads, toilets, and faucets.

14.1.2 Features of Water Conservation

Water conservation is important for the management of our limited water resources. Here are several strategies for conserving water:

Residential Water Conservation Install Water-Saving Fixtures: Make use of low-flow faucets, toilets, and showerheads. These can save water use considerably without compromising functionality. Fix Leaks: Fix leaking pipes, running toilets, and dripping faucets. Over time, even tiny leaks can waste a significant quantity of water. Efficient Kitchenware: Select water-saving appliances, such as dishwashers and washing machines. Seek out the Energy Star or WaterSense labels. Intelligent Landscaping: Employ xeriscaping, a technique that employs plants resistant to drought, and utilizes mulch to hold onto soil moisture. To reduce evaporation, water plants, and lawns in the early morning or late at night. Rainwater Harvesting: To gather rainwater for outdoor cleaning and other uses.

Agricultural Water Conservation Drip Irrigation: Reduce evaporation and runoff by applying drip irrigation to the plants. Soil Moisture Monitoring: To make sure crops receive the proper amount of water, use soil moisture sensors to optimize irrigation schedules. Crop Selection: Choose drought-resistant crop varieties and adjust planting schedules to align with rainfall patterns. Efficient Irrigation Practices: Implement irrigation scheduling based on weather conditions and crop needs to avoid over-watering.

Industrial Water Conservation Water Recycling and Reuse: Recycle water within industrial processes. Treat and reuse wastewater for cooling and other non-potable purposes. Closed-Loop Systems: Implement closed-loop cooling and heating systems to minimize water usage. Efficient Equipment: Invest in water-efficient equipment and regularly maintain it to prevent leaks and inefficiencies. Process Optimization: Optimize industrial processes to reduce water consumption and improve overall efficiency.

Municipal Water Conservation Infrastructure Maintenance: Maintain the water sources for prevention of leaks, etc. Public Awareness Campaigns: Inform people about the importance of water saving. Water Pricing: Implement the methods to conserve water pricing. Regulations and Incentives: Enforce water-saving regulations and offer incentives for households and businesses that adopt water conservation measures. D.Policy and Governance.

Integrated Water Resource Management (IWRM): Implement IWRM practices considering the holistic management of water resources across various sectors. Water Rights and Allocation: Develop equitable water rights and allocation systems to ensure sustainable usage and prevent over-extraction. Climate-Resilient Planning: Incorporate climate change projections into water management planning to ensure future water availability.

Personal Habits and Lifestyle Changes Shorter Showers: Reduce shower time to save water. Turn Off Taps: Turn the tap off when not brushing, etc. Full Loads Only: Use the washing machine when fully loaded. Use a Broom: Use a broom instead of a hose to clean driveways and sidewalks.

14.1.3 Analysis of Per Capita Water Demand

Per capita water demand is a critical metric for water resource planning and management. It represents the average amount of water used by one person in a specific area, typically measured in liters or gallons per day. Key factors influencing per capita water demand include:

Residential Usage Water used for drinking, cooking, bathing, cleaning, and landscaping.

Economic Activity Industrial and commercial water use varies significantly based on the type of industry and economic activities predominant in the area.

Climate Regions with hotter climates may have higher per capita water demand due to increased needs for irrigation, cooling, and hydration.

Population Density Higher density can lead to more efficient water use due to shared resources and infrastructure, but it can also increase demand for local water supplies.

Cultural and Lifestyle Factors Differences in lifestyle, cultural practices, and public awareness about water conservation can impact water consumption patterns.

Analyzing per capita water demand involves:

Data Collection Gathering data from household surveys, water utility records, and censuses.

Trend Analysis Examining historical data to identify trends and patterns in water usage.

Forecasting Using statistical models to predict future water demand based on population growth, economic development, and climate change projections.

Benchmarking Comparing per capita water usage across different regions or countries to identify best practices and areas for improvement.

14.1.4 Desalination Plants

Desalination plants are facilities that remove salts and other impurities from seawater or brackish water to produce fresh water suitable for drinking and irrigation. There are two primary methods of desalination:

Thermal Desalination Includes processes such as multi-stage flash (MSF) and multiple-effect distillation (MED), where seawater is heated, and the vapor is condensed to produce fresh water.

Membrane Desalination Involves reverse osmosis (RO) and electrodialysis, where seawater is forced through semi-permeable membranes that filter out salts and impurities.

Key Components and Process Some of the key components and processes are as follows:

Intake Seawater is drawn into the plant through screened pipes to prevent large debris from entering.

Pretreatment The water undergoes pretreatment to remove suspended solids and reduce fouling of the membranes or evaporators.

Desalination The core process of removing salts. In RO, high-pressure pumps push water through membranes. In thermal methods, water is boiled, and the steam is condensed.

Post-treatment The desalinated water is remineralized and disinfected to ensure it meets drinking water standards.

Brine Disposal The concentrated salt solution (brine) is managed to minimize environmental impact, often discharged back into the sea, and carefully diffused to avoid harming marine life.

Benefits Reliable Water Source: Provides a consistent water supply independent of rainfall, critical for arid regions and islands.

High Quality: Produces very pure water, which can be blended with other water sources.

Challenges High Energy Consumption: Desalination is energy-intensive, contributing to high operational costs and carbon emissions.

Environmental Impact: Discharge of brine can harm marine ecosystems if not managed properly.

Capital Costs: High initial investment for building desalination plants and associated infrastructure.

14.2 Literature Survey

Asgari and Nemati concluded that although DLT has a lot of promise to change smart water systems, there are a number of practical, legal, and technological issues that must be resolved in order to fully realize this potential. To overcome these obstacles and prove the practicality of DLT in water management, more study and experimental projects are needed.

Smart water systems can increase their sustainability, efficiency, and transparency by utilizing DLT's advantages, which will improve the management of this vital resource [1].

The authors concluded that blockchain technology holds significant promise for the sustainable management of electricity and water consumption. However, realizing this potential requires overcoming technical, regulatory, and integration challenges. Continued research, policy development, and collaborative efforts are essential to fully harness the benefits of blockchain in these critical sectors [2].

The paper explores how the combination of blockchain and IoT technologies can be utilized to develop intelligent water management systems that enhance efficiency, transparency, and sustainability. The integration of IoT for real-time data collection and blockchain for secure data management and automation forms the basis of the proposed intelligent system [3].

Industrial wastewater management is crucial to preserving the health of many ecosystems because improper disposal of industrial waste pollutes water and land. Before the leftover water is released into the environment, wastewater treatment aims to clean and preserve the water as well as eliminate contaminants and toxicants. Because industrial wastewater poses a major hazard to aquatic life and the surrounding ecosystem, its disposal is a matter of great importance today. Wastewater must so be appropriately treated before being released into bodies of water [4].

Water has become an urgent theme in the anthropology field also as the worldwide need to provide adequate supplies of clean water to all people becomes more challenging. Anthropologists contribute by seeing water not only as a resource, but also as a substance that connects many realms of social life. They trace the different forms of valuing water, examine the often unequal distribution of water, explore the rules and institutions that govern water use and shape water politics, and study the multiple, often conflicting knowledge systems through which actors understand water. They offer ethnographic insights into key water sites-watersheds, water regimes, and waterscapes-found in all settings, though with widely varying characteristics [5, 6].

Since water is one of the most valuable resources in our life, there is a steady increase in interest in water management systems. One of the main issues with urban water distribution is how to create reliable systems that make it easier to monitor water flows while encouraging customer participation. Using incentives and rewards, crowdsourcing solutions help people participate in social media platforms to raise awareness of the value of water resources. Among the technology that has gained popularity over the past several years is blockchain. Many options and methods for creating contemporary applications are provided by the potential to use this architecture in so many different industries while including cutting-edge ideas like crowdsensing, the Internet of Things, serious gaming, and decision support systems [7].

Blockchain technology has been applied to various sectors of industry and academics, including the water domain, to digitalize data management and physical asset management procedures. In the field of hydrology and water resources, its potential as an immutable data storage system and smart contract integration has produced a multitude of use cases and utilities. This comprehensive analysis looks closely at how blockchain technology is being used in hydrology and water resources [8].

Blockchain is a very popular technology that is being used more and more in many different sectors because of its benefits in distributed storage, data openness, and traceability [9].

This article begins with the current issues surrounding the protection of water resources and then goes into great detail about the features of blockchain technology, as well as the scenarios and ways in which blockchain can be applied to the field of protecting water resources, including the storage of data about water bodies, multi-sectoral collaboration, increased public participation, and more. It also discusses the reasons why the existing blockchain cannot be used extensively or in the field of water preservation, such as disparate standards, resource consumption, and a lack of appropriate human technological base [10–13].

WSDM, or water supply and demand management, is crucial to the growth of sustainable communities and cities. Only when approached from the standpoint of a comprehensive system knowledge that takes into account the social, environmental, hydrological, and economic (SEHEc) sub-systems can WSDM be effectively implemented. Researchers studying water resources advise using System Dynamics Modeling (SDM) since it simulates the biophysical and socioeconomic systems. The proposed work of the evaluated articles took into account the modeling methodology and the SEHEc sub-systems. This analysis showed that only 58% of the research used the causal loop diagram (CLD) for problem conceptualization [14–17].

The water sector must transition from its current business-as-usual methods to sustainable frameworks due to the increased importance of the environment and society at large. Due to the industry's reliance on traditional techniques, service delivery and the achievement of the Sustainable Development Goals are now lacking. Although they have been put into practice, sustainable tactics are not expected to pay off for some time. The industry's state of disarray has made it necessary to incorporate sustainable efforts like Industry 4.0 technologies and the circular economy [18].

14.3 Methodology

In the proposed work, InterPlanetary File System (IPFS) and blockchain are used in a hybrid strategy that combines IPFS's distributed file storage capabilities with the immutability and security of blockchain technology to streamline IoT-driven data. The main issues with managing IoT data, such as data security, scalability, traceability, and effective data storage, are addressed by this methodology. The three main parts of the proposed architecture are IPFS storage, blockchain infrastructure, and Internet of Things devices. Data is gathered by IoT devices and sent to a blockchain network for safe storage and verification. The distributed file system IPFS is used to store the actual data content, while the blockchain is used as a ledger for data hashes and metadata to guarantee immutability and integrity. The layers in the suggested methodology are as follows.

14.3.1 Network Layer of the Internet of Things

There are two classes of devices at this tier. First, Internet of Things devices with limited computing, networking, and storage power. Second, IoT data streaming devices with adequate processing, networking, and storage capacity.

14.3.2 Blockchain Layer

Blockchain operates as a decentralized network by using blockchain storage entities. There is an exact duplicate of the entire system for each of these items. It takes a lot of throughput and storage capacity to store IoT data files directly on the blockchain because they are often huge—many megabytes in size. Consequently, the fixed-size hash value—which is many kilobytes—is the only value stored on the blockchain.

14.3.3 Distributed Storage Layer

It can be challenging to use blockchain technology and guarantee privacy and transparency at the same time. Comparing IPFS to more established suppliers, the advantages are evident. First of all, it eliminates single points of failure, avoids node trust, and ensures globally distributed data storage. Web methods and IPFS file preservation and retrieval is comparable. Files that are uploaded are given unique hash IDs, just like URLs. Blockchain file storage, on the other hand, prioritizes transparency, which makes it unsuitable for large data sets. In order to store and retrieve data off-chain for public blockchain, this study uses SCs. After authentication, IPFS leverages blockchain SCs to grant file access when users request actions on specific resources. IoT devices gather data from their specific settings thanks to a variety of sensors on board. At the edge, this data undergoes pre-processing that includes encryption, compression, and data filtering. The pre-processing step ensures that only relevant and secure data is sent to the blockchain network, reducing the overall data load and preserving confidentiality. Once data is collected and pre-processed, it is stored in IPFS, which uses a distributed hash table (DHT) to ensure efficient retrieval and sharing. Each stored file or data block on IPFS is assigned a unique hash, which is a cryptographic representation of the data's content. Figure 14.2 shows the proposed framework using IoT sensors and blockchain.

14.3.4 Steps Used in the Proposed Framework

The blockchain component stores metadata pertaining to the IoT data stored in IPFS, serving as a secure ledger. On the blockchain, a transaction is created for every IPFS data block that is stored. The IPFS hash, timestamp, and pertinent metadata (such as device ID, data type, and location) are all contained in this transaction. This structure guarantees the integrity and validity of the data and enables the blockchain to act as a source of truth for the provenance of the data. On the blockchain, smart contracts are used to automate procedures and enforce data access guidelines.

Conditions for data exchange, such as device authentication, user authorization, and data retention guidelines, can be specified in these contracts. Furthermore, smart contracts can automate workflows by setting off alarms or messages in the event that particular criteria are satisfied in the IoT data as shown in Fig. 14.3. Users or apps query the blockchain to get the pertinent IPFS hashes in order to get data. These hashes enable speedy data retrieval from IPFS. A mismatch between the stored hash and the returned data would indicate tampering, thus the distributed ledger of the blockchain ensures that the data is checked for integrity and validity. Privacy and security are of paramount importance.

Data integrity and resistance to manipulation are ensured by the decentralized and encrypted nature of blockchain. Sensitive data saved on IPFS can be encrypted, and smart contracts can be used to provide access control measures. Furthermore, IPFS's

Fig. 14.2 Proposed methodology

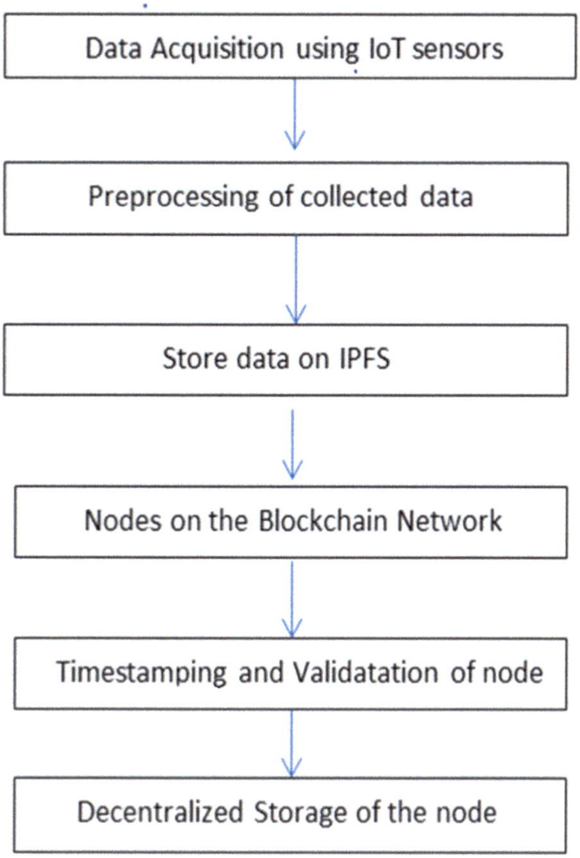

distributed architecture lowers the number of single points of failure, improving system reliability overall. Figure 14.3 shows the snippet of code for the data acquisition using IoT sensors.

The Internet of Things (IoT) ecosystem's integration of blockchain technology and the InterPlanetary File System (IPFS) provide a strong answer to many of the problems associated with IoT data management. Ensuring the security and integrity of data as it flows through the system is one of the main problems in IoT. IPFS and blockchain offer strong mechanisms to deal with these problems. The intrinsic immutability of blockchain technology helps to maintain the security of the network. The backend server receives data from the IoT sensors, stores it on IPFS, and then records the IPFS hash on the blockchain as shown by Fig. 14.4.

The smart contract stores the IPFS hash on the blockchain. Figure 14.5 shows a Solidity smart contract.

Next step is to deploy the Solidity contract to a blockchain network to a local blockchain like Ganache. This setup provides a robust solution for managing water quality data using IoT, IPFS, and blockchain. The IoT devices collect data, which

```
import time
import Adafruit_DHT  # For temperature and humidity sensor
import Adafruit_ADS1x15  # For analog to digital conversion (e.g., pH
sensor)
# Initialize the sensors
DHT_SENSOR = Adafruit_DHT.DHT22
DHT_PIN = 4  # GPIO pin
adc = Adafruit_ADS1x15.ADS1115()
GAIN = 1

def read_temperature_and_humidity():
    humidity, temperature = Adafruit_DHT.read_retry(DHT_SENSOR,
DHT_PIN)
    if humidity is not None and temperature is not None:
        return humidity, temperature
    else:
        return None, None

def read_ph():
    ph_value = adc.read_adc(0, gain=GAIN)
    return ph_value

def main():
    while True:
        humidity, temperature = read_temperature_and_humidity()
        ph_value = read_ph()

        if humidity is not None and temperature is not None:
            print(f"Temp: {temperature:.2f} C  Humidity: {humidity:.2f}%
pH: {ph_value}")

        # TODO: Add code to send data to a backend server
```

Fig. 14.3 Code snippet for data acquisition using IoT sensors

is then stored on IPFS. The IPFS hash is recorded on the blockchain via a backend server, ensuring data transparency and immutability.

```
from flask import Flask, request, json ify
from web3 import Web3
import ipfs http client
app = Flask(__name__)
# Connect to blockchain (example using Ganache local blockchain)
web3 = Web3(Web3.HTTPProvider('http://127.0.0.1:7545'))
contract_address = '0xYourContractAddress'
contract_abi = '[...]' # Contract ABI
contract = web3.eth.contract(address=contract_address, abi=contract_abi)
# Connect to IPFS
ipfs = ipfshttpclient.connect('/ip4/127.0.0.1/tcp/5001')
@app.route('/data', methods=['POST'])
def receive_data():
   data = request.get_json()
   temperature = data.get('temperature')
   humidity = data.get('humidity')
   ph_value = data.get('ph_value')
      # Store data on IPFS
   res = ipfs.add_json(data)
   ipfs_hash = res['Hash']
      # Store IPFS hash on blockchain
   tx_hash = contract.functions.storeWaterData(ipfs_hash).transact({'from': web3.eth.accounts[0]})
   web3.eth.waitForTransactionReceipt(tx_hash)
      return jsonify({"status": "success", "tx_hash": tx_hash.hex(), "ipfs_hash": ipfs_hash})
```

Fig. 14.4 Code snippet for IPFS storage

```
pragma solidity ^0.8.0;
contract WaterQuality {
   struct WaterData {
      uint256 timestamp;
      string ipfsHash;
   }
   WaterData[] public data;
   event DataStored(uint256 indexed timestamp, string ipfsHash);
   function storeWaterData(string memory ipfsHash) public {
      data.push(WaterData(block.timestamp, ipfsHash));
      emit DataStored(block.timestamp, ipfsHash);
   }
   function getData(uint256 index) public view returns (uint256, string memory) {
      WaterData memory waterData = data[index];
      return (waterData.timestamp, waterData.ipfsHash);
   }
}
```

Fig. 14.5 Solidity smart contract

14.4 Conclusion

The future path of water sustainability, a crucial worldwide issue, includes a variety of tactics and inventions intended to efficiently manage and save water supplies. Using IoT, AI, and big data to monitor and manage water resources in real time is known as "smart water management." In addition, to ensuring effective water use, smart sensors can improve irrigation and detect leaks. Improvements in desalination technology to make it more economical and energy-efficient. Desalination and Water Recycling increasing the recycling of wastewater for industrial and agricultural uses. Integrated Water Resource Management (IWRM) encourages comprehensive strategies that take into account the full water cycle and involve a variety of stakeholders in the decision-making process. The future path of water sustainability, a crucial worldwide issue, includes a variety of tactics and inventions intended to efficiently manage and save water supplies.

References

1. Asgari, M., Nemati, M.: Application of distributed ledger platforms in smart water systems—A literature review. Front. Water **4**, 848686 (2022)
2. Alrammal, M., Abu-Amara, F., Ismail, Z., Nadeem, M.: Blockchain technology for sustainable management of electricity and water consumption. Eng. Proc. **59**(1), 223 (2024)
3. Dogo, E.M., Salami, A.F., Nwulu, N.I., Aigbavboa, C.O.: Blockchain and internet of things-based technologies for intelligent water management system. In: Artificial Intelligence in IoT, pp. 129–150 (2019)
4. Hakak, S., Khan, W.Z., Gilkar, G.A., Haider, N., Imran, M., Alkatheiri, M.S.: Industrial wastewater management using blockchain technology: architecture, requirements, and future directions. IEEE Internet Things Mag. **3**(2), 38–43 (2020)
5. Orlove, B., Caton, S.C.: Water sustainability: anthropological approaches and prospects. Ann. Rev. Anthropol. **39**, 401–415 (2010)
6. Liu, J., Yang, W.: Water sustainability for China and beyond. Science **337**(6095), 649–650 (2012)
7. Pahontu, B.I., Petcu, A., Predescu, A., Arsene, D.A., Mocanu, M.: A blockchain approach for migrating a cyber-physical water monitoring solution to a decentralized architecture. Water **15**(16), 2874 (2023)
8. Satilmisoglu, T.K., Sermet, Y., Kurt, M., Demir, I.: Blockchain opportunities for water resources management: a comprehensive review. Sustainability **16**(6), 2403 (2024)
9. Xia, W., Chen, X., Song, C.: A framework of blockchain technology in intelligent water management. Front. Environ. Sci. **10**, 909606 (2022)
10. Wu, G., Li, E., Wang, M.: Application and prospect analysis of blockchain technology in water resources protection. In: 2022 International Conference on Blockchain Technology and Information Security (ICBCTIS), pp. 182–187. IEEE (2022)
11. Naqash, M.T., Syed, T.A., Alqahtani, S.S., Siddiqui, M.S., Alzahrani, A., Nauman, M.: A blockchain based framework for efficient water management and leakage detection in urban areas. Urban Sci. **7**(4), 99 (2023)
12. Sundaresan, S., Kumar, K.S., Kumar, T.A., Ashok, V., Julie, E.G.: Blockchain architecture for intelligent water management system in smart cities. In: Blockchain for Smart Cities, pp. 57–80. Elsevier (2021)

13. Mohammed, M.A., Lakhan, A., Abdulkareem, K.H., Abd Ghani, M.K., Marhoon, H.A., Kadry, S., et al.: Industrial internet of water things architecture for data standardization based on blockchain and digital twin technology. J. Adv. Res. (2023)
14. Wang, Z., Wang, K., Wang, Y., Wen, Z.: A data management model for intelligent water project construction based on blockchain. Wirel. Commun. Mob. Comput. **2022**(1), 8482415 (2022)
15. Furones, A.R., Monzón, J.I.T.: Blockchain applicability in the management of urban water supply and sanitation systems in Spain. J. Environ. Manag. **344**, 118480 (2023)
16. Dondjio, I., Themistocleous, M.: Blockchain technology and waste management: a systematic literature review. In: European, Mediterranean, and Middle Eastern Conference on Information Systems, pp. 194–212. Springer International Publishing, Cham (2021)
17. Naeem, K., Zghibi, A., Elomri, A., Mazzoni, A., Triki, C.: A literature review on system dynamics modeling for sustainable management of water supply and demand. Sustainability **15**(8), 6826 (2023)
18. Silva, J.A.: Implementation and integration of sustainability in the water industry: a systematic literature review. Sustainability **14**, 15919 (2022)
19. https://medium.com/@blockchain_simplified/the-blockchain-approach-for-a-better-water-management-system-716fd9682eac